17.5D

WHY IS THERE NO SOCIALISM IN THE UNITED STATES?

Why is there no Socialism in the United States?

WERNER SOMBART

Translated by

Patricia M. Hocking
Head of German, Lockleaze Comprehensive School, Bristol

and

C. T. Husbands
Lecturer in Sociology, University of Bristol

Edited and with an Introductory Essay by C. T. Husbands
and with a Foreword by Michael Harrington

iasp

International Arts and Sciences Press, Inc.
White Plains, New York

This work was originally published in 1906 by the Verlag von
J. C. B. Mohr (Paul Siebeck) of Tübingen under the title
Warum gibt es in den Vereinigten Staaten keinen Sozialismus?
It was slightly revised from a series of articles that had
appeared in the *Archiv für Sozialwissenschaft und Sozialpolitik*
[*Works in Social Science and Social Policy*], XXI (1905)

English translation © Patricia M. Hocking and C. T. Husbands 1976
Editor's introductory essay and editorial material © C. T. Husbands 1976
Michael Harrington's foreword © The Macmillan Press Ltd 1976

First published in the United Kingdom 1976 by
THE MACMILLAN PRESS LTD
London and Basingstoke

First published in the United States in 1976 by
International Arts and Sciences Press, Inc.
901 North Broadway, White Plains, New York 10603

Library of Congress Catalog Card Number: 76–8031

International Standard Book Number: 0–87332–083–2

Printed in Great Britain by
WESTERN PRINTING SERVICES LTD
Bristol

Contents

INTRODUCTION

SECTION ONE

The Political Position of the Worker

SECTION TWO

The Economic Situation of the Worker

SECTION THREE
The Social Position of the Worker

Preface to the Original German Edition

The studies of the workers' movement and of Socialism in the United States of America published in this book first appeared in more or less identical form in Volume XXI of the *Archiv für Sozialwissenschaft und Sozialpolitik*.[1] I have departed from the original text only by introducing some new numerical data and a small amount of additional illustrative material.

I decided upon a special edition of the work only after I had become certain that the principal points of my argument were correct. The verdict of American experts on the subject assured me of this, and not only have my middle-class American friends told me that they agree with me, but the leaders of the Socialist parties have also recognised the correctness of my interpretation – something that seems to me to be even more conclusive. The *International Socialist Review*, the official scholarly journal of the Socialist Party, has even reproduced my articles for its readers, mostly in the full text.[2]

This study can serve as a supplement to the chapters of my book, *Sozialismus und soziale Bewegung*, where I have already attempted (in the last edition) to present a concise sketch of Socialism in the U.S.A.[3]

W.S.

Breslau, 14 August 1906[4]

Foreword

MICHAEL HARRINGTON

The questions raised by Werner Sombart in 1906 about the absence of Socialism in the United States are relevant to American politics in the 1970s.

A number of factors and events are converging and it is clear that this decade will be a period of political realignment or political disintegration.[1] The energy crisis, the great recession-inflation of the seventies, a growing sense of ethical and spiritual malaise, and many other trends all point to such a development. It can be argued, I think, that the nation is at one of those turning points which then fix the outlines of an entire era to come. In the past, there were the rise of Jacksonian Democracy in the 1820s, the Civil War and the triumph of Northern capitalism, the emergence of the corporate and imperial structure under the direction of the Republican Party in the 1890s, Roosevelt's welfare-state politics of the thirties. Now it seems that another moment of change is on the agenda.

In Europe, Socialism became a mass movement during the transition from *laissez-faire* to organised, imperial capitalism (that is to say, between the 1890s and the First World War), although England, as the Editor points out in the introductory essay, is something of a special case. In America, the Socialists failed. The ongoing relevance of the fact in the seventies – and of Sombart's attempt to account for it – is that its explanation requires one to understand social forces and structures which are at work to this very moment and which will profoundly influence the realignments of the seventies and eighties. Thus, *Why is there no Socialism in the United States?* is not a scholarly curiosity, but a book which poses the issue of American 'exceptionalism', an issue which is quite pertinent in the present crisis.

I will not for a moment attempt to survey the literature on the subject. That is well done in the introductory essay (even though, as will be seen in a moment, I have my interpretive differences with it). Rather, I will concentrate on a few of the themes raised by Sombart, and stressed by the Editor, which are important to the present and future as well as to the American past.

First of all, I think that the notion of the 'civic integration' of the American working class is extremely important. Sombart treats it, of course; but I would place even more of a stress upon it than he does. The continental-European Socialist movement, it must be remembered, began around a civil-rights, rather than an economic, question: the exclusion, or systematic undercounting, of the workers in the political process. In almost every instance, the psychological, emotional basis of the anti-bourgeois struggle was the demand for bourgeois equality. Even in the case of the partial exception in England, there is a striking fact that the first politically organised workers' movement, Chartism, had the same characteristic, even though it did not lay the ground-work for a mass Socialist party.

In the United States there was universal manhood suffrage almost from the very beginning. This led to the phenomenon, first brilliantly formulated by Leon Samson, of 'Americanism' as a substitute for Socialism.[2] American capitalism, Samson argued, is the Socialist form of capitalism, i.e., it preaches an egalitarianism, a denial of the reality of class society, which is unlike anything one would have found in France or Britain. Therefore a worker in America could express his drive for equality in terms of, not in counterposition to, the prevailing ideology.

The ongoing impact of this ideological factor can be seen in one of the anomalies of the seventies: that the most regressive tax in America is also the most popular. The Social Security levy does not allow for deductions or take into account family size, and it is an outrageous bargain for the rich, who get publicly subsidised retirement insurance on cheaper terms than anyone else. But Social Security retains the myth of being an insurance programme, i.e., of providing the recipient with benefits which he or she has already paid in. In fact, there is a large element of welfare in Social Security but that fact is known only to statisticians and experts. The public, with its Americanist, individualist, self-help ideology, is relatively enthusiastic about this highly regressive tax.

Secondly, the Editor points out the complexity of the 'roast beef and apple pie' theory of the failure of American Socialism. The evidence, incredible as it may seem, is still in dispute. Seymour Martin Lipset has pointed out that social mobility in America was not that different from Europe, but there are many, many complicating factors. Stephan Thernstrom has done some ingenious research in trying to deal with the quantitative question, and a lively summary of the state of the debate can be found in *Failure of a Dream?*, a volume edited by Lipset with John H. M. Laslett.[3] But what concerns me here is not the issue of the numbers but how one interprets them.

There is an easy assumption, as the Editor points out in his introductory essay, which underlies much *embourgeoisement* analysis: that higher living standards are anti-radical. In fact, the period of the greatest growth of the German Social Democracy, from the abolition of the anti-Socialist laws to the First World War, was a time of relative prosperity for the working class. Moreover, as Adolph Sturmthal has pointed out, many of the statistical comparisons of the American and European living standards in this period omit the value of the Bismarckian (or, in England, Lloyd George) social programmes.[4] So one cannot assume that poverty is radical and affluence conservative, since the reverse is often true. Indeed, in the sixties the New Left movement, which had a certain impact upon American politics, particularly with regard to the war in Vietnam, was based upon the children of prosperity. And clearly one of the important issues to be settled in the realignment of the seventies is whether this stratum is going to move permanently to the Left (and whether, in doing so, it will repel the trade-union welfare-staters who have been the mass constituency of economic reform for a generation).

On this count, then, Sombart is somewhat simplistic with regard to the past, and not too useful in terms of the future. His slighting of the importance of the immigrants is another flaw, one which the Editor notes. I will only add that the Wisconsin labour historians, Selig Perlman in particular, understood how crucial this aspect of the American working-class experience was. The strong tendencies towards the adoption of a Socialist political perspective in the American Federation of Labor in the 1890s aborted, in some considerable measure, because of the anti-Socialism of the Irish Catholics, then as now strongly entrenched in the building trades.

But finally, let me raise the most critical point about Sombart's book as it relates to the future. I would argue – and have done so at length in my book, *Socialism* – that there *is* a social-democratic movement in the United States today.[5] That is, Sombart's belief that eventually America would produce such a movement has been confirmed, albeit in a hidden and disguised fashion. There is a growing recognition in Europe, as the Editor notes, that social democracy and Socialism are not synonymous. Let the former term stand for a movement that mobilises workers on behalf of State intervention, planning and social priorities within capitalism, and the latter be a description of a political movement which seeks to transform capitalism fundamentally.

Given that definition, a labour party – a social democracy – appeared in the United States during the Great Depression. Its peculiarity was that it organised *within* the Democratic Party. Yet it is a distinct entity, with class criteria (only union members can participate in the work of COPE, the AFL-CIO political arm) and a social-democratic programme not that different from the immediate programme of the German or British social democracy. If, as I believe, structural change is on the agenda in the late seventies and early eighties, a basic question concerns whether or not this invisible social democracy will become Socialist – or whether, as not a few American conservatives hope, it will turn sharply to the Right in the name of the 'social issue' (race, abortion, feminism, sexual politics, and the like).

Obviously Werner Sombart did not anticipate the problems and possibilities of contemporary America. But he did, as this book shows, ask the right questions and sometimes give the right answers, and his concern with what it is that makes America exceptional in the capitalist world, and whether or not that exceptionalism would continue un- abated, is quite relevant to the issues of the 1970s.

List of Tables

Editor's Introductory Essay

Werner Sombart's *Why is there no Socialism in the United States?* was published in 1906 and has enjoyed a distinctive place in English-language sociology, although it has never before been fully translated into English. Passages from it have been quoted in a variety of sociological contexts, and it has been cited and sometimes misrepresented just as frequently. The book has had a significant impact not only upon attempts to explain the failure of an organised Socialist movement in the United States but also upon more general attempts in contemporary sociology to understand both the class structure of advanced industrialised societies and the types of working-class consciousness to be found in such societies. Recent theories about the effects of affluence, social mobility, and civic integration upon social and political stability derive very directly from themes found in this work by Sombart.

This is one reason why an English translation of the book is now appropriate. However, it is also hoped that this translation contributes to the growing literature that has been spawned by the American New Left of the 1960s on the 'Old Left', much of it having been written by authors heavily influenced by the politics and values of the New Left. Sombart's book is like much of this literature in that it seeks what might be regarded as global reasons for the failure of American Socialism – reasons that are derived from the experience of Socialism in the national context.[1] Local or state-wide studies of the American Socialist movement have tended to be less frequent, although the ones that exist complement the findings of those that focus on the national context.[2]

Werner Sombart's political and intellectual development was a complicated one, but, as has been documented at length in a recent work by Mitzman, his political orientation became progressively more reactionary as he grew older.[3] Born in 1863, he attended the Universities of Pisa and Berlin, and was awarded a Doctorate of Philosophy from the latter institution in 1888. From 1888 to 1890 he was a business agent at the Chamber of Commerce in Bremen, after which he became an Extraordinary Professor (a rank below a full professor) of Economics at the University of Breslau, which was considered an academic backwater when compared with some other German universities of the time. Yet because of his political sympathies he was denied

promotion to full professorship at Breslau, and his first full professorship was at the Berlin Handelshochschule [Commercial University],
where he went in 1906 – shortly after the completion of *Why is there
no Socialism in the United States?*. In 1917 he became a full professor
at the University of Berlin at the age of fifty-four. He was made a
Professor Emeritus in 1931 and died in 1941.

Sombart was never a Socialist within any of the traditions of the
German Social Democrats, but during the 1890s he expressed considerable sympathy towards Socialist ideals and, according to his own
confession, was strongly influenced by Marxian ideas. As a *Katheder-
sozialist* [academic Socialist] he played a prominent role in the influential Verein für Sozialpolitik [Association for Social Policy], on to
whose committee he was co-opted in 1892. He maintained a participating role in the Verein during his own subsequent changes in
political orientation, becoming its Deputy Chairman in 1930 and its
Chairman in 1932.

All commentators on Sombart remark on his progressive alienation
from left-wing ideals and the consequent differences in interpretation
and viewpoint between those of his works written in the 1890s and
those written in the 1920s and 1930s.[4] He made considerable accommodation with Nazism, although he was never wholeheartedly accepted
by the Nazi régime; nonetheless, it is only with considerable good
nature that one can refrain from calling him a Nazi during the last
years of his life. Mitzman, whose discussion of Sombart is generally
fair and accurate, though highly critical, identifies the crucial final
turning point in his road to the Right as the publication of *Der
Bourgeois* in 1913:

> Sombart's special sensitivity to the spiritual malaise of the German
> bourgeoisie, and his total disillusionment with the regenerative
> power of socialism, led him to a proto-fascist mentality two decades
> before the collapse of the bourgeois economic order spread such an
> attitude among the masses of his compatriots.[5]

However, Mitzman also goes further and discerns the beginnings of
this orientation in the disillusionment with capitalism and with its
specific social product, the proletariat, that was expressed by Sombart
in a book he published in 1906, *Das Proletariat*.[6] Although Mitzman's
analysis does not in fact discuss *Why is there no Socialism in the
United States?*, this book does fit quite well into his chronological
exposition of Sombart's political and intellectual development. *Why is
there no Socialism in the United States?* combines Sombart's longstanding interests in both capitalism and Socialism. He is extremely
critical of capitalism as an economic institution and of its effects: its
penchant for reducing human modes of thought from the refined, the
abstract, and the qualitative to the debased, the concrete, and the

quantitative; the inequalities in the distribution of wealth that are capitalism's necessary corollaries; capitalism's reduction of all relations to cash terms; and the ability of successful capitalism to seduce the working class from its true political interests by economic inducements. It is this last feature of capitalism that relates directly to Sombart's view of the working class, for its necessary implication is that the working class is by nature venal and willing to be suborned by affluence. In various passages of the present work Sombart makes clear he feels that this is potentially true of the working class of all capitalist countries, not merely of that in the United States. The rapid growth and success of American capitalism meant merely that the American working class was historically the first to be seduced in this way from its true interests. On the other hand, there is some ambivalence about Sombart's views on this matter, and in other passages of the book this negativism about the working class is tinged by a definite nostalgia for left-wing ideals, as in the passage where Sombart describes how he developed his political interests as a child.

Sombart begins his work from the initial axiom that the growth of capitalism leads to the growth of a Socialist movement among the working class, from which it should follow that the country with the most advanced capitalist development has the largest and most active Socialist movement. At the outset he wants to explain the United States as merely a deviant case, but (although he is not fully explicit about this) the final result of his analysis is merely to throw doubt on the acceptability of his initial axiom. Writers since Sombart have come to recognise that the level of economic development of a country is not positively correlated with the growth of Socialist class consciousness within its working class. Numerous other factors are more significant and, as Bottomore has recently observed, the relationship with economic development tends to be a negative one.[7] Even as early as the 1860s, Marx himself, following the same initial axiom as Sombart, had been troubled by the same problem that Sombart subsequently set himself with regard to America, although Marx's concern was with the failure of the *English* working class to produce an indigenous Socialist movement.[8] Indeed, as we shall see, two of Marx's explanations of this – rising wages and a quasi-democratic form of government – are partly taken up by Sombart.

The present essay by the Editor makes no attempt to present a review of the entire gamut of literature on American Socialism since Sombart, nor to compile a comprehensive list of the large variety of reasons to which the failure of American Socialism has been attributed. Instead, it gives the essential points of Sombart's argument, putting them in the context of later sociological writing not only on the topic of Socialism but also on the nature of social structure in advanced capitalist societies; then it assesses Sombart's emphasis on the economic factors that allegedly impeded the growth of Socialism in America; and finally it attempts to integrate some of the more recent discussions of voting behaviour and the dynamics of party systems with the emphasis that Sombart also places on the role played by specifically American political factors in preventing the success of a Socialist movement in the United States.

SOMBART AND SOCIAL DEMOCRACY IN AMERICA

Recent generations of political sociologists, schooled in the lessons of the twentieth-century experience about the realities of working-class politics, would undoubtedly wish to alter the grandiloquent title that Sombart gave his essay to something more modest, perhaps to 'Why is there no Social Democracy in the United States?' or 'Why is there no labour party in the United States?'. Sombart wrote the present work before the full implications of Lenin's revision of Marx's ideas both on the practice of revolution and on the type of political consciousness needed for a successful proletarian revolution had been explicitly assimilated into political analysis.[9] Before writing this book, Sombart had apparently believed, as Marx and Engels had also done,[10] that the economic conditions of capitalist production would necessarily tend to produce a militant and revolutionary working class, although it could be argued that some elements of Lenin's distinction between class political consciousness and spontaneous trade-union consciousness were incorporated by Sombart, implicitly and perhaps unconsciously, into some of his later work.[11] Social Democracy, as currently defined, is not to be equated with Socialism, as Miliband[12] and (more recently) Coates[13] have had occasion to lament, and the experience of those industrialised countries where labour parties have flourished shows very clearly that, even in the political consciousness of most of the working-class supporters of these parties, Social Democracy and Socialism are not the same. Moreover, Sombart assumes that militance by such organisations as trade unions almost necessarily corresponds to left-wing radicalism, although numerous historical instances could be given where this correlation does not obtain.[14]

The historical preconditions for Social Democracy, that is, for a parliamentary political party based on the working class, are clearly different from, and in one sense less demanding than, those for a fully fledged Socialism, and a revolutionary Socialist consciousness is not necessary for the former. Sombart apparently believed that, at least in the American context, a spontaneous trade-union consciousness would be a sufficient prerequisite for a labour party, provided that the organised trade-union movement were then to respond in a manner favourable to the development of a working-class political party and that political conditions were otherwise propitious. In this model, therefore, the attitude taken by the trade-union movement towards party politics is a crucial factor. However, it must be recognised that a correspondence between economically oriented goals of the kind pursued by instrumental trade-unionism and goals pursued in the political arena is not an automatic one; instead, it is contingent, and is affected by pragmatic considerations. Moreover, as Lane has recently argued in the British case, even when trade-union leaderships support a social-democratic movement, either through inclination or because they are forced or cajoled into doing so by the demands of their union members, the specific character of their method of opposing capitalism in the work situation necessarily constrains the movement they support into a reformist mould; such trade-union leaderships therefore tend to stultify any attempts to change a social-democratic movement in a more radical direction.[15] Even when the question posed by Sombart is reduced to seeking reasons for the lack of Social Democracy in the United States, it nonetheless still requires answering. No amount of apologia or quibbling about deviant cases can really contradict the hard fact that social-democratic attitudes, let alone a successful political party representing these attitudes, did not take permanent root in the United States. Nor were such attitudes ever held by more than a minority of the working-class electorate, even in the period of the Socialist Party's zenith – which was in fact in the years after Sombart's essay was written.

What then are the reasons given by Sombart for this lack of success? He is not always fully consistent, but there are a number of fundamental arguments that he makes, and some of these have become standard tenets of more recent attempts to explain the class structure of advanced industrialised societies.[16]

Sombart's major points are:

1. *The favourable attitude of the American worker towards capitalism*
This attitude allegedly derived intrinsic support from the legacy of motivations that had fostered early immigration to America, a legacy that prevailed even among those Americans who by the end of the nineteenth century would have been considered native stock. The worker maintained a favourable attitude towards capitalism, firstly because of its success in supplying his material needs, and secondly because of his economic integration into the capitalist system; this type of integration was achieved by various sorts of bonus and profit-sharing schemes and by the use of advantageous systems of piece-rate payment in many enterprises.

This particular argument by Sombart finds some later echo in Bell's attempt to explain the failure of the American Socialist Party by its allegedly irrelevant ethical absolutism in the period after its greatest

Presidential election success in 1912.[17] Similarly, Schumpeter explained the failure of Socialism in America in terms of the worker's supposedly distinctive attitude to capitalism: 'The average competent and respectable workman was, and felt himself to be, a businessman. He successfully applied himself to exploiting his individual opportunities.... He understood and largely shared his employer's way of thinking.'[18] Potter too, in discussing the effect of America's wealth on her national character, advances arguments that are consistent with this way of thinking.[19]

2. *The favourable attitude of the worker to the American system of government and the unusual degree of his civic integration*

This theme is a common one in recent literature on the sociology of nation-building, and it has been applied to a variety of historical contexts besides that of the United States to explain the development of comparatively stable political systems. Lipset, for example, has argued that universal male franchise and the Constitution based on Enlightenment principles were central to the development of the United States as a stable polity after it had emerged as the first new nation.[20] Marshall[21] and Bendix[22] have developed similar arguments regarding the depressing effects upon working-class radicalism of successful attempts by ruling élites to incorporate the working class into political discourse, and Roth has applied this perspective in an analysis of the development of the German Social Democratic Party.[23] Even the explanation offered by McKensie and Silver for working-class support for the British Conservative Party, while based on the supposed existence of a deferential political consciousness, recognises how important was the extension of the franchise in 1867 to large sections of the working class in the process of civic integration required for this deference to be perpetuated in working-class voting.[24]

3. *The difficulty of mounting a new political party in an ongoing two-party system*

This factor has been used by a number of Socialist writers, such as Norman Thomas,[25] in explaining the lack of the Socialist Party's success, although it is probably better known as one of the arguments made by Hofstadter for the failure of the People's Party.[26] The more conservative major parties in America have frequently stolen the thunder from third parties by incorporating as their own parts of the platforms of these more reform-oriented third parties. Of course, this process has been made easier by the fact that any shift in a reforming direction imposed by circumstances upon the major parties has only had to be fairly marginal precisely because of the merely reformist character of the parties that have managed serious attempts to break into the two-party system during most of recent American history.

Thus, the major parties have not been required to violate any funda-mental ideological principle in the process of shifting their appeal to co-opt the support of threatening minor parties.[27]

4. *The buying off of the potential radicalism of the American working class by the material rewards that American capitalism was able to provide*

According to Sombart, the crucial dynamic in this respect has been the affluence of the American working class relative to that of the European working class. Sombart assumes that the superior material situation of the American worker has prevented the development of oppositional, social-democratic tendencies within the American proletariat. This part of Sombart's argument is based on the assumption that the American worker sees himself as being in a superior position because he uses the material position of the European working class as his referent for comparative purposes. However, Sombart also clearly feels that the absolute level of affluence among the American working class, irrespective of any comparisons with Europe, has an additional incre-mental impact in repressing the growth of social-democratic attitudes. Money-income above a given absolute amount, in providing access to particular consumer durables and to a standard of living higher than some critical level, produces quasi-middle-class attitudes and orienta-tions within the working class. This can occur, Sombart assumes, despite real and even growing differentials in wealth between this bourgeois-oriented working class and the real middle class; thus, at the level of the individual worker and his family, income of more than a certain absolute amount impedes the development of social-democratic attitudes, even if – as may well have been the case in America at the turn of the century – the total distribution of society's wealth is becom-ing more unequal.

An argument of this sort assumes that the world view of the worker is restricted to his personal circumstances, and it is an obvious precursor of the crudest examples of the so-called *embourgeoisement* thesis that was promulgated in European and American sociology in the period of apparent general affluence after the Second World War. Writers such as Crosland, and Butler and Rose[28] were predicting the permanent demise of left-oriented political parties that derived mass electoral support in the working class because, so it was argued, access to luxuries on a hitherto unprecedented scale was eroding the traditional working-class support for these parties and was consigning them slowly to minority status and then to oblivion. Goldthorpe and his colleagues disposed of this argument in the British case,[29] and Hamil-ton has recently published a comprehensive attack on this and similar orientations in America sociology.[30]

5. *The greater opportunities for upward social mobility available to the American worker*

Although only one paragraph in the final section of the book is devoted directly to this topic, Sombart emphasises that it is of 'the very greatest importance in accounting for how the [American] proletarian psyche has evolved'. Sombart has a very generalised notion of the type of social mobility that was occurring in the United States to repress the development of working-class consciousness; he talks of workers going 'to the top or almost to the top' of the capitalist hierarchy, as well as their having greater opportunities than in Europe to become petty-bourgeois entrepreneurs.

Some references in English to *Why is there no Socialism in the United States?* even go so far as to say that this is the only argument of significance in the book. Dahrendorf, for example, calls it 'the cardinal thesis of Sombart's brilliant essay'.[31] In *Social Mobility in Industrial Society* Lipset and Bendix incorporate this particular argument by Sombart in introducing a discussion of the belief that American society has traditionally been more open than European societies; however, they do confuse their discussion by introducing into the same context a quotation from Sombart's subsequent analysis of the effects of the frontier on the level of working-class consciousness.[32]

The degree and nature of social mobility and particularly its effects upon working-class attitudes towards radical social change and to the social structure in general have been major themes in contemporary political sociology and sociological theory.[33] Of course, the subject has also had considerable significance in popular American culture. Still, it has a sociological history that predates Sombart. In 1852 Marx had remarked on the fluidity of American class structure: 'though classes already exist, they have not yet become fixed, but continually change and interchange their elements in constant flux.'[34]

6. *The effect of the existence of an open frontier in reducing the militance of the American worker*

Sombart espouses the least refined of all versions of the famous 'frontier thesis'. He argues that there was a safety-valve effect preventing the development of radicalism because, with 'no capital or hardly any', large numbers of workers from the East settled free land in the West as independent farmers. This crude version of the frontier thesis is associated most prominently with the name of Frederick Jackson Turner (whose first paper on the subject was published in 1893,[35] but is not cited by Sombart), and although there has been some cavilling among historians about whether Turner's views were quite as unsophisticated as this depiction, the consensus now is that they were. In any case, Sombart's argument is amenable to no other interpretation, so unambiguously is it stated.

Sombart regards the existence of the frontier as providing the American worker with the opportunity of 'escape into freedom' if the constraints of working under capitalism should become too oppressive. With no attempt at justification or elaboration, Sombart passes over the patent inconsistency between his argument on the effects of the frontier and some of his earlier statements on the American worker's attitude to capitalism. However, if the American worker 'loves capitalism' and 'devotes his entire body and soul to it', as Sombart argues at one point, one cannot but wonder why he should want to escape from it to the chilly winters and other rigours of the American prairie. It is precisely this inconsistency that was pounced on in the highly critical review of *Why is there no Socialism in the United States?* that appeared in *Vorwärts* [*Forward*], the newspaper of the German Social Democratic Party, shortly after the book was published:

> One must then ask oneself why under such circumstances the American worker 'escapes into freedom' in such large numbers – that is, withdraws from the hubbub of capitalism by settling on hitherto uncultivated land. If capitalism is so good to him, he could not help but feel extraordinarily well-off under its sceptre. Instead of this, no less than five million people have gone from the Eastern states to 'freedom' in the West during a single generation up to 1900, and it is precisely this fact that Sombart sees as one of the most powerful reasons countering the growth of Socialism. There is clearly a glaring contradiction here.[36]

It should also be added that at the very end of his book Sombart tries to hedge his bets and he argues in a single sentence that the factors which have hitherto prevented the development of Socialism in the United States are losing their impact and are about 'to be converted into their opposite'. Although Sombart does make occasional hints throughout the book of possible changes in the future that would favour the growth of American Socialism, the emphasis in his conclusion is, to say the least, a little surprising, since he has gone to great lengths in most of the book to paint a picture of a bourgeois-oriented working class that is totally hostile to Social Democracy. Indeed, his final sentence is less than fully consistent with his apparent conclusion in the last part of Section Two that a social-democratic movement in America was unlikely, in view of the fact that one had not arisen by the time he was writing.

SOMBART AND THE THEORY OF 'EMBOURGEOISEMENT'

Of the various individual arguments in Sombart's book, the one receiving most attention is that which asserts the deradicalising effects of the economic rewards that American capitalism was able to provide for its workers. In fact, the overall picture of a universally affluent working class that Sombart gives in Section Two of this work is a considerable distortion, and it fails to acknowledge the existence of tremendous poverty among substantial parts of both the native-born and immigrant working-class populations. This is all the more surprising because Sombart himself was well aware of the considerable contemporary literature documenting the extent of poverty in America,[37] and in his Introduction he quotes extensively from one of the most famous of the books published in this era on the subject, Robert Hunter's *Poverty*.[38] Nowhere is the inconsistency explained or defended, and it is clearly an embarrassment to the point that Sombart wants to make.[39] The source of the discrepancy, however, is clear enough; in giving obsessional emphasis to *average* working-class wage levels in the United States, Sombart ignored the considerable dispersion in the wage-distributions that he examined. Although one cannot seriously query Sombart's general contention that average levels of both real income and money-income were considerably higher for American workers than for their German counterparts in this period, one must at the same time recognise that variation around the average was sufficient to place many American families on the margin of subsistence. Thus, even when it is considered only in terms of income, the American working class at the turn of the century was a relatively heterogeneous grouping – far more so than is apparent from Sombart's account – and contained not only substantial numbers in poverty but also a large aristocracy of labour, which was concentrated in specific industries. The measures of dispersion supplied by the Editor for the various American and German income-distributions introduced as evidence by Sombart almost all show (at least for male wage-earners) that there was substantial absolute economic inequality *within* the American working class and that this inequality was in turn greater than in the corresponding German case.

It is only fair to note that Sombart, who had visited the United States in 1904, was far from being the only European observer to be impressed by the apparently universal affluence of the American worker. H. G. Wells, who followed Sombart to America in 1906, held a similar opinion, although his book also included discussion of contrary tendencies:

Now, there can be little doubt to any one who goes to and fro in America that, in spite of the huge accumulation of property in a few hands that is now in progress, there is still no general effect of impoverishment.... New York has, no doubt, its effects of noise, disorder, discomfort, and a sort of brutality; but to begin with, one sees nothing of the underfed people, the numerous dingily clad and greyly housed people who catch the eye in London. Even in the congested arteries, the filthy back streets of the East side, I found myself saying, as a thing remarkable, 'These people have money to spend.' In London one travels long distances for a penny, and great regiments of people walk; in New York the universal fare is two-pence halfpenny, and everybody rides. Common people are better gloved and better booted in America than in any European country I know, in spite of the higher prices for clothing; . . .[40]

One must wonder where some of these European observers made their observations since their accounts compare badly with more data-based contemporary descriptions, and Bettmann's recent book also contains sufficient indication that in this period public transportation, for example, was definitely not accessible to all.[41]

In its unrefined form then, Sombart's *embourgeoisement* argument should undoubtedly be rejected, partly at least because it cannot be made to apply to a large section of the American working class. Moreover, even when considering the circumstances of those workers who were relatively well-off, one should beware of any automatic equation of possession of luxuries with lack of social-democratic attitudes. Such an equation does not adequately specify the inter-vening psychological processes, or it may reflect a spurious relationship, or – even if appropriate – it may well tend to be contingent on further sets of circumstances. None the less, Sombart's conclusions regarding the importance that economic factors may have in establishing and maintaining a bulwark against the development of a working-class-based political movement can still be modified and adapted to the specific circumstances of the American working class.

Sombart, of course, was not the first to argue that economic well-being, measured in absolute monetary terms, has some bearing on the development of Socialist consciousness, and Engels for one came to explain the lack of a Socialist movement among the English working class in the second half of the nineteenth century in terms that are essentially those employed by Sombart. During the 1840s Marx and Engels vacillated between two subtly different viewpoints of the source of Socialist consciousness in the working class. In *The Communist Manifesto* they asserted that increasing absolute deprivation would be the crucial factor, the particular dynamic being sheer want and the frustration that it was supposed automatically to produce.[42] However, at least in one point of *Wage Labour and Capital* (written in 1847) Marx entertains the possibility that it could also be the relative deprivation of the working class *vis-à-vis* the bourgeoisie which would produce Socialist consciousness.[43] Thus, the working class would, it was assumed, use the economic position of the bourgeoisie as a referent when assessing the acceptability of their own economic position and would become aggrieved that they were falling progressively behind the bourgeoisie, despite any absolute increase in working-class affluence. Towards the end of his life Engels for one was forced to accept that neither of these models was fully acceptable. He came to reject the notion of increasing poverty that had been axiomatic to the first model, but he retained a belief in the negative correlation between wage levels and the development of a Socialist perspective that was implicit in this model. In the Preface to *The Condition of the Working Class in England* written in 1892 Engels quotes from an article he had written in 1885 to account for the quiescence of British workers in the years of the country's capitalist expansion after 1850:

> 'The truth is this: during the period of England's industrial monopoly the English working class have, to a certain extent, shared in the benefits of the monopoly. These benefits were very unequally parcelled out amongst them; the privileged minority pocketed most, but even the great mass had, at least, a temporary share now and then. And that is the reason why, since the dying out of Owenism, there has been no socialism in England. With the breakdown of that monopoly, the English working class will loose that privileged position; it will find itself generally – the privileged and leading minority not excepted – on a level with its fellow-workers abroad. And that is the reason why there will be socialism again in England.'[44]

Sombart himself accepted this later position of Engels when he too was attempting to account for the lack of a large-scale indigenous Socialist movement in England in the nineteenth century.[45] More recently Hobsbawm has accepted Engels's viewpoint not only for the years to about 1890, but has even suggested the extension of the same notion to account for the slow development of a labour party in Great Britain in the first decades of the twentieth century, when he argues that the British working class benefited from Britain's position as an imperial power.[46]

It is undoubtedly reasonable to apply a similar viewpoint to some of the better-off parts of the American working class at this time in order to account for their limited receptivity to electoral Socialism, although it would perhaps be more precise to regard economic factors as having had predisposing or contributing effects, rather than as being uniquely important in explaining the lack of social-democratic attitudes. Moreover, the relatively greater absolute economic inequality already mentioned within the American, as opposed to the German, working class, is consistent with the fact that most American trade unions at this time were exclusionist and craft-oriented, and were disposed to regard the bulk of new industrial workers (many of them immigrants) as a threat to their own livelihood. If this situation had continued for any period of time, it would be reasonable to expect some sort of radicalism to have arisen from what would have been a permanently dispossessed underclass of immigrants. In fact, the situation did not continue. American capitalism had been granted an abundance of resources and was able to expand at a considerable rate, especially in the politically crucial years after 1896 or so. Such was the rate of industrial expansion and the associated economic incorporation of erstwhile immigrants that within a generation of their arrival the latter came to have the same aggregate economic characteristics as the native-born. Peter Roberts, for example, quotes wage data in 1911 for immigrants, the children of immigrants, and the native-born.[47] While immigrants were undoubtedly relatively worse-off, the children of immigrants had a wage structure that was in virtually every statistical respect the same as that for the native-born. As long as this sort of economic integration was occurring, some consideration of economic factors to account for the lack of Social Democracy in the United States is a legitimate one, even if Sombart's original crude formulation of the argument in terms of the *embourgeoisement* of the entire working class needs refinement. Many immigrant arrivals did doubtless appreciate their longer-term prospects for economic integration, and this was partially responsible for repressing any propensity that they might otherwise have had to embrace social-democratic attitudes, at least when taken in conjunction with their immediate political circumstances and the privatised attitudes towards work and towards their ethnic peers that they brought with them.

IMMIGRANTS AND AMERICAN SOCIAL DEMOCRACY

One would think that the constant stream of immigrant voters entering the American political system at the turn of the century contained a considerable potential for change of some sort, even if not necessarily in a social-democratic direction. Yet the direct contribution of immigrants to electoral realignments at the national level, at least after 1896, was marginal. Sombart says surprisingly little about the effect of the presence of large numbers of immigrants in assisting or restraining the development of Social Democracy, although he clearly assumes that most of them do not become Socialists and that, if they had been such in their land or origin, they ceased to be so in America where, as he ironically expresses it, they 'are immune to the Socialist bacillus'.

In fact, the political propensity towards Socialism of America's arriving immigrants was a subject of considerable debate at the time, and it continues to play an important role in academic discussion about the character and ultimate failure of the Socialist Party of America.[48] Following Sombart, we must dismiss the assertion that 'those who in America pass as Socialists are a few broken-down Germans without any following'. There may have been a kernel of truth in some less pejorative form of this statement in the 1880s, when Engels was castigating the exclusivism of the Socialist Labor Party (the more doctrinaire predecessor of, and later competitor with, the Socialist Party of America), especially its insistence on holding its meetings in German.[49] However, after the turn of the century – as research by Weinstein has shown[50] – the Socialist Party was supported by substantial numbers of native-born workers and immigrant support was tending to be left behind. Besides the possible effect of the economic integration that has been mentioned already, the reasons for this are twofold: firstly, the immediate political circumstances that immigrants encountered in the machine-dominated cities in which they tended to settle; and secondly, the largely privatised orientations that they brought with them to America.

As Portes has recently argued on the basis of a study of Chilean workers, the acceptance of Socialist doctrines, or even the development of social-democratic attitudes, is not a galvanic and spontaneous process, but one that requires political education and leadership in the appropriate direction.[51] Yet what sort of political education did most immigrants receive? It was usually managed by the frank old rogues who ran the urban political machines at the turn of the century, of whom George Washington Plunkitt may have been the most voluble. Plunkitt's well-known advice to hold an election district ('you must study human nature and act accordin'') was heavily oriented to the immigrant poor, of whom he said:

> I fix them up till they get things running again [after a fire]. It's philanthropy, but it's politics, too – mighty good politics. . . . The poor are the most grateful people in the world, . . . The consequence is that the poor look up to George W. Plunkitt as a father, come to him in trouble – and don't forget him on election day.[52]

Handlin remarks on the predominantly local orientation to which the immigrant was constrained by his social and economic circumstances.

> The local issues were the important ones. . . . To the residents of the tenement districts they were critical; and in these matters the ward boss saw eye to eye with them. *Jim gets things done!* They could see the evidence themselves, knew the difference it made in their own existence. (Emphasis in original)[53]

The consequence of machine control was clear:

> The failure of socialists and anarchists to win an important position in the associational life of the immigrants prevented them also from using these groups for political ends. And with few exceptions –

Henry George for a time was one – American radicals met the stubborn opposition of the foreign-born voters.[54]

H. G. Wells said the same thing in more critical terms. After a visit to one of the saloons of Chicago's famous aldermanic figure of the time, Hinky Dink Mike Kenna, he wrote of the clientele:

> ... they were Americanized immigrants. ... They have no ideas and they have votes; they are capable, if need be, of meeting violence by violence, and that is the sort of thing American methods demand....[55]

If social-democratic attitudes are in fact learned rather than directly implanted by objective economic and social conditions, what chance did they have of being nurtured in these circumstances?

However, the dispositions of many immigrants included not only subservience to the power of the leaders of urban political machines but also other orientations that in American circumstances were equally inimical to the development of social-democratic attitudes. One was a tendency to favour ethnic-based subcultures at the expense of wider allegiances at the class level.[56] Another was a tendency in many cases to oppose capitalists rather than capitalism itself in pursuing instrumentally oriented economic objectives. This characteristic was noted by commentators of the time and was interpreted by the more faint-hearted and unperspicacious employers as indicative of Socialist propensities, but, however patronisingly it may be expressed, there is doubtless some truth in Peter Roberts's view of the Slavs:

> The Slavs will join the union and fight for higher wages and better conditions, ... they will follow a labor leader with a devotion that is religious; they have patience and can suffer in the cause they champion; but all that is done from economic motives. The Slav loves the dollar, and will keep it when the conflict is over. Let men try to lead him along the road of socialism, and he will not go; ...[57]

TWO-PARTY SYSTEMS VERSUS MULTI-PARTY SYSTEMS IN THE
GENESIS OF SOCIAL DEMOCRACY

However, the limited development of social-democratic attitudes in America is not to be explained only by the inclinations and political circumstances of its immigrant population, especially in view of the several recent studies showing support for the Socialist Party of America among the native-born. All the same, the particular political constraints that may have acted most strongly on the urban immigrant did also impinge in a more general manner on all members of the American working class; this is due to the operation of the ongoing two-party system that the Socialist Party sought to break open. Sombart's argument about the role of the party system in accounting for the limited success of the Socialist Party in the United States is possibly his strongest. In this lies what is perhaps the most basic reason for the failure of the Party, and the other reasons adduced by Sombart are then to be regarded as contributing factors, even among those population groups and for the respective time periods for which they can be shown to be valid. The failure of the Socialist Party has to be considered in the light of political trends and realignments in American politics at the end of the nineteenth and beginning of the twentieth centuries.[58]

Even without necessarily accepting Sombart's contention that American workers were elated by the radical-democratic character of the country's system of government and therefore lacked a realistic political perspective because of the feeling of power that the Constitution conferred on them as ordinary citizens, one may none the less expand and refine Sombart's conclusion about the effects on voters' attitudes of the two-party system by reference to subsequent research findings on the social psychology of voting behaviour. Not only is it the case that it is intrinsically difficult for a third party to break into a two-party system; such a system may mean that further parties are unnecessary if, as may have been true in the American context, groups of voters of a significant size who wish merely to maximise their net advantage can play one party off against the other. Furthermore, major parties in America were traditionally able to co-opt the support of third parties by adopting parts of the latters' platforms.[59] Yet, in addition to these considerations, the comparatively rigid two-party system of the United States at the turn of the century (which had survived the stress of the Populist upsurge of the 1890s and whose electors held highly stable affiliations in the periods before and after that decade) had long since socialised the majority of voters into party affiliations which, as subsequent research on voting behaviour tells us, must have had an affective as much as a cognitive basis. In the task of political socialisation the party system was building on over a century of universal male suffrage which had long preceded the development of the open and recognised hostility between capital and labour. It was this hostility that in Europe gave Socialist parties their initial impetus and also frequently coincided with the extension of the franchise to the working class.[60]

As recent research has shown, even in two-party political systems that supposedly have issue differences between parties, much voting in support of a particular party occurs for affective reasons or – at most – group-oriented ones, and a full articulation of an issue-constrained structure of political attitudes is a comparative rarity.[61] As Converse would argue, individual voting behaviour is largely predicted by party identification, which develops cumulatively in the individual by the reinforcement process that is involved in voting for the same party at successive elections.[62] This process is obviously facilitated in a situation where the same two parties have repeatedly fought elections to the virtual exclusion of any minor parties, as happened in the nineteenth century in America. There is plentiful evidence that during most of the late nineteenth century political alignments tended usually to be highly stable,[63] and from this it may be inferred that political attachments formed early in life progressively determined most voting in America in the crucial period when the Socialist parties were seeking viability. Even the realignment in the critical election of 1896, which was important and sizeable in American terms and whose bearing on the argument being advanced here is discussed in the next section of this essay, was the work of only a minority of voters. Electoral realignment of any sort (and this is what the successful intervention of the Socialist Party would have amounted to) is likely to be infrequent in a two-party system because voters are not usually disposed psychologically to break their longstanding commitments to one or the other of the major parties; it is for this reason that third parties tend to be most successful amongst younger voters, particularly those without a strongly partisan upbringing, among whom voting for a third party induces less psychological conflict with previous behaviour.[64] Significant electoral realignment occurs only in response to a substantial jolt to the political system.[65] It is almost certainly no accident that the Socialist Party's greatest success in a Presidential race occurred in 1912 (6.0 per cent of votes cast), when one of the major parties was split and the psychology of customary allegiances was in disarray. By 1916 the two-party *status quo* had been restored and the Socialist Party's share of the total vote declined to 3.2 per cent. Nor is it an accident that considerable parts of Socialist Party strength were in rural areas among native-born workers – rural areas were less likely to have been closely controlled by the political apparatus of the major parties.

In America then, there was no pattern of incessant fissions and fusions among bourgeois political parties, as one finds in Germany, for example, in the last quarter of the nineteenth century. Germany had both a multi-party system and numerous bourgeois parties that tended to fracture on very slight political pretexts. The party that had started out in 1861 as the Deutsche Fortschrittspartei [German Progress Party] underwent four different processes of split or fusion by 1910, when it emerged as the Fortschrittliche Volkspartei [Progressive People's Party].[66] Because of such instability there was never any real danger to the incipient Socialist movement that the German working class would develop much affective identification with any of the bourgeois parties from cumulative voting for them. It is easier to break open a political system whose elements are in constant flux, and German Social Democracy was able to establish a foothold in German politics by this partially fortuitous characteristic of the system to which it sought entry. Universal male suffrage in Germany from 1867 (coinciding with the development of a salient cleavage between capital and labour) and the ill-advised attempt by Bismarck to suppress the Party between 1878 and 1890 under the Socialist Law provided the political conditions for the Party's success, especially after the Socialist Law became inoperative.[67] Moreover, even the German party came to be dominated by reformist tendencies that caused the radical Michels much anguish.[68] One major effect of the Socialist Law, as historians of the Party now recognise,[69] was to contribute to the inevitable onset of reformism. The real split between reformists and revolutionaries became obvious only in the early twentieth century, but, although the triumph of reformism belies some nineteenth-century views on the supposed revolutionary character of the German working class, the readiness of this class to embrace social-democratic attitudes cannot be denied.

In Great Britain the incipient Labour movement faced political hurdles that were very similar to those faced in America. There was an entrenched two-party system that largely maintained its two-party facade to the British electorate – even if it had sometimes been prone to show irregular fissures at the parliamentary level, in part because of the behaviour of Irish Nationalists. Britain also had a trade-union movement which, despite any marginal change that may have been introduced from the late 1880s onwards by the general labour unions, was still largely opposed to overt political action by the working class, as distinct from economic action by privileged parts of it.[70] The level of social-democratic awareness in this period among the British working class must have been nugatory, and Hobsbawm even goes so far as to say that 'between 1850 and 1880 it would have been hard to find a British-born citizen who called himself a socialist in our sense, let alone a Marxist'.[71] In 1887 one writer – clearly far from sympathetic to Socialist aspirations, but probably correct in his assessment of the situation – remarked on the pronounced German presence in the leaderships of some Socialist groups in London and asserted further that, even in areas of the East End of London where they had some popular support, Socialist groups dared not risk measuring their popularity, or their lack of it, in an election.[72] Also in 1887 another writer described the population of England as 'decidedly the most strongly anti-Socialist in the world'.[73] Robert Roberts depicts the political consciousness of the working-class population of Salford in 1906 and its attitude to the general election of that year in terms that speak volumes for the lack of political awareness among the population to whom Socialism was supposedly directed:

Our district voted solidly Conservative except for once in the famous election of 1906, when fear that the Tories' tariff reform policy might increase the price of food alarmed the humble voter. A Conservative victory, it was widely bruited, would mean the 'little loaf', a Liberal win, the 'big loaf'. These were politics the poor could understand! ... The overwhelming majority of unskilled workers remained politically illiterate still. The less they had to conserve the more conservative in spirit they showed themselves. Wages paid and hours worked might spark off discussion at the pub and street corner, but such things were often talked of like the seasons – as if no one could expect to have any influence on their vagaries. Many were genuinely grateful to an employer for being kind enough to use their services at all. Voting Conservative, they felt at one with him.[74]

In fact, by 1898 there was the first labour majority on a local borough council – in West Ham, where control was taken by a coalition of Radicals, the Irish and the Social Democratic Federation[75] – and labour candidates did have some significant successes in parts of London from the turn of the century. Even so, these successes were in a sense exceptional, and Hobsbawm attributes them to the fact that, somewhat unusually, the working class of the poorer sections of east London moved from an apolitical consciousness to one that encouraged support for Labour candidates, but without passing through the phase of Liberal Radicalism (often based on religious dissent) or Labour Sectarianism that in the English context characterised the political development of more affluent and settled parts of the working class in the late nineteenth century. Hobsbawm says that areas south of the river Thames were slower to support Labour candidates and remained loyal to Liberalism till the 1920s.[76] The similar reluctance of Durham miners to depart from their Liberal Dissenting traditions to follow Labour, as recently reported by Moore, is another example of the slowness with which social-democratic attitudes followed objective class conditions.[77]

Thus, the dilatory pace at which the Labour Party established itself on a large scale in Britain is at least partly a result of the same situation that condemned the American Socialist movement to such electoral travail in the early years of this century – the difficulty of breaking down the dispositions that had been instilled into voters by an ongoing two-party system. On the one hand, it is impossible to dispute the fact that social-democratic perspectives were barely developed in the British working class at a time when they were apparently well established in the working classes of, for example, Germany and – in different form – France and Italy. On the other hand, however, it is unfair to interpret this as being entirely due to some innate spirit of deference in the British working class, as opposed to the alleged radical nature of the German working class; Marx and (especially) Engels were frequently inclined to make condescending remarks to this effect.[78] However, German writers such as Michels[79] and (elsewhere) Sombart himself[80] were much less sanguine about the revolutionary perspectives of the German working class, and it must be remembered that in Britain neither the political system nor the trade-union movement did much to encourage the development of social-democratic attitudes, let alone Socialist ones.

It is therefore indisputable that a considerable crisis was needed to break the power that a two-party system had to repress the expression of social-democratic politics and, although the actual role of the First World War in explaining the final success of the Labour Party in Britain is still a contested one,[81] even a sceptic of the war's effect would probably be ready to agree that it played a contributing role, if not necessarily the crucial one, in promoting conditions that bred support for the British Labour Party. The war's impact was certainly such that never again was the British working class the captive of the sorts of imperialist and jingoistic attitudes that, as Robert Roberts argues, were so powerful in shaping its political orientations before 1914.[82]

Even in emphasising the effect of the war, it should not be forgotten that the Labour Party received considerable assistance on its road to viability from the collapse of the Liberal Party. However, whether it was the war or the Liberals' split that enabled the Labour Party finally to succeed, one or both of these factors did provide the vital dislocation of the previous two-party arrangement that was a prerequisite to success.[83] In America, on the other hand, the Socialist Party was favoured with no such similar good fortune, and during the make-or-break period when the Party had either to succeed or to go under, the two-party system always recovered from any threats to its equilibrium.

THE NATURE OF ELECTORAL REALIGNMENT IN THE UNITED STATES, 1896–1916

The British experience therefore validates the argument that a profound crisis of some sort – whether the dislocation be economic, social or political – is needed before a social-democratic party can take root in an ongoing two-party system which is already buttressed by a developed network of alignments and by a stable pattern of affiliations. While, as has been pointed out, the American political system had a high degree of stability, it would be a mistake to imply that it was totally static. During the 1890s, and culminating in the Presidential election of 1896, the political system underwent a substantial electoral realignment, at least at the Presidential level.[84] Although this of course occurred before the Socialist Party of America was formed as a viable political force, it is instructive to explore the possibility that this realignment had some subsequent effect on the Party's failure.

In the 1890s the United States experienced just the sort of economic crisis that provided an opportunity for a radical movement to attract and maintain support, but Populism, the movement that actually benefited from this crisis, represented a type of radicalism that was difficult for the average urban worker to accept. While this is not the place to enter into the extensive debate on the nature of Populism,[85] it can be asserted unequivocally that this was an agrarian movement with its strongest support among impoverished farmers of the South, hard-pressed farmers in the western states of the Middle West such as Kansas and the Dakotas, and in the silver-mining Mountain states. More important, whether or not one subscribes to Hofstadter's view concerning the intolerant features of Populism, there is overwhelming evidence both of the movement's strength among Protestants[86] and of a tendency towards religious fundamentalism on the part of some of its leaders. The fundamentalist views of William Jennings Bryan, who ran on a joint Populist-Democratic ticket in the 1896 Presidential election (as well as on the Democratic ticket in the Presidential races of 1900 and 1908), are well known.[87] Moreover, when Silver Democrats captured the Democratic Party for Bryan during Grover Cleveland's second term, they stamped on it a character that it was to retain with little change almost for the next thirty years.[88] The organised Democratic Party became largely a repository for rural provincialism and Protestant fundamentalism until at least 1924. In the 1896 election the effect of the capture of the Democratic Party by this particular interest was dramatic. As one author has written:

> The presidential race in 1896 produced equally strong shifts in sentiment. Western states, customarily with large Republican majorities, veered to the Democrats by twenty or thirty percentage points, while eastern states, especially in the cities, swung towards the Republicans by almost as much. . . . The agrarian-oriented Democratic party gained in western silver-mining states, in the wheat belt, and in many rural sections even of the East; it lost heavily in the cities and in other areas of large industrial employment such as the upper peninsula of Michigan. The Republican gains of 1894, which continued over into 1896, were largely urban. The precise nature of this new strength is not yet clear, but it appears to have been composed largely of workers and immigrants who blamed the Democrats for the depression and who were suspicious of the economic interests and the nativist tinges of the farmers.[89]

Other writers have documented how Bryan's brand of radicalism, with its agrarian and fundamentalist bias, alienated numerous Roman

Catholic voters, often in urban areas, and pushed them towards the
Republican Party.[90] Thus, because what passed in the 1890s as
American radicalism had a specific character that urban workers often
found hard to accept[91] and because it became associated with the
Democratic Party through the events of 1896, the paradoxical result
was that many of these workers were driven to support the more
conservative of the two major parties in 1896. It can be argued that
the peculiar character of the 1896 realignment increased the already
parlous difficulties that the Socialist Party had in appealing to the
large urban and immigrant vote that would be crucial to its success.
The reason for this is not that the Populist-Democratic episode of
1896 gave radicalism an unsavoury reputation but rather that it made
significant numbers of potential Socialist voters additionally wary of
departing from their Republican partisanship through a fear that such
a move might permit a Democratic victory. It is fair to argue that the
average Catholic immigrant voter would be reluctant to vote for a
Socialist ticket at the best of times, especially given the anti-Socialist
bias in his religion,[92] but he would be even more reluctant to do so if
the short-term result might be to elect to office some avenging fundamentalist like Bryan.

While the electorally crucial majority of potential Socialist voters
were frightened off by this prospect, there is plenty of evidence that
numerous old Populists found their way into the Socialist Party,
especially in the South.[93] However, these were a minority and did not
amount to the vital electoral base that the Party needed if it was to
succeed. It is almost as if the Socialist Party tried to break open the
two-party system during just the period when this system was least
vulnerable.

Alignments formed in 1896 persisted at the national level till at least
1912, when the Socialist Party achieved its greatest Presidential success.
However, in 1916 – when for the first time Eugene Debs did not run as
Socialist Presidential candidate and the little-known Allan L. Benson
headed the ticket – Woodrow Wilson managed to capture crucial
proportions of the labour vote in his bid for re-election.[94]

THE SOCIALIST PARTY OF AMERICA AND THE FIRST WORLD WAR

What of the event that in Britain, as it was argued, substantially
contributed to the growth of social-democratic attitudes and to the
consequent rise of the Labour Party? Why did it not play a similar
dislocating role in the United States?

In the short term the First World War did bring the Socialist Party
some considerable boosts in electoral support. Among German-Ameri-
cans, even those who were normally of the most conservative political

dispositions, the Socialist Party on some occasions collected considerable numbers of votes because of its opposition to America's participation in the war.[95] However, such successes were transitory and may have contributed something to the Party's problems after the war. For the war did not produce in America the profound changes of mood and social structure that occurred in Britain. America's participation was too short-lived for the full impact of the war's horrors to be felt there. It was as if America's late entry meant that the war was over while the country was still in a jingoistic, patriotic frame of mind and, indeed, several writers have used the image of *coitus interruptus* to describe the fact that the country was still fired with militant patriotism but had no war to fight.[96]

When it was combined with the widespread fear among the American middle class that foreign radicals would attempt to bring about the sort of revolutionary situation that had occurred in Russia and was attempted in Germany, this situation paved the way for the post-war period of repression of the Left from which the Socialist Party was never able to recover. The Party, in any case already split by now into various factions, was totally unable to mount effective resistance against the repression represented by the Red Scare of 1919 and 1920.[97] The American working class and its leaders were powerless against the repression represented by the Red Scare of 1919 and the rise of a working-class labour party, the First World War paved the way in America for middle-class nativist intolerance[98] in what Higham calls 'the tribal twenties'.[99] The political phenomenon in these years was not the rise of a labour party, even if Robert M. La Follette's 1924 Progressive Party candidacy did attract some of the old Socialist Party vote;[100] the political event of note was the rise and success of the Ku Klux Klan. It was a long way removed from Socialism.

C.T.H.

Translators' and Editor's Notes and Acknowledgements

Some comments must be made on the numerous conventions followed by us in translating and presenting some of the less straightforward aspects of Sombart's text.

1. Sombart introduces numerous passages or phrases quoted from English and, in doing so, he follows variable practices. Some are quoted in English, while others have been translated by him into German from their English sources. There is usually no obvious reason why Sombart should have followed one usage rather than the other in any particular case, and almost all such passages or phrases have been given in English without editorial comment on whether Sombart's text gave them in their original English or translated into German.

2. Sombart is also given to introducing occasional words or phrases in quotation marks; some of these are in English, while others have been translated into German from a parent English word or phrase. Some of them are attributable to particular sources, while others are not so attributable or are merely stock phrases. Furthermore, in common with frequent German practice in this period, Sombart often uses quotation marks to imply irony or sarcasm. We have treated these various phrases as follows: all such phrases are given in English; if a phrase is attributable to a particular source, it has been enclosed in quotation marks, but no distinction has usually been made in the treatment of English phrases quoted by Sombart in English and those that he has translated into German, nor has any editorial comment been made on this; if Sombart has quoted a phrase in English or in German that is not obviously attributable to a particular source, we have usually included it in our translation without quotation marks, which would normally have added nothing to its meaning – the only major exception to this being those phrases that clearly have a distinctive or restricted usage and that Sombart then goes on immediately to expand upon or define in some way. Those special cases where Sombart has used quotation marks to imply irony or sarcasm have usually also been rendered in the translation with quotation marks, although nouns so affected have also sometimes been preceded by 'so-called' and the quotation marks may then have been omitted; the translators' judgement about readability and a desire to be as consistent as possible

with normal English punctuation convention were the criteria by which one rather than the other procedure was followed in any particular case.

3.   Sombart's text is plentifully endowed with spaced type, which is the earlier German equivalent of italicisation. Because spaced type was used much more frequently in German texts of the period in question than italics would have been in equivalent English writing, we have ignored many of Sombart's uses of it, although his emphasis has sometimes been incorporated into the diction of the translation. Sometimes, where the occasion seemed to call for it (and such occasions were few), we resorted to italics in our translation.

4.   Sombart also has an irritating *penchant* for introducing words and phrases from what seem like half the dead and live languages of Europe: French, Spanish, Italian, and Latin in particular. Most such usages seem pure *hubris* and pretension (calling the 'free land' of the unsettled West *terra libera*, for example), and so their English translations have been given without any indication of the form of the original. In very rare cases the original has been retained in the translation; where the word in question is now accepted as an English word (for instance, torero), it is used without italics, and where it is not so accepted, it has been italicised.

5.   Whether or not and how to translate German titles into English are not the simple issues they might seem; standard translations do not always exist, and when they do not, confusion can be caused by the use of one particular word rather than another in the English title. (The German *freisinnig* is a good example of a word that is found in various titles and is amenable to different English translations.) We have therefore preferred to retain German names where possible and the titles of major German political parties, of what we considered were comparatively well-known organisations of various sorts, of journals, and of magazines, are given throughout in German, although our English translation of their titles is given in brackets when they are first mentioned in the text or notes. It was considered that items of these sorts are well enough known by their German title to most interested English readers, even to those not reading German. They accordingly receive their primary index entry under their German title, while under our English translation of their title there is a secondary entry that refers the reader to the primary entry. On the other hand, personal occupational titles, any titles of German government departments that occur in the text, and titles of some lesser-known German trade unions have been given in English translation in the text, since their native form is less likely to be generally recognised. Correspondingly, their primary index entry is under their translated English title and the secondary one is under their German title.

6. Those places in what is now Poland and was in 1906 part of the German Empire whose names have both a German and a Polish form have been named throughout in the German form. However, the Polish name is given in parentheses when the place is first mentioned. Further, many of the places unlikely to be known to most English readers receive a short editorial notation where it was considered this would be of assistance to them.

7. Sombart's original contains numerous references in a comparative context to *bei uns* [literally, 'among us'] – usually meaning 'in Germany' or occasionally 'in Europe'. We have translated most such references as either 'in Germany' or 'in Europe' in order to avoid any confusion for British or American readers that might have arisen from a literal translation. The reader should bear in mind the extensive geographical area covered by Germany, or the German Empire, in 1906. *Drüben* and *da drüben* ['over there'] have been translated as 'in America'; similarly *die Union* has mostly been translated as 'America' or 'the United States', since its literal meaning of 'the Union' would usually have sounded very odd to English ears. (Incidentally, it is perhaps slightly ironic that in the contemporary German of the Federal Republic *drüben* has become and still is a euphemism for the German Democratic Republic!)

8. The book version of *Why is there no Socialism in the United States?* was apparently transcribed and printed by the publishers without any of the editorial changes that would have been necessary to hide the fact that its source was a series of discrete essays in the *Archiv für Sozialwissenschaft und Sozialpolitik*. Thus, the book makes an occasional cryptic reference to 'our journal' (i.e., the *Archiv*) and talks of completing the work 'in later issues of this journal'. In the translation such phrases have been rendered by something more appropriate to a book.

9. A few of the phrases and sentences in Sombart's text (some of them given in parentheses) which he added to embellish or clarify some point he was making have been reduced by the Translators to the status of notes, when their inclusion in the main body of the translation would have impeded readability.

10. In Sombart's original all tables are presented without serial numbering in a manner that intends them to blend into the flow of the text. In conformity with present conventions, all but the least intrusive smaller tables have been extracted from the text, sequentially numbered, and given a separate title. References to specifically numbered tables have been added to the translation.

11. Sombart's occasionally careless system of referencing has been rationalised, updated in style, and made to conform as much as possible to contemporary English literary practice. Page numbers have frequently been added in cases where Sombart himself did not bother.

12. In the Notes following the translation Sombart's original footnotes and those added by the Editor have been arranged sequentially together according to the order of their appearance in the text, since this procedure seemed most convenient to the prospective reader. All notes added by the Editor begin with '*Ed. –* ', with the exception of notes on the Editor's Introductory Essay, where such notation is clearly redundant. Notes of comment appeared by the Editor to some of Sombart's original notes are enclosed in brackets and have ' *– Ed.*' immediately before the final bracket. Similar conventions have been applied to the notation of tables in the translation.

13. The final comment should be on the modes of presenting different currencies. Sombart, of course, uses both American dollars and German marks, sometimes converting the former to the latter and sometimes not. The Editor has therefore added conversions of dollars in marks where such conversions were considered to be of likely assistance to the reader. The capital M abbreviates for marks both in the tables and in those places in the text where readability required that conversion values be presented as unobtrusively as possible. It is hoped that the British reader will not be aggrieved that sterling equivalents have not also been added; this would have been too cumbersome. If that reader wishes to make the necessary calculations, he or she may wish to know that at the time Sombart wrote this book £1 sterling was worth about 20 marks and about $4·80. Would that it still were!

Numerous people have generously assisted us in several ways, either with the preparation of the translation and the editorial notes or by commenting on the initial draft of the Editor's Introductory Essay. We should especially like to thank Geoffery Windsor of the Department of German, University of Bristol, for his valuable advice on occasional problematic passages of Sombart's text, as well as the Editor's father, Gerald Husbands, for his extensive comments on an initial version of the translation; whatever merit in terms of style and diction the final version may have is due partly to him, although he is in no way responsible for any remaining errors or inelegancies of style. In addition, thanks for assistance on particular matters are due to: Bernard Alford of the Department of Economic and Social History, University of Bristol; Gerald Cullinan of the National Association of Letter Carriers, Washington, D.C.; Lawrence M. DeBreto of the Minnesota AFL-CIO, St. Paul, Minnesota; Glen E. Holt of Washington University, St. Louis, Missouri; Iris Minor of the Department of Economic and Social History, University of Bristol; Robert W. Newell of the American Flint Glass Workers' Union of North America, Toledo, Ohio; Maxwell Powers of Greenwich House, New York; Joseph P. Ricciarelli of The Granite Cutters' International Association of America, Quincy, Massachusetts; Dr. Ritter of the Bundesarchiv, Coblenz; Diane Weissman of Cambridge, Massachusetts; and various members of the Department of Sociology, University of Bristol – especially Kieran Flanagan, who made various particularly useful contributions to the final product.

Certain members of staff of the Wills Memorial Library, University of Bristol, have been of unfailing assistance in tracing fugitive references; in this regard we should like to thank Clive Ward, divisional librarian for social sciences, and Michael Taperell, divisional librarian for modern languages. The staff of the Inter-Library Loan Service were extremely helpful in securing highly recondite source material. Many of these services seemed to us to be above and beyond the call of duty, although the people concerned performed them with enthusiasm and alacrity. In addition, we should also like to thank the staffs of the following libraries, which were all visited to consult necessary source material: the Universitätsbibliothek, Tübingen, Federal Republic of Germany; the Nationale Forschungs- und Gedenkstätten der klassischen deutschen Literatur in Weimar, German Democratic Republic; the British Museum Library; and the British Library of Political and Economic Science at the London School of Economics and Political Science.

Patricia Lees, Sandra Richards and Margaret Rowe have between them typed several versions of the manuscript with skill and devotion. To them final thanks are due.

P.M.H.
C.T.H.

Bristol, July 1975

INTRODUCTION

1 Capitalism in the United States

The United States of America is capitalism's land of promise. All conditions needed for its complete and pure development were first fulfilled here. In no other country and among no other people was capitalism favoured with circumstances that permitted it to develop to the most advanced state.

In no other country is it possible to accumulate capital so rapidly. There are several reasons for this. The United States is rich in precious metals: North America produces a third of all the silver and a quarter of all the gold in the world. It is rich in fertile soils: the Mississippi Plain comprises about five times as much as the best humus soil as do the black earth districts of southern Russia and Hungary together. It is rich in abundant deposits of useful minerals that today give three times as much output as any European deposits. As a result of these characteristics and by virtue of the developed state of its man-made technology, America is more suited than any other country to provide capitalism with the means for conquering the world. The United States now produces almost as much pig iron as all other countries in the world put together – in 1905 twenty-three million tons as against twenty-nine and a half million tons produced by the rest of the world. The United States is more suited than any other country for capitalist expansion. The Mississippi Plain is ideally positioned for economically viable agriculture and for the unlimited growth of transportation: it is an area of 3.8 million square kilometres, therefore approximately seven times the size of the German Empire,[1] without any barrier to communication and, by way of a bonus, it is already provided with several natural means of transportation. On the Atlantic coast there are fifty-five good harbours that have waited thousands of years for capitalist exploitation. The United States therefore has a vast market area, and compared with America a European state is scarcely more than a medieval city and its dependent territory. The striving after endless expansion, so fundamental to every capitalist economy, can be freely fulfilled for the first time in these North American expanses that stretch far beyond where the eye can see. Such striving found itself constantly checked within the restrictive confines of Europe, and doctrines of free trade and trade agreements could always only be poor substitutes for it. One can truly say that if one wanted to construct the ideal country for the development of capitalism on the lines required by this economic system, such a country could take on the dimensions and particular characteristics only of the United States.

And what of the people? Men have been moulded for centuries as if in a task of conscious preparation, and the most recent generations of them were appointed to pave the way for capitalism's invasion of the virgin terrain of America. Finished with Europe, they moved over to the New World with the will to carve themselves a new life based on principles of pure reason. They had left all remnants of their European character behind in their former homes, together with all superfluous romanticism and sentimentality. They had left everything of their feudal artisan existence, as well as all sense of traditionalism, and had taken across with them only what was necessary and of service to the development of a capitalist economy, namely a powerful, unremitting energy and an ideology that turned activity in the pursuit of capitalist aims into a duty, as if it were a response to a command from God to the faithful. Max Weber has demonstrated in our journal[2] the close connections that exist between the postulates of the puritan Protestant ethic and the requirements of a rational capitalist economy. Furthermore, as a resource to those leading the implementation of this new economic system came wage labourers from a population apparently also made in order to develop capitalism to the most advanced form. For centuries labour was scarce and therefore expensive, which compelled employers to devise its most rational utilisation and thereby fully to control how their businesses came to be organised. It compelled them also to think systematically of making labour superfluous by means of 'labour-saving machinery'. Thus began a drive towards the highest technological perfection, something that was never able to happen to the same degree in a country with an old civilisation. Following that, when the most advanced forms of economic and technological organisation had been created, endless multitudes of people poured in, who could increasingly be used only as resource material in the service of capitalist interests, as the possibilities of existence outside the capitalist nexus were reduced. It is known that during recent decades at least half-a-million people have entered the United States each year and that the number of arrivals has risen to three-quarters of a million or more in many years.

In fact, nowhere on earth have the economic system and the essence of capitalism reached as full a development as in North America.

Nowhere else is acquisitiveness as clearly seen as it is there, nor are the desire for gain and the making of money for its own sake so exclusively the be-all and end-all of every economic activity. Every minute of life is filled with this striving, and only death ends the insatiable yearning for profit. Making a living from anything other than capitalism is as good as unknown in the United States, and an economic rationalism of a purity unknown in any European country serves this desire for gain. Capitalism presses forward remorselessly, even when its path is strewn with corpses. The data that provide us with information on the extent of railway accidents in the United States are merely symbolic of this. The [New York] *Evening Post* has calculated that from 1898 to 1900 the number of people killed on the American railways was 21,847, which is equal to the number of Englishmen killed in the Boer War during the same period, including those who died of illnesses in military hospitals.[3] In 1903 the number of people killed on the American railways was 11,006, while in Austria in the same year it was 172. If one standardises these figures per hundred kilometres and per million passengers, one finds that accidents happened in America at a rate of 3.4 per hundred kilometres, as opposed to 0.86 in Austria, and that they happened at a rate of 19 per million passengers in America, compared with one of 0.99 per million passengers in Austria.[4] This economic and industrial system and its accompanying technology are employed relentlessly to guarantee the highest profit. While in Germany we see public indignation when a colliery shuts down one mine or another, year in and year out the management of the American trust determines with great equanimity which enterprises are to be worked and which left idle. In this way capitalism readily creates the economic organisation after its own image: this is shown in location of industry, structure of individual businesses, size and shape of factories, organisation of trade and commerce, and in co-ordination between production and marketing of goods. When one knows that everything has been deliberately made for a rational purpose, one is obliged to conclude from this that everything has been deliberately made to suit capitalist interests.

The financial rewards of this could not fail to appear. In terms of her capital base – that is, the amount of her capital accumulation – the United States (despite her comparative youth) is today way beyond all other countries. The yardsticks by which one can measure the state of the capitalist surge are the numbers of bank returns. In 1882 7304 banks reported to the Comptroller of the Currency, but in 1904 there were 18,844 of them. The banks of 1882 had capital assets of $712,100,000 and those of 1904 had assets of $1,473,904,674. In 1882 bank deposits amounted to $2,785,407,000, and in 1904 they were $10,448,545,990.[5] The total banking power of the United States, made up of capital, surplus profits, deposits, and circulation, is estimated by the same source to be $13,826,000,000, while the corresponding figures for all the other countries in the world taken together are reckoned to amount to only $19,781,000,000.[6] The amount of capital that has flowed into industry alone within the last twenty years should not therefore surprise us. According to the Census, the amounts of capital invested in manufactures in 1880, 1890 and 1900 were as follows:[7]

1880 : $2,790,272,606
1890 : $6,525,050,759
1900 : $9,831,486,500

It is known also that the United States is the country where the model of the Marxist theory of development is being most precisely fulfilled, since the concentration of capital has reached the stage (as described in the famous penultimate chapter of *Capital*) at which the final cataclysm of the capitalist world is near at hand.[8] The most recent statistics on the number and size of the trusts give the following striking picture.[9]

There are seven 'greater' industrial trusts into which have been combined 1528 concerns that were formerly independent of each other. The capital concentrated in them amounts to $2,662,700,000. The largest of these seven giants is the United States Steel Corporation with nominal capital assets of $1,370,000,000, and the second largest is the Consolidated Tobacco Co. with only $502, 900,000. These are followed by 298 'lesser' industrial trusts that control 3426 plants and together have at their disposal capital assets in excess of $4,055,000,000. Thirteen industrial trusts with 334 plants and $528,000,000 in capital assets are at present in the process of being formed, so that the total number of industrial trusts amounts to 318, with 5288 plants and $7,246,000,000 in capital assets. To these should be added 111 of the 'greater' franchise trusts (such as telephone, telegraph, gas, electricity, and street-car operations) with 1336 individual subsidiaries and $3,735,000,000 in capital. And now comes the *pièce de résistance*: the group of the large railroad concerns. There are six of these, of whom none comprises less than a thousand million dollars. Together they have at their disposal over $9,017,000,000, and they control 790 subsidiaries. Finally, we have yet to mention the 'independent' railroad companies with capital assets of $380,000,000.

If one adds together all these giant combinations, within which by far the largest part of American economic life is included, one arrives at the enormous total of 8664 'controlled' subsidiaries and $20,379,000,000 in capital assets. Just think! Eighty-five thousand million marks concentrated in the hands of a few capitalists![10]

Perhaps one may best recognise how dominant the capitalist system is by examining the American social structure, which no longer contains any feature of non-capitalist origin. Nowhere do we meet residues of the pre-capitalist classes whose presence in greater or lesser degree gives every European society a characteristic feature. There is no feudal aristocracy, and instead the capitalist magnates have the field to themselves. The time that Marx could foresee only in his imagination when he wrote *Capital* has already arrived in the United States. Here the 'eminent spinners', the 'extensive sausage makers', and the 'influential shoe black dealers', as well as the railway barons, force the people to pay them homage. James Bryce has written: 'When the master of one of the greatest Western lines travels towards the Pacific on his palace car, his journey is like a royal progress. Governors of States and Territories bow before him; legislatures receive him in solemn session; cities and towns seek to propitiate him, for has he not the means of making or marring a city's fortunes?'[11]

There is no half nor wholly feudal peasantry or class of artisans. In their place is a versatile group of farmers and a handful of petty capitalist entrepreneurs in trade and industry. Both of these classes have been heavily tarred with the capitalist brush. They are both led on by a search for profit, as they build up their businesses rationally and with due regard for economy. Also, the organisation of this entire labour force into jobs following the dictates of present-day capitalism lets the occupational sectors at the centre of the capitalist nexus predominate more as the years go by. Today agriculture, even in a country that is still half a colony, makes up a smaller part of the occupational structure than in Germany, and the proportion in trade and transportation, which is now considerably larger than in Germany, is increasing quickly. From 1880 to 1900 the proportion of the gainfully employed population in agricultural pursuits in the United States fell from 44.3 to 35.7 per cent (as compared with 36.12 per cent in Germany), and the proportion of persons engaged in trade and transportation rose from 10.8 to 16.4 per cent (as compared with 11.39 per cent in Germany).[12]

At the same time the entire life-style of the people increasingly adopted a manner suited to capitalism.

Today the United States is already – and I repeat, despite its youth – a country of cities, or more exactly, a country of large cities.[13] I do not mean this only in the numerical sense, although the statistics also make the extent of its urbanisation clearly recognisable. Actually, calculating for the country as a whole, the urban proportion of the population today is not quite as great as in Germany: for example, in 1900 41.2 per cent lived in places of over 2500 inhabitants in the United States, as against 54.3 per cent living in places of over 2000 inhabitants in Germany. However, this is not the complete picture. First, the proportion of the population of the United States living in large cities of over 100,000 inhabitants is already greater today than anywhere else in the world, with the exception of England. At 18.7 per cent it approaches a fifth of the entire population. Second, the shifting of the population towards the cities is taking place at a rapid pace; between 1890 and 1900 the urban portion of the population rose from 29.2 to 41.2 per cent, as mentioned above. Third, the low total number is explained by the numerical domination of the South, where there are relatively few towns. If one considers only the Eastern states of the country, one finds there only 31.8 per cent of the population living in rural areas, as against 35.8 per cent in large cities of over 100,000 inhabitants.[14] However, when I say that the United States is a land of cities, I mean it in a deeper and inner sense that particularly expresses why I am relating urbanism and capitalism. I mean it in the sense of a type of settlement that differs from spontaneous growth, rests on a purely rational basis, is defined from purely quantitative perspective and represents as it were the deeper meaning of the word 'urban'. Only in the most infrequent cases does the European city fully incorporate this idea. The latter has mostly grown spontaneously, and yet it is basically only an enlarged village, the essence of which is reflected in its appearance. What has Nuremburg in common with Chicago? Nothing, except the superficial characteristic that in both places many people relying for their sustenance on supplies from outside live concentrated next to one another. In matters of the spirit there is no resemblance. The former is a village-like, spontaneous formation, while the latter is a real city artificially set up according to principles of rationality, in which (as Tönnies would say) all traces of *Gemeinschaft* have been extinguished and pure *Gesellschaft* has been established. However, if in old Europe the city takes after the countryside (or rather has done till now) and has brought the character of the latter to itself, in the United States, on the contrary, the flat countryside is basically only an urban settlement that lacks cities. The same rational intelligence that created the box-like cities has gone out across the countryside with a surveyor's chain, and following a single uniform plan, has divided this entire enormous area into exactly equal squares. From the first moment on this could not but rule out any idea of natural and spontaneous settlement.

Nor, for that matter, does the United States lack the feature that has always been conspicuous in the structure of a society resting on capitalist foundations – namely, the tremendous contrasts between wealth and poverty. The United States does not have any exact statistics on income and wealth, but we do possess several attempts to estimate the distribution of wealth which, though not to be regarded as perfect statements, may none the less lay claim to some value since they have been undertaken conscientiously and with regard for all available material.[15] According to these sources, out of total private wealth, which was estimated at sixty billion dollars in 1890,[16] thirty-three billion, or 54.8 per cent, was in the hands of 125,000 families, who represented 1 per cent of all families, while 6,250,000 families (50 per cent) were without property.

At the present time the ultimate distribution of total wealth may still be taking shape, but it may be said indisputably that the absolute contrasts between poor and rich are nowhere in the world anything like as great as they are in the United States. Above all, this is because the rich over there are so very much richer than the same group in Germany. In America there are certainly more people who own 1,000,000,000 marks than there are people owning 100,000,000 marks in Germany. Anyone who has ever been in Newport, the Baiae of New York,[17] will have picked up the impression that in America having a million is commonplace. There is certainly no other place in the world where the princely palace of the very grandest style is so obviously the standard type of residence, while anyone who has wandered once through Tiffany's department store in New York will always sense something akin to the odour of poverty in even the most splendid luxury businesses of large European cities. Because Tiffany's also has branches in Paris and London,[18] it can serve excellently for drawing comparisons between the extravagance and therefore the wealth of the top four hundred families in the three countries concerned. The managers of the New York head office told me that most of the merchandise they offer for sale in New York comes from Europe, where it is made specially for Tiffany's of New York. However, it is completely out of the question that a store in Europe – even Tiffany's own branches in Paris and London – would stock merchandise at prices such as it would fetch in New York. Only in New York are the dearest items said to be brought in for the woman shopper.

On the other hand, the misery of the slums in the large American cities finds its real equal only in the East End of London. Robert Hunter's book, *Poverty*, recently appeared and, although this is not up to the quality of Engels's *The Condition of the Working Class* (despite what Florence Kelley has stated in a review[19]), it is none the less excellently suited to fulfil the purpose that it sets itself – which is to throw light into the depths of the misery in America's large cities. The author has lived for years as a settlement worker in the most infamous quarters of various large industrial cities, he has therefore gained his own impressions, and also he knows how best to give life to the rich literary and statistical material on which he has drawn. He estimates now that the number of people in the United States living below the poverty line, that is, those who are underfed, underclothed or badly housed, totals in times of average prosperity ten million, of whom four million are public paupers. In 1897 over two million people in New York may have received relief.[20] In times of economic expansion, as in 1903, 14 per cent of the population of that city lives in distress, and in bad times, as in 1897, the figure is 20 per cent. From this it may therefore be estimated that, if one also counts the deserving poor, the number living in poverty in New York and in other large cities would seldom – so the author thinks – fall below 25 per cent. In Manhattan, the main part of New York, in the notably prosperous year of 1903, 60,463 families (14 per cent of the total) were evicted from their homes.

One in every ten persons who die in New York is buried at public expense in Potter's Field.[21]

Finally, however, there is yet another infallible sign of the highly developed state of capitalism in the United States; this is the distinctiveness of its national character.

Does the American national character show features that are found universally throughout the entire country? One might doubt it in view of the enormity of the area the country covers, and people who set themselves up as so-called experts on American conditions warn against saying that there is something common to everyone in the country. They say that the differences are as great as those between the individual peoples of Europe and that the American nation really inhabits a continent and not a single country. This wisdom is only superficial. It is true that everything which concerns the character of the countryside is extraordinarily varied in the United States. On the other hand, all institutional matters and in particular the character of the people display a quite startling uniformity. This has been established often enough by real experts, such as Bryce and others, and to anybody who come into contact with American life and who has the opportunity to look under the surface it must stand out as a special characteristic of the nation. Bryce has convincingly set forth the reasons for this striking conformity in all public institutions in the various individual states of the Union, but what is the source of the homogeneity of the American national character? Or should we not look for an explanation of it, but satisfy ourselves with hypothesising an idiosyncratic 'American spirit' that dropped out of the blue on to this chosen people for no particular reason and contrary to principles of social causation? We shall be all the less ready to accept this when we cannot really believe in the uniqueness of that exquisite 'American spirit'.[22] On closer inspection, we think that we recognise it as an old acquaintance who is so familiar to us on Lombard Street or in Berlin West.[23] Over in America, however, this acquaintance has grown into a purer type and is of more imposing dimensions. We realise that we must seek its source in particular environmental circumstances, as these developed first in Europe and later, but more fully, in America. At the same time we shall thereby explain its uniformity.

However, anybody who examines closely the peculiarities of the American national character must see that its particularly distinctive features have their roots in the capitalist organisation of economic life. I want to try to make this credible.

Without doubt and as often recognised, life in a capitalist milieu accustoms the mind to reduce all transactions in the sphere of economic life to money or to para-economic relationships, as is a requisite of this type of economic organisation; that is, one takes monetary value as the criterion of measurement, particularly in the evaluation of things and of people. It is evident that, when conduct of this kind becomes adopted and continues for generations, sensitivity for merely quali- tatively determined value must gradually diminish. As far as objects are concerned, feeling is lost for anything that is merely beautiful or perfectly formed – that is, for anything which is specifically artistic and which cannot be defined, measured or weighed in quantitative terms. When evaluating things Americans demand that they be either functional and pleasant (as implied by the word 'comfort'), or obviously expensive. Their taste for things of material value is borne out by the fact that all décor in the United States is overdone; this applies to everything from ladies' clothes to the reception areas of a fashionable hotel. If the amount of money that something cost is not immediately evident, then, without more ado, one includes the numerical money-value in one's allusions to the valued object. 'Have you seen the $50,000 Rembrandt in Mr X's house yet?' is an often heard question. Or, in a newspaper report, 'This morning Carnegie's $500,000 yacht arrived in the harbour from such and such a place.' Among human beings it is natural that one's financial property and income should form the basis of how one is evaluated. Feeling for the unmeasureable uniqueness of personality and for the essence of the individual disappears.

However, one cannot now overlook the fact that this habit of destroying all qualities by relating them to their measurable monetary value also influences judgements of value in situations where – with the best intentions – it is no longer possible to apply the monetary standard. This habit cannot but evoke a high regard for quantity as such, as an attitude of mind that is encountered in the very centre of the American soul. The perspicacious Bryce calls this 'a tendency to mistake bigness for greatness'; there is admiration for every large quantity that is measurable or weighable, whether it be the number of inhabitants of a city, the number of parcels transported, the speed of railway trains, the height of a monument, the width of a river, the frequency of suicides, or whatever. Some people have wanted to explain this 'craze for bigness', which is so characteristic of modern Americans, by means of the sheer size of their country, but why then do the Chinese or the Mongolians from the uplands of Asia not have the same characteristic? Why did the Red Indians not have it, even though they lived on the same vast continent? I put forward the view that, wherever ideas of bigness develop among such primitive peoples, those ideas have a comical character. They are based on the endlessness of the starry sky, on the boundlessness of the steppe, and what distinguishes them is precisely the fact that they cannot be quantified. The estimation of size in terms of numbers has been able to take root in man's heart only through the medium of money as em- ployed by capitalism (not through money itself, as Simmel erroneously believes[24]). The huge dimensions of the American continent have certainly encouraged this characteristic, but the feeling for numbers had first of all to be awaked before it was possible to transform geographical ideas into sizes comprehensible in numerical terms.

Anyone who has been accustomed to value only the quantity of a phenomenon will be inclined to compare two phenomena with each other in order to measure one against the other and thus to attribute to the bigger one the higher value. If one of two phenomena becomes the bigger one during a certain period of time, we call that being successful. Unfortunately the German language cannot express the ideas of both 'bigness' and 'greatness' in a single word, but the sense of something being big in quantitative terms necessarily goes hand in hand with a high estimation of its success; again, this is a conspicuous feature of the American national character. Being successful, however, means being ahead of others, becoming more, achieving more, and having more than others: in short, of being 'greater'. According to this principle the success that is valued most is that which can be expressed purely in terms of numbers, i.e., the accumulation of riches. Furthermore, even the non-merchant is assessed first of all on the strength of *how much* he has known how to make of his talent. If this test does not result in a satisfactory income, there is no alternative but to take the amount of his fame as the measure of his worth.

The particular emotional reactions being dealt with here are shown perhaps most clearly by the position that the Americans take towards sport. On this subject they are really interested only in the question of who will win. In New York I was present at a mass gathering where a match being fought out as far away as Chicago was transmitted live to the expectant crowd by telegraph as it was going on. The excitement was based only on the tension of wondering which side would win. It is the function of betting to increase this tension: by this the whole activity of sport is again cheerfully reduced to pure cash terms. Can one imagine betting in a Greek stadium? Certainly not. What above all else made everybody happy there was joy both in unquantifiable individual achievement and in personal beauty and strength, and these can be valued just as much in the loser as in the winner. Likewise, would betting be conceivable at a Spanish bull fight? Of course not. However, the women throw their jewellery and the men throw expensive clothes to the torero who knows how to deliver the lethal stroke with elegance and *grandeza*. That is artistic appreciation!

However, the particular character of judgements about value determines how the individual's will operates. If the American prays before the god of Success, he strives to lead a life acceptable to his god.[25] We therefore see in every American – beginning with the paperboy – restlessness, yearning, and compulsion to be way and beyond other people. Neither the enjoyment of life in comfort to the full nor the fine harmony of a personality at peace with itself can be the American's ideal in life; instead, this ideal is constant self-advancement. From this follow haste, restless striving, and ruthless competition in all areas, since, when all individuals are bent on success, each must aim to come ahead of the rest. Thus there begins what one might call a steeplechase, or a search for Good Fortune, as – in somewhat superficial manner – we are wont to express it. However, this steeplechase is different from all other races because the winning-post does not stay still but for ever retreats farther ahead of the advancing runners. We described this striving as restless, but perhaps limitless would be even more appropriate. Any striving after quantities must be limitless because that sort of striving recognises no limit.

This competitive psychology produces a deep-seated need for freedom of movement. One cannot view one's goal in the race of life and wish to be bound hand and foot. Hence the challenge of *laissez-faire* belongs to those American dogmas and maxims that one cannot help but encounter 'when sinking a shaft, so to speak, into an American mind', as Bryce expresses it. However, I should like to explain the general pervasiveness of this basic idea in a slightly different way from Bryce. The aversion from all official supervision from above and from all State intervention, embodied as the 'doctrine of non-interference by government with the citizen', certainly originated in a purely doctrinaire, idealistic and rational spirit among the men of 1776. Yet the modern American now cares only a little for the so-called 'exalted principles' of the framers of the constitution, since such principles have no decisive bearing upon his everyday life. If he still clings obstinately to the *laissez-faire* principle, this is because he feels instinctively that this is the only correct guideline for anyone striving for success. The American is really undoctrinaire, and he will readily sacrifice this principle if doing so does not block the path of his advancement. This may be seen from the fact that the same Americans who have written on to their national standard the 'unabridged activity of the individual'[26] sometimes have not the slightest hesitation in limiting in a quite inconsiderate manner the freedom of the individual,[27] or in setting up communist arrangements, the sight of which would make the hair of every liberal Lord Mayor in Germany stand on end.[28]

For the average American being successful means first and foremost becoming rich. This explains why that restless striving, which we recognised as an essential part of the American national character, is applied before all else to economic life. In America the best and most energetic people apply themselves to financial careers, whereas in Europe[29] they go into politics. In the mass public an excessive valuation of economic matters develops for the same reason, namely because people believe that in this sphere they can most easily reach the goal for which they strive. By economic matters I mean the capitalist economy whose symbol as it were is the stock certificate that is traded on the Stock Exchange. By participating in speculation on stocks and commodities, the mass public seeks to grab hold of the wheel of fortune where the lucky winnings are found. There is no other country on earth where the public is so involved in the business of speculation as in the United States; there is no country where the population so thoroughly wants to enjoy the fruit of capitalism.[30]

Our observations have now completed a full circle. We started with the subject of capitalism, from which we tried to derive essential elements of the American national character. We see now how the action of this national character itself contributes to the strengthening and development of the capitalist system; thus the unique American spirit is always being reborn from itself, and it is always being transformed into a purer manifestation of the *spiritus capitalisticus purus rectificatus.*

2 Socialism in the United States

What I have presented in the preceding pages was definitely not intended to describe the American economy (I hope to find the opportunity for this in later studies), and even less was it intended to depict American civilisation: furthermore, I never had any intention of giving a full portrayal of the American national character. Of course, much broader foundations would be needed for all those matters. In fact, the only purpose of those lines was to show circumstantial evidence of the existence in the United States of capitalism in an extraordinarily highly developed state. I hope that this is now regarded as having been demonstrated successfully, even if the 'sympathetic reader' has not been ready to follow me on all the digressions.

Quite the contrary, this evidence is merely meant to serve as the starting point for some observations that I want to make on the American proletariat. We know that the position of the wage-labouring class is conditioned by the character of capitalist growth and in particular we have learned both that all social movements have their origin in the situation created by capitalism, and also that modern Socialism is only a response to capitalism. We should therefore obviously start from a consideration of the economic situation if we want to obtain an explanation of the mode of existence of the proletariat in any country. However, this procedure proves itself especially fruitful in the case of the United States. That is to say, in this way we arrive most easily at a clear statement of the problem and are thus saved from the risk of writing without a plan on everything and anything. Let us then proceed.

If, as I have myself always maintained and often stated, modern Socialism follows as a necessary reaction to capitalism, the country with the most advanced capitalist development, namely the United States, would at the same time be the one providing the classic case of Socialism, and its working class would be supporters of the most radical of Socialist movements. However, one hears just the opposite of this asserted from all sides and in all sorts of tones (of complaint if by Socialists, of exultation if spoken by their opponents); it is said that there is absolutely no Socialism among the American working class and that those who in America pass as Socialists are a few broken-down Germans without any following. In fact, an assertion of this kind cannot fail to awaken our most active interest, for here at last is a country with no Socialism, despite its having the most advanced capitalist development. The doctrine of the inevitable Socialist future is refuted by the facts. For the social theorist as well as for the social legislator nothing can be more important than to get to the root of this phenomenon.

To begin with, we must ask whether the statement that there is *no* Socialism in the United States, especially no *American* Socialism, is actually correct. Now, if taken as absolutely as that, it is undoubtedly false.

First of all, there is one or, more precisely, there are two social-democratic parties, in the sense understood throughout continental Europe, that are by no means supported only by Germans. At the Unity Convention of the Socialist Party at Indianapolis in 1901 only twenty-five of 124 delegates, i.e., about 20 per cent, were foreign-born.[31] At the last Presidential election this party achieved 403,338 votes,[32] to which are to be added perhaps 50,000 votes for the Socialist Labor Party. Thus, in the United States in 1904 there were about as many social-democratic votes cast as in Germany in 1878,[33] or as were cast for the Freisinnige Vereinigung [Liberal Alliance] and the Anti-Semites together in the last election for the Reichstag.[34] However, this figure of the Socialist votes in America undoubtedly represents a minimum of the workers with Socialist sympathies, the reasons for which will be given later. Contrary to the situation in Germany, the number of such workers is considerably greater than the votes cast in elections.

What cannot be denied, however, is that the assertion that the American working class does not embrace Socialism is largely true.

This is the primary significance of the election statistics just quoted. One may add considerably to these figures in order to obtain the actual number of Socialists, but even so one will still be dealing with a disappearing minority. The votes cast for the Socialist Presidential candidate in 1904 amount to about 2.5 per cent of the total number of votes, and moreover that is the result of only the most recent election. In the 1900 election the Socialist Party achieved only 98,417 votes. Added to this is the fact that these Socialist votes are by no means stable. They fluctuate quite considerably from one year to another, as is evident from the following examples. Votes cast for certain candidacies of the Socialist Party are shown in Table 1.[35]

I shall also try later to give an explanation for the quite remarkable phenomenon of the unpredictable rising and falling of these election figures. For the time being it need only be pointed out, in order to show on what weak foundations the Socialist Party in the United States rests at the moment, even where it has already gained ground.

However, the conclusion suggested by the election figures is now confirmed as being correct by a series of indubitable supporting facts.

TABLE I Votes cast for and percentages of the vote received by various candidacies of the Socialist Party of America (sometimes called the Social Democratic Party) in selected states and cities from 1900 to 1905[a]

	1900 (President)	1902 (Governor)	1903 (Treasurer)	1904 (President)	1905
Alabama	928 (0.6)	2313 (2.4)	—	853 (0.8)	—
Colorado	684 (0.3)	7431 (4.0)	—	4304 (1.8)	—
Massachusetts	9716 (2.3)	33,629 (8.4)	—	13,604 (3.1)	—
Pennsylvania	4831 (0.4)	21,910 (2.0)	13,245 (1.6)	21,863 (1.8)	—
Texas	1846 (0.4)	3513 (1.0)	—	2791 (1.2)	—
City of Chicago	—	—	—	44,331[b]	23,323[c]
Greater New York[d]	—	—	—	24,600 (3.8)	12,000[c]

Notes

[a] *Ed.* – The percentages of the vote received by the Socialist Party candidates and the designations of the offices concerned have been added by the Editor after consultation with data on election results given in *The World Almanac and Encyclopedia*, 1902–5 (New York, 1902–5). In some cases there are slight, but usually insignificant, discrepancies between Sombart's vote-totals and those of the *Almanac*. Sombart himself must have taken several results in this selection from the *Almanac*. Most of the others almost certainly were taken from a compilation by A. M. Simons called 'The Socialist Outlook' in *International Socialist Review*, v (1904–5) 203–17.

Whether Sombart has been particularly fair in his selection of examples for this table might be a subject for considerable debate. With the possible exception of Massachusetts none of the states chosen had or came to have any great reputation for Socialist strength. On the other hand, Illinois cast 6.4 per cent of its Presidential votes for the Socialist candidate in 1904. In Milwaukee County, part of which is conterminous with the City of Milwaukee, the Socialist Presidential percentage was 26.0 per cent in 1904.

[b] *Ed.* – Neither the relevant issue of the *Almanac* nor the compilation in the *International Socialist Review* gives results for the City of Chicago only, but in 1904 the Socialist Presidential candidate received a total of 47,743 votes in the whole of Cook County, where Chicago is located; this is 16.9 per cent of Cook County's Presidential vote in 1904.

[c] *Ed.* – Because access to appropriate sources could not be secured, it was not possible to calculate the percentages of the total vote represented by the 1905 totals nor to ascertain the offices for which these votes were cast, although in each case it was probably for the Mayoralty.

[c] The vote-totals for Greater New York have been rounded to the nearest hundred.

The assertion with which we began therefore gains credibility: namely, the broad cross-section of the American proletariat, and precisely those holding an instrumental orientation both among the wage labourers and in particular among the skilled workers, do not embrace Socialism, nor do the most important of their leaders, who (among the more renowned leaders of the national unions) are the great majority. However, this too is to be taken with a grain of salt.

Not embracing Socialism does not mean that, like the old English pure trade-unionists, they are disposed to free-trade and free-market principles [*manchesterlich*] and abhor all State intervention or State-socialist reforms.[36] Today the vast majority of organised workers and their leaders rather favour 'political action', that is, an autonomous workers' politics. Among the demands that the American Federation of Labor[37] wants to be made law are the following:

3. the introduction of a legal work-day of not more than eight hours;
8. the municipal ownership of street-cars, water-works, and gas and electric plants;
9. the nationalization of telegraphs, telephones, railroads, and *mines* [Sombart's emphasis – *Ed.*]; and
10. the abolition of the monopoly system of landholding, and the substitution therefor of a title of occupancy and use only.[38]

This programme does indeed mean a serious shaking of the 'foundations of our existing social order'. It also raises the question of the sense in which I then feel that those asserting that the American working class does not embrace Socialism are right. If I did not fear causing misunderstandings by employing the recently much used and admittedly somewhat ambiguous word, I should answer that the American worker does not embrace the 'spirit' of Socialism as we now understand it in continental Europe, which is essentially Socialism with a Marxist character. However, I prefer to explain in detail what I mean.

1. One feels that the American worker (a phrase still being used as a short form for the 'modal' American worker whose views are dominant in the bulk of the working class and among its leaders) is not on the whole dissatisfied with the present condition of things. On the contrary, he feels that he is well, cheerful and in high spirits – as do all Americans.[39] He has a most rosy and optimistic conception of the world. Live and let live in his basic maxim. As a result, the base of all those feelings and moods upon which a European worker builds his class consciousness is removed: envy, embitterment, and hatred against all those who have more and who live extravagantly.

2. There is expressed in the worker, as in all Americans, a boundless optimism, which comes out as a belief in the mission and greatness of his country, a belief that often has a religious tinge. The Americans think themselves to be God's chosen people, the famous 'salt of the earth'.[40] As he so often does, Bryce hits the nail on the head when he says: 'Pessimism is the luxury of a handful; optimism is the private delight, as well as public profession, of nine hundred and ninety-nine out of every thousand, for nowhere does the individual associate himself more constantly and directly with the greatness of his country.'[41] This means, however, that the American worker identifies

himself with the present American State. He stands up for the Star-Spangled Banner. He is 'patriotically' inclined, as it would be expressed in the German sense. The disintegrative force that leads to class separation, class opposition, class hatred and class conflict (i.e., the dissension that was characterised above) is weaker in America than in Europe, while the integrative force that both compels the affirmation of the national political community and of the State and that also brings out patriotism is stronger. Among American workers one therefore finds none of the opposition to the State that is to be found in continental-European Socialism. I think that John Mitchell, the well-known leader of the miners, expresses the view of the vast majority of American workers today when he says:

> 'The unions who do oppose the militia fail to recognize that they, as unionists, are a part of the State,...vested with the right of determining in part the policy of the State. The trade union movement in this country can make progress only by identifying itself with the State.'[42]

It does not need to be emphasised here that Mitchell (who I suppose is most representative of the 'average worker', of the type standing midway between the extremes) already sees it to be necessary to make concessions to the existence of class consciousness and to the beginning of class antithesis, nor that he has therefore already been reproached by more conservative social legislators for preaching among the workers a 'narrow and exclusive solidarity'.[43] We are not yet concerned with the issue of establishing 'developmental trends' (which will be the major subject of exposition in later sections), but rather with gaining a picture of the situation that mirrors as faithfully as possible the present *status quo*.

3. The American worker is not opposed to the capitalist economic system as such, either intellectually or emotionally. Again I should like to quote what Mitchell says on this point. The passages in his book in which he calls the standpoint of the trade unions towards capitalism purely opportunist run as follows:[44]

> Trade unionism is not irrevocably committed to the maintenance of the wage system, nor is it irrevocably committed to its abolition. It demands the constant improvement of the condition of the workingmen, if possible, by the maintenance of the present wage system, if not possible, by its ultimate abolition.

Mitchell's personal conviction, however, is that this 'abolition' does not necessarily need to come about, for 'the history of trade unionism in the past seems to indicate that by the aid of the State and by the concerted efforts of workingmen, a vast and wide-spread amelioration of their condition can take place under the present system of wages'.

Other noted workers' leaders positively emphasise the community of interests of capital and labour. One such leader has said that 'they are partners and should divide the results of industry in good faith and in good feeling', that if 'laborers in their madness destroy capital such is the work of ignorance and evil passions', and that the future will again produce the full harmony between capital and labour that is now only temporarily disturbed.[45]

However, I believe that the relationship between the American worker and capitalism is even more intimate than is expressed by these manifestations of friendship and demonstrations of respect. I believe that emotionally the American worker has a share in capitalism: I believe that he loves it. Anyway, he devotes his entire body and soul to it. If there is anywhere in America where the restless striving after profit, the complete fruition of the commercial drive and the passion for business are indigenous, it is in the worker, who wants to earn as much as his strength will allow, and to be as unrestrained as possible. Hence, only rarely do we hear complaints about the lack of adequate protection against dangers at work; instead, the American worker is ready to go along with these dangers, if protective arrangements might diminish his earnings. We therefore encounter restrictions of output and disputes about piece-work or technical innovations much more rarely than in England, for example. I shall demonstrate still more exactly but in a different context that the American worker puts much more into his work and accomplishes more than his European counterpart. However, the greater intensity put into his labour by the American worker is only the extension of his fundamentally capitalist disposition.

Young Edward J. Gainor, a member of the Executive Committee of the National Association of Letter Carriers, certainly speaks from the heart as far as the great majority of the members of his class are concerned, when – in a lecture on 'The Government as Employer' – he expresses his principled aversion to workers being public officials; in doing so, he introduces the following reasons for not favouring the situation of the public official:

1. the public official has no prospect of achieving a 'social position' by his own labour, in other words, of managing to become rich;
2. after attainment of the maximum wage or salary, no further increase of efficiency occurs, for in the absence of recognition for his success only an idiot will exert himself more than is strictly necessary;
3. the public official is more restricted as to how he can organise his private life; and
4. the public official is barred from a political career, described by Gainor as an 'avenue of human endeavour that offers great attractions for all ambitious Americans'.[46]

The particular way in which the working class is organised provides the best evidence that the outlook which we come across in the foregoing and similar statements really is that of the bulk of the American working class, which is ruled by the spirit of business.

As is generally known, four different groups or types of workers' organisations exist today in the United States. Of these, one – the Knights of Labor[47] – has only a past. The heyday of this organisation, which was more related to a guild of freemasons than to a modern trade union, was in the middle of the 1880s. For reasons that are not pursued here, the membership of the Knights of Labor rose from 52,000 in 1883 to 703,000 in 1886, only to drop to almost half the latter figure in 1888. As already stated, the Knights were not a trade union in the modern sense; they did not encourage unions within particular sectors of the economy and they abhorred the strike and similar measures. Today they are on their last legs.

Another group of workers' associations has at best only a future. This is made up of those Socialist-inclined trade unions of the West that are united in the American Labor Union.[48] Their membership is still small. They represent an oppositional minority and we are not therefore considering them at this point.

A third group has neither a past nor a future, and is also insignificant in the present. This is the Socialist Trade and Labor Alliance, which was founded by Daniel De Leon in 1895 and 1896 in opposition to the trade unions.[49]

Finally, the fourth group, by far the most significant and the only one needing to be considered at present, is made up of the trade unions united in the American Federation of Labor. The number of organised workers finding their place in the American Federation of Labor has risen enormously during the last ten years. In 1896 membership was 272,315, in 1900 it was 548,321, and in 1904 it was 1,676,200, which is more than four-fifths of all organised workers in America.

The character of the trade unions bound together in such a large association is not, of course, homogeneous. Since workers with Socialist opinions who belong to the Socialist Party also participate in the trade-union cause with great eagerness and since a large number of organisations dominated by them are also affiliated to the American Federation of Labor, purely social-democratic viewpoints have a chance to be heard at the annual conventions, as well as ultra-conservative ones on the other side. None the less, as I have already pointed out, the leadership of the Federation lies in non-Socialist hands and the great majority of unions united within it favour the distinctly American viewpoint about the position of the wage labourer that I have sketched above.[50] This specifically American spirit is therefore reflected in their politics.[51] They rely on a purely business approach and this leads them to protect the interests of the occupational groups whom they represent by remaining exclusive and by seeking monopolies, without much regard for the proletarian class as a whole and with even less regard for the underclass of unskilled workers.[52] Consequently, they have a strong tendency to guild-like isolation[53] and so produce what is essentially a vertical structuring of the proletariat, the union of which into a single closed class acting for itself is naturally retarded. This politics of business finds its purest expression in the combinations of the monopolistic trade union and the monopolistic employer in the so-called 'Alliances', which are organisations aimed at the common exploitation of the public through a union of the employers and workers of a particular sector of the economy. One can describe these sorts of trade unions as capitalist and can contrast them with the Socialist trade unions; the former are carved from the same wood as capitalism itself and, in both their inclinations and their effects, they are directed to the maintenance and strengthening of the capitalist economic system, rather than to its overthrow. The politics of the Socialist trade unions are also tailored to success in the present, but at the same time they do not lose sight of the proletarian class-movement against capitalism.

Enough has been said to establish that the heart of the American trade-union movement has a capitalist character. 'Trade unionism is the business method of effecting the betterment of the wage earner under the highly organised conditions of the modern industrial world.'[54] 'Collective bargaining is a business matter.' In such statements made by those best acquainted with the American trade-union movement is that movement's spirit unambiguously expressed.

Finally, the attitude of the leading trade-unionists to the efforts of the bourgeois social reformers that have been apparent for some years in the United States shows that the former really do want to lead a hard struggle 'for the betterment of the wage earner', but without thereby intending to forsake the capitalist economic system. The very different spirit of the American working class, in comparison with European or at least continental-European workers, shows itself here. American workers feel that they are very much in opposition to the employers as far as the establishment of working conditions is concerned, but they are none the less ready to stand shoulder to shoulder with those members of the bourgeoisie who want to support them in their fight. Furthermore, workers' representatives dine freely and frequently with those employers who are willing to come to an understanding with their workers on the basis of equal rights. Among American workers there is none of that oppositional consciousness specific to proletarian Socialism which characterises the great majority of German workers. Let us say that the relationship of Germany to America is therefore as follows. In Germany it is the minority, and certainly not the élite of the working class, that seeks contact with bourgeois social reformers – say in the Gesellschaft für Soziale Reform [Society for Social Reform][55] – while the great majority of organised workers remain in unremitting class conflict with all bourgeois so-called 'friends'. In America the reverse is true. The leading trade-unionists (and behind them undoubtedly stand the élite of the organised working class) commune with non-partisan social reformers and with reformist employers in the National Civic Federation,[56] which roughly corresponds to our Gesellschaft für Soziale Reform, and it is only a small fraction that stands resentfully on the side, whereas in Germany it is the majority.

In this sense one is therefore justified in saying that there is no Socialism in America.

From the theoretical as well as the practical point of view, the interesting problem that follows from this conclusion may now be formulated like this: the United States is the country with the most advanced capitalist development, so that its economic structure represents our future. What Marx correctly stated about England in 1867, we may now apply to America. *De te fabula narratur, Europa* [About you, Europe, is the story being told],[57] when we are reporting about conditions in America, at least as far as capitalist development is concerned. The country representing our own future now has a basically non-Socialist working class. Does this phenomenon therefore represent our future *too*? Were we wrong to regard the rise of Socialism as a necessary phenomenon in the wake of capitalism? The answer to these questions demands an examination of the reasons that have led to the distinctive mode of thought of the American worker. The conception that we have of the nature of scientific method prevents our being satisfied in explaining this by reference to a specifically 'American spirit'. Instead we shall seek to trace the reasons for its existence by making it our business to establish first of all the conditions of life peculiar to the American proletariat – as viewed from a historical, a political, an economic, and more generally, a social perspective. Once we have understood those conditions and have succeeded in using them to explain the disposition of the American worker, a further question faces us. On what substructure do these conditions of life rest? Is this substructure to be regarded as permanently established, and will it support for ever the structure that is rising on it today; or does it threaten to totter, and along with it the superstructure? To state the matter plainly: are the conditions of the American worker lasting and permanent – either as being specifically American or as lying in the general direction of capitalist development – or are those conditions linked to postulates that are subject to alteration? If the latter is the case, will the alteration be such that the conditions of life turn out to be the same as or similar to those in Europe (which have already produced Socialism), so that the ground in America will be prepared for Socialism? Stated more generally, is there a tendency towards unity in the modern social movement, or must we deal with movements taking different forms in different countries? If there is a tendency towards unity, is this in the direction of Socialism or away from it? Will the future social structures of Europe and America turn out the same or different? Is America or Europe the 'land of the future'?

The purpose of the series of studies that I propose to present in the following sections of this work is to introduce some material that answers the questions raised above.

SECTION ONE

The Political Position of the Worker

1 Politics and Race

In what follows I want to try to explain the reason for there being no Socialism in the United States (in the sense developed in the previous chapter) by specifying the particular conditions in which the American proletariat lives. First of all, I want to deal with the character of political life, since that is what every observer considers most obviously distinctive.

Before doing this, however, I must mention a way of thinking that is occasionally encountered when the matters under discussion here are argued over. I dare say one has heard the opinion expressed that the lack of Socialism in America is based not on the character of American life but rather on the special characteristics inherent in the Anglo-Saxon race, from which most of the American proletariat is held to be drawn. These characteristics are said to make the American proletariat unreceptive to everything that looks like Socialism. This reasoning is false in two respects. Firstly, the so-called Anglo-Saxon race is not 'by nature' unsusceptible to Socialist ideas. The proof of this is the Chartist movement in England in the 1830s and 1840s, which had a strongly Socialist flavour, and the pattern of political development in recent years in the Australian colonies[1] and even in the mother country. Secondly, the North American proletariat does not consist exclusively or even predominantly of members of the Anglo-Saxon race. If, as may be largely the case, it is permissible to infer the composition of the proletariat from general statistics of the numbers of immigrants and foreign-born inhabitants,[2] the following picture is obtained.[3] Of the population that had immigrated into the United States at the 1900 Census, only 8.1 per cent came from England, 2.3 per cent from Scotland, as against 25.8 per cent from Germany, 15.6 per cent from Ireland, 7.8 per cent from Russia and Poland, and so on.[4]

The situation regarding persons of foreign parentage is similar. In 1900 their proportion of the working population amounted to 38.4 per cent. England and Wales contributed only 3.6 per cent to this percentage, and Scotland only 1.0 per cent, compared with 11.3 per cent from Germany and 8.4 per cent from Ireland. Specifically for manufacturing and mechanical pursuits, the proportions of persons of foreign parentage was 56.2 per cent, of whom 5.8 per cent were from England and

Wales, and 1.6 per cent from Scotland, compared with 16.1 per cent from Germany and 11.7 per cent from Ireland.[5] None the less, even if one takes into consideration the total immigration in the nineteenth century, the proportion of Anglo-Saxons is less than one is generally inclined to assume. It amounts to only 33.58 per cent, even when it includes the Irish (who certainly make up more than half of the Anglo-Saxon total), as against 24.16 per cent contributed by German immigration.[6]

There are therefore millions of people in America who during the last generation have immigrated from countries where Socialism flourishes. In 1900 Germans or working Americans of German parentage alone amounted to 3,295,350, of whom 1,142,131 were employed in manufacturing and mechanical pursuits; thus, the greater part were certainly wage labourers. If one wants to argue that it is the Anglo-Saxons who are immune to the Socialist bacillus, the question why these millions of Germans are not also Socialists in America must still be answered.[7]

In explaining the circumstances of interest to us, we must therefore exclude any argument based on racial membership. Instead, the explanation is more likely to be found in the variegated mixture of the American population, which at the same time exhibits extremely homogeneous developmental characteristics, the determining factors of which are to be sought in the features of American life. I have already said that I wished first of all to investigate how these features shape political life.[8]

2 The Political Machine

Given the extent to which public life in modern states is being organised on a more complicated basis and the extent to which the democratisation of the system of government is increasing, it is becoming more and more difficult for political ideas to be put forward otherwise than in the framework of a party organisation. This is undoubtedly closer to the truth in the United States than it is in any other political commonwealth. The United States is certainly the only large state with a really democratic system of government where political affairs are made even more complicated by its being federally organised.

To say it is a large state means that it is twenty times as large as the German Empire. To say it has a really democratic system of government means that universal suffrage now exists as the rule in every state of the Union. The restrictions still existing are not worth considering. From such universal suffrage come not only the legislative bodies, as in the European states (with the exception of Switzerland), but also – and this is the point – almost all higher administrative officials and superior judges. Everywhere the highest state official, the Governor, is chosen by election, with his period of office amounting to two or four years – those states with a two-year period being about the same in number as those with a four-year one. The majority of states also elect the Lieutenant-Governor, who is the Governor's deputy. In two-thirds of the states – in fact, in all the Western and Southern ones and also in New York, Pennsylvania and Ohio[9] – the superior judges are popularly elected for short terms. It is well known that the country's highest official and representatives are chosen by public elections.

However, to these federal and state elections there should now be added the elections for the county boards and city councils, as well as the elections of various local administrative officials, especially the Mayor.

A conscientious citizen can therefore spend a good part of his life concerned with elections. We have only to make it clear how many election opportunities can occur in, for example, a state like Ohio. The following offices are elective.[10]

1. *Federal offices:* once every four years, the President; and once every two years, the members of the House of Representatives.
2. *State offices:* once every year, members of the Board of Public

Works[11] (for three years), and members of the Supreme Court (for five years); once every two years, the Governor of the state of Ohio, the Lieutenant-Governor, the Secretary of State, the Treasurer, the Attorney-General, the State Senators (members of the upper house of the Ohio state legislature), and the Representatives (for the House of Representatives, the lower house of the Ohio state legislature); once every three years, the Commissioner of Common Schools, and the Clerk of the Supreme Court; and once every four years, the Auditor.

3. *District offices:* once every two years, the Circuit Judge (for six years) and the Judge of the Court of Common Pleas (for five years); and once every ten years, the members of the Board of Equalization,

4. *County offices:* once every year, the County Commissioners (for three years), and the Infirmary Directors (for three years); once every two years, the Treasurer, the Sheriff, and the Coroner; and once every three years, the County Auditor, the Recorder, the Surveyor, the Judge of Probate, the Clerk of the Court of Common Pleas, and the Prosecuting Attorney.

5. *City offices:* once every year, members of the Board of Police Commissioners in most cities, members of the Board of Infirmary Directors (for three years), the Trustee of Water Works (for three years); and once every two years, the Mayor, the City Clerk, the Auditor, the Treasurer, the Solicitor, the Police Judge (in the larger cities), the Prosecuting Attorney of the Police Court (in larger cities); the Clerk of the Police Court (in larger cities), the City Commissioner (in cities of the second class), the Marshall (not in the larger cities), the Street Commissioner, the Civil Engineer, the Fire Surveyor, and the Superintendent of Markets. The city council has power to determine whether the three last-named offices shall be appointed by them or be elected at the polls. Otherwise, however, the long list of officials set out here is elected directly by the people. Even then, those offices that are found only in one of the two great cities of Cincinnati and Cleveland are omitted. None the less, this still results in the following numbers of elections: seven are held annually, twenty-one to twenty-six biennially, eight triennially, two every four years, and two every five or ten years.

As a result there is an average of twenty-two elections that every citizen has to go through in the course of a year. This does not mean that he would have to go to the polls on twenty-two separate occasions, because elections for different offices are often held on the same day. Yet each year he must still elect twenty-two men whom he deems qualified for their respective offices.

The demands that these polling activities make on the efficiency of the average citizen have only to be stated for one to recognize that they cannot be fulfilled. Just consider, for example, the fact that a considerable number of the elections take place throughout a single large area.[12] One should also consider the fact that, if there is not to be complete confusion, an agreement about the candidates to be nominated must be reached among the inhabitants of a city, county or state (and, in the Presidential election, among those of the whole Union), added to which is the canvassing that must be done for the candidates nominated. One need not then ponder for any length of time to appreciate that the individual voter cannot possibly be left to his own resources in election procedures, but that there must instead be people who make it a career to concern themselves ceaselessly with the problem of elections, whether to discover suitable candidates, to draw up uniform lists or to promote the election of the candidates nominated.

In the beginnings of American democracy, when the numbers both of voters and of elective offices were still small (till about 1824), the masses of voters were guided by the legislatures themselves. These formed committees among themselves – the Congressional or Legislative Caucus – by whom the candidates recommended to the people for election were nominated.

Then, when the democratic tidal wave arrived at the beginning of the 1820s, the function of giving guidance to the masses of voters was also democratised, that is, displaced from a high to a low level. First of all, in the steadily growing city of New York with its motley mixture of population there were some demagogues who endeavoured to take possession of the electoral machinery for themselves – the name of the well-known Aaron Burr is foremost among these – and who, with the help of a crowd of servile lackeys, organised the notorious guild of professional politicians in whose hands the business of politics in the United States has rested ever since. Their domination became all the firmer as the electoral machinery became more complicated and as respectable society withdrew more and more from participation in politics.

The work (if it may be so designated) of the professional politicians is now in fact quite enormous. The election machinery, as it has gradually developed, is roughly as follows.[13] In each election district nominating meetings are summoned by the party organisers when needed; these meetings are called 'primaries'. Here delegates are chosen – at the command of the party organisers, of course – and these delegates go forward together to conventions where the nominating of the candidates takes place. When a slate has been confirmed, canvassing has to be done on its behalf, and on election day the mass of voters, who appear on the scene only then,[14] have to be dragged to the polls. The number of delegate conventions that now have to meet is the same as the number of geographical areas of jurisdiction operated over by the offices to be filled. Commonly a delegate convention – the State convention, for example – can nominate a whole number of candidates: Governor, Lieutenant-Governor, Secretary of State, Treasurer, Attorney-General, members of the State Supreme Court, etc. Often, however, the geographical areas of jurisdiction of the offices to be filled are not conterminous, so that several delegate conventions have to be arranged. Thus, in some circumstances, the chain of conventions is very long. There is then a county convention; a ward convention (in larger cities);[15] a city convention; an Assembly district convention; a convention for the senatorial district, in which the members of the upper house of each state are elected; one for the congressional district, in which Congressmen are elected; one for the judicial district; and finally the State convention, which has been mentioned already, and the national convention for the Presidential election. For some of these conventions members are chosen directly in the primaries, but for others (i.e., the State and national conventions) members are chosen by the conventions held lower in the hierarchy in the Assembly districts.

If this giant Machine is to function at all well, a vast number of highly organised professional politicians have to be ceaselessly at work. In every district a staff of trained party workers must be at the disposal of the actual 'wire-pullers', who in their turn are kept up to the mark by the 'head wire-pullers'.[16]

Finance must correspond with the amount of manpower available, so that the adequate functioning of the Machine is made possible. A few figures make this evident. Bryce puts the costs of elections in New York in an ordinary (not Presidential) year at $7,000,000, of which $290,000 is borne by the city.[17] The mayoralty election campaign in New York had the following outlays of labour and money. Tammany, the organisation of the Democratic Party, held 3700 meetings, and the Fusionists, its opponents, held 4000. Tammany employed 1500 speakers and its opponents 2500, The former spent $60,000 on printing, and the latter $10,000 less. For processions and other demonstrations for electoral purposes $25,000 was spent by both parties. In all, the election campaign cost Tammany $900,000, and the Fusionists $500,000.[18] The total expenses for the Presidential campaign are estimated at $5,000,000.[19] These then are the outlays that a party in America must be able to afford in order to fight for its 'ideas', if that is the appropriate descriptive word. It can immediately be seen what difficulties for the foundation and success of a workers' party of a social-democratic type must result from this situation, even if one is considering only the beginning of the party's political life. In addition, it is a fact that the political Machine has for years rested in the hands of the old-established parties. The difficulty for a new party is therefore doubled. It has to battle with old parties that are already in control. The special constraints upon the development of an independent, Socialist party organisation that result from these circumstances deserve closer consideration.

3 The Monopoly of the Two Major Parties

From the very beginning of the Republic two large, almost equally strong parties have dominated public life in the United States. Their names have changed. Until the beginning of the 1820s they were called Federalists and Republicans (or Democratic Republicans); then came the National Republicans (later the Whigs) and Democrats. Since 1856 they have been Republicans and Democrats. In a later passage I shall discuss what they entail, and there I shall also try to answer why there have always been only two significant parties in the United States. Here I want only to investigate the reasons for the monopolistic position of the two dominant parties and thus to account for the strong hold that they have.

The first fact to be considered is that they have disposition over the necessary finance to maintain the giant election Machine in working order, and the facts stated on the previous pages have already given an idea of this Machine's complexity.

The finances with which the American parties work come from three sources:

1. Voluntary contributions from rich party members and general public subscriptions, as in Germany. The only difference is that capitalists in America, because they see directly the immediate results, are more inclined to support with large sums the party that promises the most assistance. As we shall see, it is a basic feature of party organisation in the United States that one and the same capitalist concern gives subsidies first to one and then to the other of the two major parties. The big trusts finance party organisations everywhere, and the Standard Oil Company, like other such big companies, gives its money to the Democratic Party in New York and to the Republicans in Pennsylvania, these being the parties that are directly in control of the respective states or have the prospect of being so in the near future. It is adequate to make the point that the parties are always in a position to acquire great sums from the rich people of the country.[20]

2. Assessments on officials in employment furnish the party organisations with the second possibility of securing necessary finance for themselves. A certain percentage of salary is levied for party purposes. Bryce reckons that at the end of the 1880s the annual salary

of New York city officials was $11,000,000, while that of the 2500 Federal officials, who were also assessed if belonging to the same party, was $2,500,000. An assessment of 2 per cent of these amounts brings $275,000, or roughly 1,250,000 marks, to the party treasury. Even policemen, messenger boys, and ordinary workers in government establishments are assessed by their parties in this way.[21]

3. Finally, the taxation of the candidates for individual offices also brings in still more finance. There is the custom that everyone who has his eye on a position and wishes to be nominated as the candidate pays his party a 'contribution to expenses', which is quite considerable. For the most part it takes up an entire year's income, and more than that for salaried offices. In fact, in many cases it is greater than the full regular income that the official draws during his tenure of office.[22] The size of the amounts that are paid over to the party treasury in this manner are varied. According to a price-list the rates of which one often finds being quoted,[23] the following prices apply in New York: a judgeship, $15,000; a seat in Congress, $4000; an aldermanic position, $1500; election to the Assembly, $600 to $1500; and so on. From these sums Tammany receives an annual income of $125,000, and the opposition party almost $100,000.

The election purposes for which all these funds are levied are primarily the purchase of votes, purely and simply. Most of the Negro votes, as well as the votes of many uneducated immigrants from half-barbarian countries and the votes of the *Lumpenproletariat* in the big cities, are notorious for being able to be bought, and are notoriously bought. The price fluctuates and the average for a Negro vote, for example, is reckoned at $3.00.

Of course, most of the votes, even those of the lower classes, are not to be acquired in this heavy-handed way. However, the party leadership knows how to make itself popular among broad sections of the poorer population by helping those who are in need with gifts during hardship and distress. To one person a dollar is loaned; another receives a free railway ticket; in one place coal is distributed on cold days; elsewhere a chicken is given for Christmas; medicine is bought for the sick; where a death has occurred, a coffin is provided at half-price; and so on. Along with all this solicitude there is generous treating in the saloons, where perhaps the most important part of the entire election business is transacted. Here the party's agent – the party worker who is always in every saloon and is often the saloon-keeper himself – works also on all those who are to be won over by means other than money or direct assistance of the type mentioned above. As Ostrogorski so aptly expresses it, each voter is 'taken by his weak side' by the party worker. One man wants police permission to carry on his street-vending business or to open a saloon; another has contravened the building code or has some such transgression on his conscience. The Machine puts all this right by influencing the courts deciding the case in favour of its client; in most instances the courts' judges, being themselves elected officials, are also in the power of the Machine. Alternatively, however, the matter is handled in the opposite way. The party imposes punishments on the refractory voter and so wins him back, or at least frightens others. If he is an employee in state or local government, the party sees to it that he is dismissed; if he is a factory-owner, the factory inspectorate keeps a stricter eye on him; the tax-collector examines twice as carefully the books of the trader who is out of favour and discovers that he has not paid his taxes fully; the saloon-keeper who does not adhere to licensing hours is immediately fined; and so on.[24]

The facts just stated have already made it clear what one is dealing with when confronting the American party system. The major parties have the money with which they can directly or indirectly purchase votes and with which they can pay their large staff of workers, as well as finance the other apparatus of the election machine through which the electorate is influenced. They also have control over all sorts of methods of favouring their supporters and harming their opponents. For these reasons they have a great hold over their supporters, as well as a political monopoly, whether they are actually in power or just have a firm prospect of gaining it next time. Moreover, because they have this position of power, they therefore have at their command the means to bless and to condemn; they also have access to the amounts of money necessary to keep the election machine going.

However, this closed grouping, which is so disastrous to all those not within it, is even more significant in other contexts.

First of all, there are the advantages that the ruling party offers its supporters in its role as distributor of offices. This is manifest in the case of all electoral offices. Anyone who aspires to such a position for himself or for his friends must naturally make the strongest effort to be a member of the largest party or at least of a party that does have some chance of winning. If one is hunting for jobs, it is no use being in a party whose candidates collect a tenth or a twentieth of the vote and which will have a majority perhaps only once in ten or twenty years. This reasoning applies not only to electoral offices but also to the majority of offices that are subject to appointment, for these too are allotted to the supporters of the ruling party.

The so-called Spoils System has prevailed generally in the United States since the first Presidency of Andrew Jackson from 1829 to 1833, although it had become institutionalised even earlier in some states, in particular, New York and Pennsylvania. It is based on the principle that 'to the victor belong the spoils'.[25] This basically means that offices are filled not according to qualification, but by taking into account the party allegiance of the aspirant. If one considers that this principle holds good for the highest and lowest position in Federal, state, county and local government, to Under-Secretaries of State and postmasters as well as to office boys and policemen, one can easily estimate what a huge hold is thereby exercised on the masses by the two major parties, who are seriously concerned only with the distribution of spoils.[26]

The significance in the development of party politics in America of this close connection between political party and the distribution of offices cannot be assessed too highly. It deserves attention particularly when – as here – one is seeking the reasons that account plausibly for the tiny growth of the Socialist movement, for this is the major loser under the prevailing system.

As a worker it is easy to be a social democrat if one definitely knows that, even if one belongs to a party supporting the State, one will not become a member of a trade board, a commissioner for an exhibition, or president of the Imperial Insurance Office or the Imperial Statistical Office. As a postman or a policeman, one can indulge one's social-democratic tendencies confidently, albeit secretly, when one knows it is unlikely that one will be dismissed from one's post.

In America the situation is different. Here, as we saw, the path to even the most modest offices leads through the yoke of party membership. All those who aspire to a position, however small, in the service of the state or community must give their whole selves to the party beforehand; this applies not only to election days but also to the long period before, when aspirants must be active party workers. The degree of their commitment is then put to the severest test, which most fail. The process is repeated on a grander scale in the case of the leading trade-unionists, who are the workers' leaders and to whom a richer reward is held out if they swear loyalty to the ruling party; they will be given a well-paid job, perhaps as a factory inspector or even as an Under-Secretary of State, depending on the significance attached to the person to be provided for. The practice of rendering influential workers' leaders harmless by bestowing on them a lucrative post is a thoroughly established one, and for years it has been used with the greatest success by the ruling parties. We can follow this castration process among a whole series of the best-known leaders. At the moment the President of the American Federation of Labor, whose equivalent in Germany would be Karl Legien,[27] is said to have been selected to succeed Carroll D. Wright as Commissioner of the Bureau of Labor,[28] while John Mitchell, the victorious leader of the miners and so roughly equivalent to Hermann Sachse or Otto Hué in Germany,[29] is supposed to be receiving a post as Under-Secretary of State in Washington.

It has been ascertained that in Massachusetts thirteen workers' leaders have obtained political positions in this way within the space of a few years, while in Chicago thirty have done so.[30]

Now it is not infrequent that a 'social democrat' who is demanding 'the overthrow of the existing social order' simultaneously has the picture of a fat sinecure hovering continually before his eyes. He is unselfish enough to be able to preach to his followers in the evening about the emptiness of the prevailing political order and the necessity for a Socialist movement, while in the afternoon immediately pre-ceding that evening the boss of one of the major parties offered him the candidacy for a lucrative electoral office or promised him a fat proportion of the spoils of the next election victory!

However, when influential leaders betray a really oppositional workers' movement in this way every time that they have achieved power and esteem among their fellows, this means a direct gain for the major party not only in so far as the person of the leader and the group of workers who trusted him are concerned. In a far wider sense capitalism is strengthened indirectly, because a possible independent workers' party experiences a damaging loss when its leader is lured away by the bait of office. In other words, on every occasion the major parties snatch the officers of the Socialist party organisations from under the noses of the latter while they are still being formed.

In all the cases discussed so far the individual has been driven into the arms of the major parties by self-interest or by the wish to secure some form of advantage for himself or for his close friends.

None the less, it is not merely personal motives that bind the great mass of people to the old parties. To an equally strong degree idealistic forces play a part.

Firstly, it is general 'political interest' or the wish to have a hand in the shaping of public life that often drives the individual in America to link himself to one of the major parties just because it is the major party. He follows it because only with its help can he hope to push through a reform dear to his heart, or to remove immediately some inconvenience that is distressing him. In order that this can be appre-ciated, it is essential to make clear the fundamental difference that prevails between the systems of government of European countries[31] and that of America. In European countries popular influence on the process of public life is possible even in the best arranged set-up only through the long business of forming a parliamentary majority. Repre-sentatives are elected to go to parliament in the hope that together they will there have a majority to which the government will give heed. Obviously this is a very slow and in no way always radical procedure.

While this process of transformation is being completed, fine speeches are made in parliament to enunciate party principles. These fine speeches have a significance that is in inverse relationship to their prospects of having any real influence on the conduct of affairs of State. For all that, there is some sense in electing a few representatives who do not belong to the majority, but who will sound forth with useless tirades professing their party commitment. These tirades are a consolation to the people, who are condemned to have neither power nor influence. Thus, the German Reichstag, whose decisions are tantamount to irrelevant so far as the process of public life in Germany is concerned, is the most suitable place for minority parties with fine orators. Everyone knows that everything which Arthur Stadthagen[32] says could remain unsaid without even a single important political measure being in any way different. Yet the Social Democratic voter is pleased when he reads those bloodthirsty outpourings in his newspaper and says to himself, with a smirk of furious delight, 'He's given it to them good and proper!' It is the lack of 'political will', or the will to gain immediate influence and power, that precipitates this sort of response. If one were more polite, one would describe what is being expressed here as idealism. In fact, this stance finds its most highly developed manifestation in Germany, the land of 'poets and thinkers'. For this reason we are all minority politicians from birth.

In the United States the position is just the opposite. To begin with, the purely democratic form of government induces the American masses to direct their attention to the success that is within their grasp. Because not only legislative representatives but also judges and administrative officials are popularly elected, interest is concentrated on the elections of officials and not on the elections of those going to legislatures. For reasons still to be discussed, the legislature, especially the House of Representatives in Washington, plays a very much more insignificant role than the parliament in a west European state, perhaps even a smaller part than that of the German Reichstag. On the other hand, the degree of interest in the elections of officials is very high; this is for the obvious reason that through them one can achieve much more quickly the particular success at which one is exclusively aiming. It is worth much more effort to the Americans to remove an unpopular Governor or judge than to send a fine orator to the legislature in Washington. This would be true for any people, even the Germans. Just consider the position if, during the period of the Socialist Law, it would have been possible for the workers in Berlin to sack State Prosecutor Hermann Tessendorf;[33] or if today they could remove any criminal court that is notorious for its draconian punishments of offences involved in striking; or if they could revenge themselves on a certain body of judges, say the ones who handed down the Löbtau Judgement,[34] by giving them the push at the next election!

The American worker can do that sort of thing. To be sure, it is for a price that many will find high; in fact, he must link himself to one of the major parties just because they are the major parties, since only with their help is it possible to influence successfully the result of an election.

One can quite easily follow up individual examples of how, in actions of this sort, the working class always reverts its attention to the major parties, on which it had originally intended to turn its back. Especially informative are the events at the last elections in the state of Colorado. In 1902 the Socialist candidates collected a highly respectable total of votes for themselves. Then in 1903 came the great strikes, which degenerated – as often happens in America – into a formal civil war. Bombs were thrown, buildings were set on fire, the militia were called up, battles took place between workers and the military, the best-known workers' leaders were deported by decree of the Governor of the state, all the newspapers were full of the 'civil war in Colorado', and the bitterness of the workers was greater than it had ever been.[35]

A German commentator would have said that the social-democratic vote in that state would increase enormously, but what in fact was the case? In 1904 the votes cast for the social-democratic candidates amounted to half as many as had been given two years earlier. The explanation of this outcome – so incomprehensible to us – is very simple when one bears in mind the political circumstances of the United States. The voters who had previously supported social-democratic candidates had transferred their allegiance to the Democratic Party in order to support that party actively in the fight against the hated Governor Peabody, who was justifiably seen as the mastermind behind the whole hostile posture taken by the authorities towards the workers during the great strikes. It is important to note that this tactic was successful. The Republican Governor was not re-elected, but replaced by a Democrat.[36] Even if conditions under the governorship of the new man remain unchanged, the need for revenge has none the less been satisfied and the hated enemy dealt a painful blow, which is something that always feels good, even more so than a poem by Ludwig Thoma.[37]

Alongside these rational and pragmatic considerations are a series of indeterminate sentiments that make Americans further disposed to the major parties, to which they become firmly bound.

In my introductory observations I mentioned how strongly developed in Americans is the feeling for measurable greatness and for large numbers and how this feeling leads them to overvalue the trappings of success. Such a state of mind ensures a politics of majorities. Americans find it intolerable to belong to a party which invariably receives tiny totals at the ballot box, which will not achieve any tangible successes in the foreseeable future, and which, as a consequence, is branded with the stigma of ridicule. On election days the minority politicians must stand in resignation on the sidelines with a long-suffering expression; these are the times when the excitement about the number of votes won by the major parties is at its height, when all the newspapers depict in gigantic letters the electoral successes of the candidates supported by them, and when the telephoned figures of votes cast are displayed on huge transparent screens that the large newspaper offices erect on Presidential election days. Being on the sidelines during all this activity is not something that the temperamental American can tolerate.

To continue: the feeling for something of large measurable dimensions, combined with the radical-democratic principles of the Constitution, has cultivated in Americans a blind respect for majorities. They think a majority is bound to be on the right track or it would not be a majority. How can the people *en masse* be wrong? This is what Bryce, in a telling phrase, calls 'the fatalism of the multitude'.

Along with this esteem for the great mass of voters as such goes the propensity that Americans have to join together with many others for common action; this has been called their gregariousness.[38] This disposition (which on its own would lead only to the formation of parties, some large, others small) in fact works to the further advantage of the major parties because it is linked to strong feelings of loyalty and attachment to the crowd who have previously been elected. This disposition expresses itself in a 'fanatical Party loyalism', as Ostrogorski calls it. However, in order that the heartfelt need that is expressed in this enthusiasm for party membership may be fully satisfied, it must be able to manifest itself in a large grouping of which one can be proud. It seems to me that Ostrogorski is correct when he connects all these emotions with the fact that the American is impoverished in his access to primary groups and for that reason joins the large organisations of the old parties with all the longing of an isolated being. There is much truth in the following description:

> Like the ancient Greek who found in the most distant colonies his national deities and the fire from the sacred hearth of his *polis*, the American finds in his nomadic existence everywhere, from the Atlantic to the Pacific, from Maine to Florida, a Republican organization or a Democratic organization, which recalls him to himself, gives him a countenance and makes him repeat with pride the cry of the New York politician: 'I am a Democrat', or 'I am a Republican'.[39]

Thus, many motivations – of a real as well as of an imaginary nature – come together to produce the same result: the major parties are kept large and powerful and so their political monopoly is ensured. They have this monopoly because they are major parties, and they are the major parties because they have this monopoly.

4 The Failures of All Third Parties

The old major parties of America have been correctly compared with giant trusts that control such vast capital and dominate so exclusively all areas of supply and sale that any competition against them by third parties is out of the question. If a competitor comes on the scene, the old parties summon everything to devour him. If need be, they unite for a short time in order that together they may defeat their foolhardy rival in battle.

The history of third parties in America is therefore a sad story of continual defeats that leaves little hope for the future. A quick glance at the vain attempts that have so far been made to break the monopoly of the old parties will confirm the correctness of what has been said. In the following list I am counting only the better-known parties that have been founded, and I make no claim to completeness.

1830—Anti-Masonic Party: this owed its origin to a chance event (the mysterious disappearance of a former Masonic lodge brother, who was assumed to have been murdered by his erstwhile Masonic comrades), and it generated some hostility against secret societies. The party disappeared after a few years.[40]

1840—Abolitionists (later the *Liberty Party* and the *Free Soilers*): the Abolitionists opposed polygamy and slavery. In the 1850s they became part of the Republican Party without having achieved any significance themselves.

1843—Native American Party:[41] their programme was the exclusion from public offices, etc. of all those not born in America. They gained ground only in New York, Philadephia, and some other cities. They soon collapsed, only to revive again in 1854 under the name of Know-Nothings.[42]

1854—Know-Nothing American Party: in the 1850s the Know-Nothings achieved some significance. In 1855 they elected Governors and State Representatives in New Hampshire, Massachusetts, Rhode Island, Connecticut, New York and California, and they elected a part of their ticket in Maryland. In Virginia, Georgia, Alabama, Louisiana, Mississippi and Texas the Democratic majorities were at least strongly reduced because of them. In 1856 they held their first and only convention, and for all that they won 874,534 votes in the Presidential election of that year against 3,179,433 for the two major parties,[43] although in fact they secured only the eight Electoral College votes of Maryland out of the total of 296. A few years after this the Know-Nothings disappeared.[44]

1872—Prohibition Party (Prohibitionists): their programme was: fighting 'alcoholism' through Federal, state and local action; direct election of the President; Civil Service Reform; reduction of post, railway and telegraph charges; female suffrage; a sound currency with redeemable paper money. Their vote total rose from 5608 in the first year to 246,876 in 1888, and since then it has fluctuated around that total. The party continues to exist; in 1904 it received 260,303 votes.

1874—Greenback Party: originally this was a party whose sole aim was currency reform – the withdrawal of national bank notes, the declaration of paper money as the only valid currency, permission for the settlement of all debts in paper money. In 1877 the party, which originally consisted only of farmers and petty entrepreneurs, received additional support from the working class. It then adopted the title of the Greenback Labor Party. Its vote-total suddenly increased from 81,740 in 1876 to 1,000,000 in 1878, only to fall again just as quickly. In 1880 it received 308,578 votes, and in 1884 175,370. Soon it was to disappear completely as an independent party, after another attempt had been made in 1886 by the Knights of Labor to revive the old Greenback Party as the Union Labor Party. In 1888 this party achieved a total of 146,836 votes at the Presidential election, and then it too disappeared.

1890—People's Party (Populists): this party was made up of representatives from the Farmers' Alliance (a radical farmers' association), the Knights of Labor, the Single-tax Clubs of Henry George,[45] and others, and it displayed essentially small-farmer and petty-bourgeois democratic tendencies. Its programme, which reached the height of confusion not found even among American party organisations, demanded among other things: free coinage of silver, State ownership of the large institutions of communication and transportation; the establishment of postal savings banks; that 'all land owned by corporations or by aliens should be handed over to actual settlers'; the introduction of the referendum; direct election of the President by the people; introduction of the legally enforced eight-hour day; abolition of the Pinkerton police; and so on.

The success of the Populists was the greatest that a third party had ever achieved in the United States. At the 1892 Presidential election it already had 1,055,424 votes and – what is still more significant – twenty-two votes in the Electoral College. Moreover, it was the first time since the Civil War that Electoral College votes were cast for a third party. In 1894 their vote-total rose to 1,564,318. In 1896 the party was already a thing of the past. The Democratic

Party (which at that time had to contend with the difficult problem of the silver controversy in its ranks) almost completely absorbed the Populists, who all voted for the Silver Democrat, Bryan. A small rump remained. In 1900 around 50,000 of these voted for Barker and in 1904 144,637 voted for Watson.

This tragic fate of all third parties has undoubtedly contributed still more to increasing the difficulties facing an independent party. It has brought third parties into disrepute. The character of third parties can be inferred from the numerous individual cases of their failure. Of course, the major parties show an active interest in propagating among the people the idea that all third parties are 'utopian', inviable, 'un-American', and so on. They derive new vitality from the lamentable downfall of their competitors, and this vitality would present a further obstacle to the strong development of an independent Socialist Party.

However, I can imagine at this point that the scrupulous reader may still not be satisfied with the reasoning put forward so far. He will ask whether it is really only the mere state of party organisation that has till now prevented the emergence of a Socialist movement. Against this hypothesis he will raise the following objection: reference to the fiasco of other parties that have been founded is not on its own convincing. Have not all these parties failed through their own weakness? Were they not inviable because they were incapable of moving clearly towards a particular goal and because they lacked a base among groups of the population with similar interests? Is not the Socialist movement different from all those other ones named precisely because it is based on homogeneous interests?

Should not a party that really pursues grand aims and really serves the common interests of the broad mass of people be able to succeed in the long run against the old parties? Even in the history of political parties in the United States we have one important example of the possibility, in extraordinary circumstances, of breaking the monopoly of the major parties and of forming a new and viable party. There is no more humble example than that of the present Republican Party, which was borne up on the enthusiasm for the abolition of slavery and knew how to maintain its quickly won position of control. Of course, at the time of the rise of the Republican Party, whose beginnings go back to 1854, conditions were considerably more favourable to the emergence of third parties. Party discipline was not yet as strong as now, and in the West, where the new party first gained ground, party organisation was very weakly developed. The effective political machine was all created just after the Civil War, and by the Republican Party itself.

It might still be said that what one party managed to do using the battle cry of 'Emancipating the Black Slaves' should be attainable by a party today, even in harder circumstances, when it has proclaimed the much more powerful and comprehensive slogan of 'Emancipating the White Slaves from the Fetters of Capitalism' and of 'Emancipating the Proletariat'. If it really were possible to unite the broad sections of the working population on this programme and in that way to awaken their class consciousness, it seems to me that no election machine, however complicated, and no monopoly of the major parties, however longstanding, would halt such a triumphal march.

If therefore one wishes to give an exhaustive account of the reasons that until now have stopped the growth of Socialism in the United States, one will have to delve more deeply into the problem and trace the more hidden causes, which I do not think are hard to find if one looks carefully. To the extent to which they are to be discussed in this context, they still lie partly in the area of politics. One must endeavour to recognise not only the outward shape but also the inner nature of American politics. This applies especially to matters concerning party politics. The reason why the old parties have their electoral monopoly is undoubtedly largely that they are the major parties and possess the most effective political machine. However, their character itself contributes to the maintenance of this monopoly. Today they are still the parties of the predominant part of the working class for all the reasons I have set forth, even though such reasons may be specious, but in spite of this they would not be so if it were not in their nature to make it easy for the wage labourer, even the class-conscious one, to belong to them. The reason for this will be explained in what follows.

5 The Inner Nature of the Ruling Parties

For the educated person from central Europe American parties are a riddle from the start. Even their names! I remember how hard I found it at the time when I first became interested in politics to make up my mind in favour of one of the two major American parties. I did not know anything about them other than their names. I liked both names equally well and therefore found the choice dreadfully difficult. While in every other country I found at least one party whose name was acceptable – the *estrema sinistra*, the *radicaux* or the *extrême gauche*, the Fortschrittspartei or even the Freisinnige Volkspartei[46] – I stood between the names of the American parties like Buridan's Ass[47] between the two bundles of hay. I found 'Democratic' just as good as 'Republican', and I could not for the life of me discover which of the parties was the more 'radical' (it being a foregone conclusion that my sympathies would go to this one). I found that 'Democrats' could just as well be to the 'left' of 'Republicans' as 'Republicans' could be to the left of 'Democrats'.

This distressing experience as a boy was quite natural. Even to someone of mature judgement the nature of the contrast between these two names must appear puzzling, and their official nomenclature must cause trouble to anyone wanting to fathom what the two parties stand for. This is because the titles that the parties bear do not in fact express any contrast or even any difference. They are simply nonsensical. One feels therefore that one will have to ignore the names and look to the programmes, in which there will be found at least some difference of viewpoint, if not a definite contrast. However, anyone who cherishes even these expectations will be bitterly disappointed. There is no trace of any fundamental difference of viewpoint between the two American parties on the most important political questions.

Usually one distinguishes them according to their respective positions towards the roles of the Federal government and the individual states. The Republicans are called centralists and the Democrats particularists. This contrast is obviously a historical one, however, and today it is at most of only theoretical significance, since there is no implication that practical politics should vary according to this criterion. For years there has been hardly any noticeable conflict between the interests of the Federal government and those of the individual states. If there were to be any, however, it would always be doubtful what stance either individual party would take. Its opinion would be decided according to whether it might expect an increase in its support in adopting one orientation rather than the other. If one were to construe the difference between Democrats and Republicans as corresponding to that between particularism and centralism, this would not be expressing the inner nature of these parties; one would be in a position similar to that of someone who wanted to explain to a foreigner the difference between Conservatives and National Liberals in Germany in the same terms. There was a difference once, but long, long ago![48]

In all other decisive political questions, however, the contrast between Republicans and Democrats is now even more reduced.

For a while the parties stood in sharp opposition to each other on the currency issue. The Democrats yielded too easily to the interests of the owners of silver mines and came out for the free coinage of silver. Today this issue no longer divides the Republicans and Democrats. The dispute over the correct currency policy, in so far as it is still continuing, has broken out much more in the ranks of the Democrats, and there are Gold Democrats and Silver Democrats.

Occasionally it seems that there is a tendency for the Democratic Party to lean more to free trade and for the Republican Party to favour protective tariffs. One should not forget, however, that the Democrats stand up for free trade, or the moderation of protectionist policies, only in opposition to the prevailing Republican policy. If they themselves were to have the power of decision, their free-trade stance would very soon be substantially moderated, for one should remember that Pennsylvania is inclined to protectionism on account of its iron industry, that northern Georgia and southern Tennessee have similar tendencies for the self-same reason, and that Louisiana demands the protective tariff in the interest of its sugar industry. The Democratic Party must defer to these important states, so that it never espouses the free-trade view too strongly, while its demands for the reduction of the tariff are made more from the viewpoint of financial policy. On the other hand, the number of free-traders in the ranks of the Republican Party is by no means small.

On the alcohol issue, which excites America so much, both parties also have to prevaricate without committing themselves. Each has to be prepared for serious losses in the event of wanting to support the anti-alcohol movement vigorously. The Irish and the Germans are drinkers *par excellence*. The great majority of the former, however, are Democrats, while most of the latter are Republicans.[49]

The position of the two parties *vis-à-vis* Civil Service Reform is just as indecisive; both are equally hostile to it and both attest their sympathies for it with equal warmth. Similarly, they are indecisive about the legal regulation of the trusts, and the railway, telegraph and telephone companies, and on the issue of State intervention in general. On all these and other points the party platforms utter mostly such vague phrases as the following: they will make it their business to give the problem their constant attention and to try to solve it in a way that would most correspond to the interests of all and be consistent with the sacred traditions of the State. In short, first there is talk around the subject, and when it comes to the point, they seek a respectable way out of it.

I think that one will do justice to the two major parties in the United States only if one first of all puts aside all ideas that one has formed on the basis of the European situation regarding what form a political party takes. This means that American parties are not to be seen as groups of people united in the representation of common political principles, although this was perhaps the case at one time when they began. It may perhaps be correctly said that in the first decades of the Republic those representing a more centralist viewpoint went into the Federalist Party, while those advocating a separatist, states' rights or anti-centralist policy went to the Republican Party (i.e., the Democratic Republicans); the former were more orientated to the ideal of Order and the latter to that of Liberty, as Bryce would like to construe the contrast. However, to whatever extent this may have been true and whatever difference of principle there may have once been, by the end of the second decade of the nineteenth century, around 1820, this distinction certainly already belonged to the past. When in 1824 Van Buren organised the opposition to the just-elected John Quincy Adams, he was in something of a dilemma as to the reason for a fight. Finally he found one in the defence of states' rights, which were allegedly in danger but were really not being threatened by anyone. As is well known, he chose Jackson as a leader and understood perfectly how to raise enthusiasm for the new man out of nothing. Jackson soon appeared as the champion of the 'sacred rights of the people', which of course his opponent honoured just as much as he did. One might now imagine that with this new type of party organisation stronger democratic tendencies would really have established themselves, but there was no further talk on the subject. Later adversaries did not think of allowing the democratic catchword to lose its value as far as they were concerned. Van Buren was to experience that himself when he was later sacrificed. He followed Jackson in the Presidency, and his opponent became Harrison. Now Harrison was brought forward as the 'man of the people' against Van Buren, as the latter had himself done with Jackson against Adams. Harrison was the 'log cabin' candidate and the man of the people who led a frugal, simple life and cultivated all the virtues of a simple man, while Van Buren lived in a palace, dined with golden knives and forks, and so on.[50]

These facts indicate that the factors which originally produced the different parties had lost their effectiveness. The *raison d'être* of the political party had disappeared. Consequently the parties would have had to disband if they had really wanted to be no more than champions of particuar political principles. However, they did not disband, thanks to their own staying power and out of a consideration for the other purpose that a political organisation can serve in a democratic commonwealth – the hunting for offices.

The organisation that had not managed to attain control now recognised that its only task was the achievement of power, so that it could distribute the spoils among its followers. The fact that the population (for reasons deriving from its particular character) was initially divided into two camps resulted in a dichotomy in political organisation that was not disrupted. With the lack of political principle to distinguish the parties, this dichotomy would not in itself have been necessary. There need have been only one bunch of job-seekers. As said already, the existence of two parties rests on historical accident.

At the time of the Civil War, however, a change occurred; the situation regarding slavery gave rise to further disputes about principles. The Republican Party emerged with a sharply defined programme whose essential point was the determined opposition to slavery. However, this basis for differentiation between the parties disappeared even more quickly than in the first decades of the Republic, and even more radically. With the abolition of slavery the Republican Party would have been obliged to disappear forthwith from the picture, but it did not disappear. The complete lack of political principle in the two major parties became quite blatant for the first time. Today, in fact, they are no more than organisations for the common purpose of hunting offices: Bryce says, 'all has been lost, except office or the hope of getting it', and Ostrogorski says, 'politics is merely a means for getting and distributing places'.[51] This emerges especially clearly from the fact that the United States – the democracy *par excellence* – none the less does not have any party government. In Congress in Washington there are really no parties any more. The strict discipline that governs elections ends on the threshold of Congress. Here the individual Congressman acts according to his own free judgement. Politics resolve themselves into an aggregation of private transactions which the individual Congressmen find it advantageous to conclude, whether with the government or with the different interest groups in the population who have their respective representatives in the Houses of Congress. Thus, even the crucial decisions are taken in the murkiness of committee sessions, while the deliberations of the full Congress have sunk to complete insignificance. To be understood in the context of these facts is the phenomenon which Europeans find so very strange, namely that the Executive and the majority in the legislature belong to different parties as often as to the same one. From Jackson's resignation until the end of the century (with the exception of the Civil War years, when the belligerent states were not however represented in Congress at all) the President and the majority of Congress have without exception not belonged to one and the same party in any single Presidential term of office. Instead – more especially after the second year of the Presidency – a majority hostile to the President is returned to Congress.[52]

The two major parties can now be differentiated from each other no more by social class than by political principles. Let us pass over the question of how far class interests originally had a voice in the formation of the political parties – it seems as if the Federalists were more the party of commercial and industrial capital in the New England states and the so-called Republicans of that time were more the party of small farmers. Certainly this distinction according to class criteria had already been obliterated in Jackson's time, since by his period we find the anti-capitalist trait equally in both parties, and the distinction was lost fully when the new Republican Party was formed at the time of the Civil War. Even if one wanted to construe the whole movement that led to the emancipation of the slaves and to the Civil War as one staged exclusively out of class interests and if one wanted to apply to that movement formulations of the fight between capitalism and feudalism that had been derived from the European experience (and one would then have to speak of the Republicans as champions of the capitalist class), such a contrast would none the less have become very feeble by today.[53] The Negro question has directly removed any class character from each of the two parties and has caused the concentration of strength to be much more according to geographical areas than class membership.

Since ('out of an old attachment to their liberators') the Negroes vote Republican almost to a man, it goes without saying that all elements of the population in the Southern states who belong to 'good society' vote Democratic – whether they be white farmers (tenants as well as property-owners) or industrial or commercial entrepreneurs, or whether they be members of the liberal professions. In other words, the ruling class, whose members in the Northern and Central states are perhaps inclined more to the Republican Party, belong to the Democratic Party in the Southern states.

Besides these geographical distinctions, differences of nationality among the immigrants play a role in the way the parties are organised. The Irish are Democrats almost to a man, whether because as Catholics they found the once strong and puritanical observance of the Republicans repugnant or because they settled first in New York when it was already in the hands of the Democratic Party. On the other hand, the Republicans are the predominant choice of the Germans, either because in natural opposition to the Irish they sought out the other party (as is one view) or because (as others correctly think) they settled as farmers in the Central and Western states where there was already a Republican majority that they simply joined.[54]

Enough has been said. One may twist and turn the issue as one wishes, but with the best will in the world it is no longer possible to discover any particular class features in America's two major parties.

The unique character of the major parties (as I have attempted to describe them in the previous pages – in terms of their external organisation, their lack of political principles and their social heterogeneity) has a decisive significance for the question that is of interest to us here. It obviously influences strongly the fundamental relations between the old parties and the proletariat. First of all, it makes it extremely easy for the proletariat to belong to the traditional parties. In attaching himself to one of the two parties, even the class-conscious worker need never go against the dictates of his intellect, because these parties do not have to be seen as class organisations and as advocates of a specific class interest; instead they may be seen as essentially neutral groupings that are united for purposes to which, as we saw, even the representatives of the proletariat are by no means indifferent – namely, hunting for offices. I said 'one of the two' parties because even the wage-labouring class is represented just as much in one party as in the other, depending on respective local contingencies.

However, the unique character of the old parties not only makes the position of the proletariat towards these parties different from what it would be in any European state. The character of the parties also influences the position that they take towards the proletariat. This means that between the proletariat and the old parties a good understanding is produced or, more correctly, the traditionally good relationship is maintained intact.

It is undoubtedly true that both major parties have a strongly populist streak in their characters. Each of them can point to periods in its history when it has outspokenly supported some oppressed social group or other. In the Republican Party's crown of glory the leaf commemorating its support for the slaves has not always withered; the Democrats have backed up the exploited farmers; and so on.

However, what is more important is that at the moment the parties have the roots of their entire organisation in the mass of the people. The activists who form the great majority of party workers have come from the lower class and have often enough risen to leading party positions. The system working here is the same as that of the Roman Catholic Church. The hierarchy of the party, by resting on a purely democratic basis, preserves popular trust in the party. This corresponds with the comparable trust produced when the worker lets a drink be bought for him in the saloon and knows that even the party boss has risen from his ranks. Trust seems to me to be the most essential factor for all party organisation. It is infinitely more important than the best-reasoned programme. It is like the situation in Germany, for example, where the great attraction of Social Democracy rests in good part on the trust that the masses place in their leaders, above all in those who are seen to have suffered on their behalf; this is the basis of the large and still continuing force of the Socialist Law as a factor in contributing to the party's strength.

Now the matter does not just rest with this emotional feeling between the people and the qualified representatives of the party. Instead the party must, for reasons of prudence, try systematically to keep the masses in a good humour, for their success in elections is naturally dependent upon the votes of the population. The chance circumstance that there are two major parties competing with each other now benefits the proletariat, as well as all lower social strata. This fact has on its own ensured that both parties have set about earning for themselves the favour of this class of voters, or else they have actively attempted to retain their support. They have operated dexterously to do this, essentially by making concessions to the wage-labouring class whose members, at least in many districts, deliver the decisive votes.

In order to exploit still further the situation in which the ruling parties are open to pressure, a quite special system has very recently been put into operation by those representing the workers' interests: this is the system of questioning candidates, which has been made disreputable by its opponents, the supporters of the Socialist Parties, with the somewhat disrespectful description of a 'begging policy'.[55] None the less, today it apparently enjoys great popularity with the large majority of organised workers in America. It consists of the representatives of the workers' interests, i.e., the leaders of the trade unions or of the large trade-union alliances, presenting to the candidate who wants the workers' vote a carefully prepared questionnaire and making their decision whether to vote for him or not dependent upon the outcome of the questioning.

As far as I know, this system was first operated in Winnetka, Illinois, in the middle of the 1890s, and it is therefore called the Winnetka System. The reason for its being brought into operation was not to promote the interests of a particular group in the population, but rather so that with its help the community might receive the supposed advantages of direct legislation by the people. The method conceived was seen as 'a system by which the people can secure the practical application of direct legislation without any change in the written constitution of the state or the local charter'. In 1901 the American Federation of Labor took up the practice, and it was decided to publish an extra number of the *Federationist* in which the system was to be explained and recommended. This number appeared in January 1902 and was widely distributed.[56]

Since then the system has been adopted in various towns and states –

ADDRESS AND QUESTIONS TO CANDIDATES FOR LEGISLATURES.

.... 1904.

Hon...

Candidate for the Legislature,

DEAR SIR:

You are asking the people of the district to select you as their representative in the Legislature. This entitles them to ask you as to your attitude on the issues in which they are interested and by which they are affected—the burning questions of the day. Preparatory to doing this permit us to outline the basis of the political evils, which we do in the accompanying address and questions to candidates for Congress, which we invite you to read, and to do so at once, that you may realize the far-reaching importance of the questions we are to ask.

SOLUTION OF BURNING NATIONAL QUESTIONS.

The burning questions of the day are *national*, for our country has developed to where the railroads and all the other great corporations are interstate, therefore nothing short of interstate law will suffice.

In the settlement of these great national issues the members of the Legislatures are vital factors. They elect United States Senators and therefore can pledge them to vote to abolish government by injunction and to install the eight-hour day in government contract work and to install the advisory initiative and advisory referendum; secondly, the members of the Legislature can *instruct* the hold-over Senators—instruct them to vote for these three measures; and, thirdly, the members of the Legislature can vote to establish by State law the machinery for verifying signatures to national petitions and for taking a referendum vote whenever Congress shall so decide. To that end we ask you, sir—

QUESTION No. 1.—If elected, will you vote only for such candidate or candidates for the United States Senate as have promised in writing to vote to abolish government by injunction, to install the eighthour day in government contract work and to install the advisory initiative and advisory referendum, the details to conform to the measures we herewith enclose, subject to such minor changes in lastmentioned

system as may beagreed to by the Legislative Committees of the A. F. of L. and the National Grange?

Answer . . . .

QUESTION No. 2.—If elected, will you vote to instruct the hold-over Senators—instruct them to vote for the above-described measures?

Answer . . . .

QUESTION No. 3.—If elected, will you help to enact a statute whereby five per cent of the voters of the State calculated on the basis of the last vote for governor, may call a special election for a referendum vote on a proposition to instruct United States Senators if one or both of them shall fail to obey the Legislature's instruction?

Answer . . . .

QUESTION No. 4.—Do you promise that if elected you will help to enact a statute that shall supply the machinery for verifying signatures to national petitions, and the taking of a referendum vote when so decided by Congress, the details to conform to the measure we herewith submit, subject to such minor changes as may be agreed to by the Legislative Committees of the A. F. of L. and the National Grange?

Answer . . . .

To each of the questions asked we would like a clear-cut "yes" or "no." If you or any other candidate refuses to come out for the people, squarely and openly, in writing, signed by yourself, we shall take the steps described in our letter to Congressional candidates.

Please let us hear from you at your earliest opportunity. A refusal to reply during the next ten days will be a negative to our questions and we shall govern ourselves accordingly.

Respectfully yours,

....

By...

Chairman Legislative Committee.

BLANK FORM FOR REPLY.
(DETACH AND MAIL.)

....

.... **1904.**

Mr....

....

DEAR SIR: Replying to the questions in your letter I desire to make the following answers:

To question No. 1, my answer is............ Question No. 2 ....
Question No. 3 .... Question No. 4 ....

I remain, sir, very respectfully yours,

....

Candidate for the Senate (House),
For the...........District of.....................

with success, it has been asserted.[57] In 1904 it was for the first time made an integral part of trade-union policy in a comprehensive way. The Executive Council of the American Federation of Labor sent to all industrial federations and local trade unions affiliated to it a circular dated 15 July, in which they were strongly urged to introduce the Winnetka System in their election districts. Two model questionnaires for members of Congress and for members of the State Legislature were attached to the document.[58] Also announced in it were the points on which the policy of the American Federation of Labor and its members was to be primarily concentrated. They are as follows:

1. the introduction of the initiative and the referendum:
2. the passing of a Federal law that would establish the eight-hour day for all jobs given by the Government on contract;
3. the passing of a law against injunctions, i.e., a law that would prevent the restriction of judicial restraining orders placed upon workers who are striking, etc.

The questionnaire for candidates to the State Legislature accordingly has the text shown in the accompanying reproduction.

Anti-Socialist trade-union leaders attach a great deal of hope to this system. They think that in this way they have permanently removed the threat and danger of an independent Socialist workers' party. Others see the introduction of this system of questioning as the beginning of the end of the old situation, taking the view that the failures which they think the workers will experience cannot fail to drive them out of the old parties, once their participation in politics as a class is sanctioned by the system. At this stage I do not have any position to take on this question, since I am not expounding about possible future developments but want only to give the reasons that *until now* have halted the growth of a strong Socialist workers' party in the United States. However, it must be remembered in the first place that the working class, even after it had begun to practise 'independent politics', lived in the belief that by skilful exploitation of the old two-party politics it could secure for itself all the advantages to which it aspired.[59] This belief, to which the working class has been socialised from time immemorial and which was nurtured by the character of American party politics already described, has now experienced only a hardening into dogma by the introduction of the Winnetka System. For this reason I have had to mention the system here, although its effects belong to the future rather than the past.

6 The Position of the American Worker in the State

I hope that everything that I have so far set out in relation to the characteristic attitude of the American worker towards politics and his distinctive position in politics accounts plausibly for the fact that the proletariat in the United States has not so far come forward to form its own party; I hope that it could be said that what I have set out explains the lack of any formal representation of the Socialist viewpoint. However, it still does not sufficiently explain why Socialist perspectives are so weakly developed in America nor why the mood, whose existence we have already acknowledged, favouring acceptance of the political and social order is dominant in the great bulk of the American working class. It would be wrong to underestimate the moral content of this mood and to attribute all manifestations of its joyful optimism purely and simply to the prospects of achieving an office in the State. On looking more deeply into the matter, we find that the strong aversion of the American worker to Socialist tendencies of the embittered sort to be found in Europe is to be explained in good part by the distinctiveness of his political situation. In particular, his love for the existing State is certainly explained by the political position that he occupies in this State.

It is a frequently observed peculiarity of the American worker that he perceives a kind of divine revelation in the Constitution of his country, and consequently he reveres it with devout awe. His feelings towards the Constitution are as if it were something holy that is immune from mortal criticism. This has been rightly spoken of as 'constitutional fetish worship'.[60]

The American worker is brought up from childhood, in school and in public life, with this orientation, and when he comes to reflect on it himself he has no reason to change the viewpoint inculcated into him in so many ways. Everything that he can reasonably demand in the way of rights is in fact guaranteed to him in the Constitution because he is part of the People.[61]

We came across individual aspects of the radical-democratic character of the Constitution earlier, when we were seeking some idea of the extent of suffrage. Over and above all these individual rights, however, the Constitution stipulates that it can always be altered by the People,

and only by the People, in a direct vote. The whole Constitution therefore rests on the basis of popular sovereignty,[62] and – as in other matters
previously mentioned – only Switzerland provides a comparable
example. The sovereign People alone decides on what law there should
be throughout the United States. The availability of this right leads to
a series of far-reaching consequences upon the character of the spirit
governing public life. First of all, it has produced what one might call
a democratic cliché and has developed it considerably.

The frequent demand upon the citizens to participate in elections has
given added impetus to this development. The call to exercise the
'sacred rights of the People' is again and again being heard, and the
simple man again and again feels that he is surrounded by the entire
exalted prestige of the 'sovereign'. 'We, the free People of America...'
'We, the People of the State of ... , grateful to Almighty God for our
freedom, ...': that kind of thing resounds into the American's ears from
childhood onwards. The last and poorest commoner has a part in the
sacred sovereignty; at least formally, he is the People and the People
are the State.

In this way there grows up in every individual an unrestrained
feeling of power, unrealistic though this may be. In his consciousness
it is an undoubted reality. 'The citizen believes that he is still king in
the State and that he can bring things to order if he only wants to.
The words of the orator speaking to the people, "If the American
People will stand up in its power and majesty", are by no means simple
clichés to his audience. Every individual amongst them believes in this
mysterious power that calls itself "the American People" and that
nothing can resist. Everyone has a mystical trust in the efficacy of the
People's will and speaks of it with a sort of religious ecstasy. This trust
often stands in striking contrast to what has really been achieved or
even only aspired to. For the most part the citizen does not lift a finger
to remove the inconveniences of public life, but lives with the firm conviction that he only has to wish that they be brought to an end for that
to happen. This conviction keeps the love of justice and the hatred of
injustice alive within him, like a fire from which one seldom sees a
spark, but which is not extinguished and can break out at any time
into a flame of enthusiasm that spreads light and warmth.'

Very closely connected with this is one final important characteristic
of political life in the United States; this is the immense significance
that 'public opinion' has for everything which takes place. This really
is a substantial governing force to which the judicial authorities defer,
as well as the executive and legislative bodies. We saw that in America
there is no party discipline in the sense that this exists in England,
France and Italy. One reason for that lies in the character of party
politics in America, but another one lies in the circumstances stressed
here that in the Constitution the People have sovereign control over all

public authorities and can send these packing at any moment. Consequently the elected representatives of the People – no matter whether they are judicial or administrative officials or members of Congress – are subject to the continuous control of the population, whose will is expressed in the mysteries of 'public opinion' when it is not being shown directly in voting.

As is well known, the President and (in most states) the Governor have the right to veto decisions of Congress and of the State Legislatures. However, they will exercise that power only when they are sure of having public opinion behind them. In such a case even the legislatures will give up putting through a particular bill, even though they can overturn a veto with a two-thirds majority. The effectiveness of public opinion is naturally increased by the short periods between elections. This predominance of public opinion cannot do otherwise than assist in increasing immensely every citizen's consciousness of power. If the general disposition of the people really is the deciding factor in the political process, this must produce in the individual citizen and therefore also in the worker an intensive feeling of participation in political activity. The worker has in every respect the same formal rights as the richest trust magnate; moreover, he knows that behind him are the mass of his fellow workers, who are the decisive factor in elections, and he is confident in the effectiveness of his constitutionally guaranteed individual rights. The comparative strength of individual social groups, which comes out, for example, in the make-up of Congress or the class membership of individual officials, is completely subsumed in public opinion. Since he is himself helping to make public opinion, the little man can imagine that by its means he is the one who in the last analysis determines the destinies of the State, despite all indication to the contrary.

In addition, there is the fact that public opinion in America – at least until recently – has always been sympathetically disposed to specific workers' interests. The worker's consciousness that he has some value in the State is therefore strengthened in a twofold manner. Ought he not then continue to be satisfied with this State system? The State after all not only grants him a full share in public life, but in addition it values him politically and socially as a full citizen. All the courts try to win his favour. In America the worker, as he sees the position, is fully entitled to strike his chest proudly and say with head held high: '*civis americanus sum*'.

To be sure, this formal equality of rights in the State is not all that matters. As was stated in the *Doléances*[68] during the French Revolution: 'The voice of Liberty proclaims nothing to the heart of a poor man who is dying of hunger.' A radical-democratic system of government can indeed attract the population to the idea of the State, but it will not be able to prevent criticism of the prevailing society, and especially of the existing economic order, if the latter does not also guarantee a tolerable material existence to the people. Reasons for the lack of a popular movement opposing the governmental and social systems cannot then be found exclusively in the character of the political position of the population. Instead, what may be referred to in general terms as economic situation must correspond with political circumstances. The task of the following section is to present evidence that the economic situation of the North American proletarian is also such – or, more correctly, was also such – as to protect the country from the entanglements of Socialism.

SECTION TWO[1]

The Economic Situation of the Worker

1 A General View

The adequate consideration of the standard of living of a person or a family means establishing how much the unit of domestic consumption in question spends upon commodities during a particular economic period. It also means placing this amount in relation to the material requirements of life; in short, it means examining whether the quantity of commodities concerned is sufficient to fulfil the conditions necessary for an existence worthy of a human being, and whether it also leaves latitude for the satisfaction of cultural and luxury needs. Examination of the standard of living of a population whose individual members have different incomes means forming groups and working out the size of the components of this population that fall into each of the several categories that comprise a graded scale of living standards; the categories of this scale can be distinguished as poverty, indigence, sufficiency, affluence, and wealth. One must especially find out how the 'bulk' of the population (the half lying between the lower and upper quartiles) lives. The comparison of the standards of living of two populations – of two nations, of two social classes inside a nation, or of the same social classes in two different nations[2] – would therefore involve examining how the two populations are divided between the categories of the scale of living standards.

Anyone who is to some extent familiar with the sources knows that to carry out such a programme for a whole country, or even for one social class within a country, encounters the greatest difficulties. One would need a complete inventory of all households to be found in a country or in a stratum of the population, and that does not of course exist. What comes closest to such an inventory is the data on individual household budgets that every country possesses in some form or other – the United States is furnished with the best of these data. One might think it appropriate to begin the enquiry here. However, one soon learns that this approach does not lead to the goal. All budgets, as well as every larger collection of budgets, lack information on the extent of their validity. In other words, the budgets say nothing about how large the percentage of a population is for which they are typical – and it is as a percentage of a population that we want for present purposes to regard the proletariat. Above all, however, these data do not permit comparisons because they do not allow one to ascertain whether they correspond with the same income-classification in any two populations that are being compared. One must therefore decide, even if unwillingly, to adopt an indirect approach, although this does bring one closer to the goal to which one aspires, since it involves the examination of money-incomes or (in our case) money-wages.

Of course, even here there are numerous obstacles. No country, not even the United States, has comprehensive and reliable wage statistics. None the less, we shall still be able to manage. The statistical material on wages that is available, particularly for the United States, is sufficient to give us an approximate picture of the structure of money-income in the working class, or at least to enable us to recognise the outlines of this picture. If one knows something of the rank-ordering of money-wages received, there are two possible ways of ascertaining the standard of living: as before, there is an indirect approach, which in this case establishes the prices of the individual commodities being consumed, and there is a direct approach, which involves the use of household budgets. The latter method is advantageous when one has been able to assign each household budget to its correct position in the ranking of total income and when therefore one has also been able to establish by particular comparisons whether any two household budgets from two respective populations or countries correspond to the same income-classification in each. Thus one can establish whether the domestic economic units being compared really have relatively similar standings.

Firstly then, I shall try to give a picture of the size and gradation of money-wages in the United States and I shall endeavour to compare the data thus obtained with those of other countries, particularly Germany.[3]

2 The Money-income of the Worker in America and Europe

The main sources of statistics on wages in the United States are the Census and the reports of the Bureaux of Labor Statistics.[4] In addition we have at our disposal a series of research works on average wages, as well as a large number of statistics classifying wages. Above all, our task is to contrast suitably selected American data with equivalent data for Europe, and particularly for Germany, that are as comparable as possible.

1. Data on average wages are given in the Census, the lame duck of official wage statistics.[5] In spite of methodological considerations tending to invalidate this research, I want to note some of its very general results.

The average annual wages of all industrial workers in 1900 are shown in Table 2.

What stands out above all else in Table 2 is the gap between the Southern states and all the others. It is therefore useful to give the averages for the United States when the South has been excluded; these were $513.96 (2158.63M) for men, $280.88 (1179.70M) for women, $167.64 (704.09M) for children, and $457.26 (1920.49M) for men, women and children together.

The figures presented here are not totally fanciful. This is borne out by the fact that on the one hand the average wages in the various economic regions of the United States do not differ too much from each other, but at the same time the averages do express fairly correctly the wage differences existing in the economy. If we wish to compare these crude figures of average wages with similar figures for European countries, the appropriate bases of comparison are the figures for average wages compiled by the German industrial associations that administer accident insurance.[6] Clearly one must compare these with American wages when the latter have been similarly partitioned into individual industries (but treating the whole country as a single unit in order to even out all local differences, as has been done with the German figures). I am choosing as the date for the German data the same year as that to which the Census figures refer (1900), which was the great boom year for the German economy. The fact that wages over 4 marks are not considered is therefore more than compensated for,[7]

TABLE 2   Average annual wages in 1900 of all industrial workers in America, by sex and region

Region	Men	Women	Children	Total
New England states	$507.12	$307.34	$187.15	$443.74
	(2129.90M)	(1290.83M)	(786.03M)	(1863.71M)
Middle states	$528.71	$280.75	$159.52	$461.52
	(2220.58M)	(1179.15M)	(669.98M)	(1938.38M)
Southern states	$334.96	$183.91	$107.20	$300.81
	(1406.83M)	(772.42M)	(450.24M)	(1263.40M)
Central states	$488.51	$249.45	$166.21	$446.51
	(2051.74M)	(1047.69M)	(698.08M)	(1875.34M)
Western states	$577.09	$273.48	$175.07	$543.98
	(2423.78M)	(1148.62M)	(735.29M)	(2284.72M)
Pacific states	$577.11	$278.09	$181.62	$526.90
	(2423.86M)	(1167.98M)	(762.80M)	(2212.98M)
United States	$490.90	$273.03	$152.22	$437.96
	(2061.78M)	(1146.73M)	(639.32M)	(1839.43M)

Source: United States Census Office, *Twelfth Census,* VII, Manufactures, Part I, Table XXXIX, pp. cxv–cxvi.

and the German data actually represent maxima. For the sake of clarity I have converted dollars into marks at a rate of 1 dollar to 4.20 marks.

In the case of the German data in Table 3 the different amounts quoted for the same industries represent differences between individual parts of the country. In the case of the American data they reflect the fact that several branches of industry correspond to each German industrial grouping, and different average wages apply to each branch. The compilation in Table 3 includes all industries for which fully comparable data may be determined. The average annual wages paid in 1900 in various industries in Germany and in the United States are now given in Table 3.

The official statistical data concerning wages of workers in the German mining industry have been derived by calculations similar to those used for the wage rates determined by the industrial associations that administer accident insurance.[8]

We can conveniently contrast them with wages for American mining that have also been calculated by the method employed by the Census.[9] Both are also average annual wages. I am giving those for the year 1902. In that year the American worker employed in bituminous coal-mining earned $629 (2642M) – with men's, women's and children's earnings calculated together. The miner[10] at the face earned $671 (2818M).[11]

On the other hand, the wages earned in the same year in coal-mining in Prussia are as follows: in the jurisdictional district of the Breslau

Superior Mining Board face workers earned on average 890 marks and all workers together earned an average of 815 marks; in the Dortmund jurisdiction the figures are 1314 and 1131 marks respectively, and in the Bonn jurisdiction they are 1199 and 1068 marks.

TABLE 3 Average annual wages in 1900 of workers in various industries in Germany and the United States[a]

Industry	Germany	United States
Clothing	621.4M	1323.0M–2276.4M
Glass	724.9M	2154.6M
Pottery	772.2M	1701.0M
Brick and tile	556.2M	1482.6M
Iron and steel	792.5M–1014.2M	1642.2M–3074.4M
Chemicals	929.4M	2070.6M
Textiles	506.0M–776.5M	1129.8M–2192.4M
Paper	714.4M–765.9M	1318.8M–2087.4M
Leather	895.4M	1436.4M–1822.8M
Wood	698.8M–821.0M	1407.0M–1801.8M
Milling	743.0M	2007.6M
Sugar	496.0M	2045.4M–2326.8M
Tobacco	541.1M	1024.8M–1663.2M
Book-printing	893.7M	1747.2M–2234.4M

Note

[a] *Ed.* – For the probable source of the German data see Note 7 of this Section. The entries in the German column are, for each *Berufsgenossenschaft* or group of them, the total amount of wages of insured persons that are chargeable in calculating contributions, divided by the number of insured persons. The entry against 'Sugar' is incorrectly given as 596.0M in Sombart's original text.

The source of the American data is United States Census Office, *Twelfth Census*, VII, Manufactures, Part I, Table XLI, pp. cxvii–cxxiii.

2.   Alongside the calculations of average wages and supplementing them are statistics on the *distributions* of wages. They are so much more valuable methodologically, and America is particularly well-endowed with them. The United States now has special wage data of unquestionable value: these are the cash-wages paid by 720 business establishments and they are systematically classified into wage-distributions.[12] However, there are also a great many valuable publications by the various Bureaux of Labor Statistics, which I have mentioned in my literature review. Unfortunately, we cannot contrast the American statistics on wage-distributions with comparable data for Germany because such data are not available in anything like the same quantity or quality. Absolutely nothing of this kind is published officially in Germany, and for that reason we must be pleased that we at least possess a series of research studies that have been capably executed by private individuals

and that contain valuable data on wages. With the help of this material we can still undertake some instructive comparisons. Having regard to the character of the comparative data, I am making selections from the large quantity of available American material with a view to maximising comparability.

The wage data cover either all or many of the industrial workers of an area, or the workers of a certain industry. Using the first of these types of data, I want to contrast the wage statistics for Massachusetts[13] and for Illinois[14] with similar statistics that we have on the workers of Stuttgart,[15] with the statistical information on the wages of industrial workers for seventeen communities around Karlsruhe that has been provided by Factory Inspector Rudolf Fuchs,[16] and also with research on workers in Hanau.[17]

I am very well aware that there are objections to such a comparative approach. However, I think this procedure is not entirely without justification and therefore has some value. I should certainly prefer to compare data on wage-distributions for the whole Kingdom of Saxony with those for Massachusetts, but at the present moment we have nothing better than the local data that I am using. There are two considerations that help to some extent to dispel the doubts that must arise, doubts that are primarily due to the difference in size of the areas whose wage structures are being compared: the first consideration is that industries of the most diverse sorts are found in all the areas being compared, and the second one is that any large differences are to some degree compensated for by the particularly wide coverage of even the private German enquiries. The Stuttgart study managed a sample of 6028 male workers, the Hanau one of 2382 workers, although the Karlsruhe study contained only something over a thousand. However, an inspection of the individual tables provides the greatest encouragement. One finds there a surprising internal consistency in the composition of the various wage categories, first within the American statistics and then within the German ones: this is evidence that one is using figures that, because of their typicality, have some degree of reliability. If one wants to be quite certain, one may increase by 10 or 15 per cent the rates of pay given in the German data being quoted for comparative purposes. (This is because they all refer to southern Germany and one of them refers to rural industries.) However, with this adjustment I strongly believe that the average wages of German industrial workers are expressed with some degree of accuracy in our tables, certainly in so far as they show those workers who do not belong exclusively to highly paid industries.

The structure of industrial wages for Massachusetts and Illinois in 1900 is shown in Table 4.

The contrasting incomes earned by the German industrial workers are as shown in Table 5.

TABLE 4 Distributions of average weekly wages in 1900 of workers in industry in Massachusetts and Illinois, by sex (in percentages)

| | Massachusetts | | Illinois | |
	Men	*Women*	*Men*	*Women*
Less than $5.00 (21.00M)	3.63	15.96	5.78	32.43
$5.00–$5.99 (21.00M–25.16M)	3.75	15.70	3.47	18.69
$6.00–$6.99 (25.20M–29.36M)	7.05	20.22	4.71	18.39
$7.00–$7.99 (29.40M–33.56M)	9.68	15.34	8.36	11.57
$8.00–$8.99 (33.60M–37.76M)	9.96	12.46	7.92	6.47
$9.00–$9.99 (37.80M–41.96M)	14.26	9.72	17.32	4.71
$10.00–$11.99 (42.00M–50.36M)	15.83	6.62	16.34	4.24
$12.00–$14.99 (50.40M–62.96M)	17.71	2.94	17.02	2.46
$15.00–$19.99 (63.00M–83.96M)	13.82	0.90	13.09	0.84
$20.00 (84.00M) or more	4.31	0.14	5.99	0.20
	100.00	100.00	100.00	100.00

Derived Descriptive Statistics[a]

Mean	$11.36	$7.25	$11.55	$6.38
	(47.71M)	(30.45M)	(48.51M)	(26.80M)
Median	$10.21	$6.90	$10.29	$5.94
	(42.88M)	(28.98M)	(43.22M)	(24.95M)
Semi-interquartile Range	$2.88	$1.53	$2.81	$1.47
	(12.10M)	(6.43M)	(11.80M)	(6.17M)
Quartile Coefficient of Variation	0.262	0.215	0.252	0.244

Note

[a] *Ed.* – In those calculations where a lower class limit of the bottom class and an upper class limit of the top class are needed, the following values have been used: the lower class limit of the bottom class has been taken as $3.00 and the upper class limit of the top class as $29.99.

If one looks at the major features of the arrays of figures in Tables 4 and 5, the following facts are to be clearly distinguished. In Massachusetts 7.38 per cent of men earned less than $6.00, and in Illinois 9.25 per cent; in Stuttgart 69.8 per cent of men earned less than 24.01 marks (the nearest equivalent in marks to $6.00), in Karlsruhe 79.6 per cent, and in Hanau 88.2 per cent. Approximately as many men in Illinois (63.77 per cent) earned between 37.80 and 83.96 marks ($9.00 and $19.99) a week as earned between 15.01 and 27.00 marks in the Karlsruhe region, the exact equivalent percentage being 67.1 per cent. Four-fifths of the men in Massachusetts, and therefore the greater majority (in fact, 81.26 per cent), earned between 29.40 and 83.96 marks ($7.00 and $19.99), while in Stuttgart and Hanau the same proportion (in fact, 79.2 per cent and 82.5 per cent respectively) earned only between 15.01 and 27.00 marks.

Only a very small number of women in the German areas where

data were collected earned over 20.00 marks; 0.8 per cent of women in Karlsruhe and 1.5 per cent in Stuttgart earned over 15.00 marks. In the American areas of data collection 84.04 per cent of women in Massachusetts and 67.57 per cent in Illinois earned $5.00 (the nearest

TABLE 5 Distributions of average weekly wages in industry around Karlsruhe and in Stuttgart and Hanau, by sex (in percentages)

	Around Karlsruhe[a]	*In Stuttgart*	*In Hanau*
Men			
Less than 12.01M	11.1	1.6	2.3
12.01M–15.00M	10.5	6.1	12.2
15.01M–18.00M	19.4	18.7	23.5
18.01M–21.00M	22.3	22.3	27.9
21.01M–24.00M	16.3	21.1	22.3
24.01M–27.00M	9.1	17.1	8.8
27.01M–30.00M	4.7	8.3	1.7
30.01M or more	6.5	4.8	1.3
	99.9[b]	100.0	100.0
Derived Descriptive Statistics			
Mean	19.50M	22.22M	19.36M[c]
Median	19.21M	21.19M	19.30M
Semi-interquartile Range	3.81M	3.57M	2.95M
Quartile Coefficient of Variation	0.197	0.167	0.153
Women			
Less than 6.01M	11.5	7.1	
6.01M–9.00M	44.8	42.7	
9.01M–12.00M	38.5	37.0	
12.01M–15.00M	4.4	11.7	
15.01M or more	0.8	1.5	
	100.0	100.0	
Derived Descriptive Statistics			
Mean	8.64M	9.57M	
Median	8.58M	9.02M	
Semi-interquartile Range	1.78M	1.90M	
Quartile Coefficient of Variation	0.204	0.207	

Notes
[a] *Ed.* – The primary source of the Karlsruhe data gives daily rather then weekly earnings. Sombart assumed a six-day working week and, perhaps a little generously, merely multiplied the daily figures by six to obtain weekly figures comparable with his other sets of data.
[b] *Ed.* – This total contains a rounding error.
[c] *Ed.* – In calculating the mean of the Hanau data on male earnings, the lower class limit of the bottom class has been taken as 8.01 marks and the upper class limit of the top class as 34.00 marks.

equivalent in dollars to 20.00 marks) or more. Four-fifths of women, who in Germany earned between 6.01 and 12.00 marks, had in Massachusetts a weekly wage of between 21.00 and 50.36 marks ($5.00 and $11.99).

Let us now see whether these results are confirmed by the wage statistics arranged according to occupational classifications.

TABLE 6 Distributions of average daily wages in 1902 of workers employed in coal-mining in the United States and in the Ruhr District of Germany (per thousand)[a]

American coal-miners (excluding anthracite-miners)	
Less than $1.50 (6.30M)	85
$1.50–$1.99 (6.30M–8.36M)	245
$2.00–$2.49 (8.40M–10.46M)	408
$2.50 (10.50M) or more	261
	999[b]
Derived Descriptive Statistics	
Mean[c]	$2.20
	(9.24M)
Median	$2.16
	(9.07M)
Semi-interquartile Range	$0.34
	(1.43M)
Quartile Coefficient of Variation	0.156
Coal-miners in the Ruhr District	
Less than 2.61M	78
2.61M–3.80M	209
3.81M–5.00M	396
5.01M or more	317
	1000
Derived Descriptive Statistics[c]	
Mean	4.33M
Median	4.45M
Semi-interquartile Range	0.82M
Quartile Coefficient of Variation	0.185

Notes

[a] *Ed.* – It was not possible to consult Sombart's sources for either of the above sets of data. However, the American figures are also reproduced in a later Census publication; see Bureau of the Census, *Special Reports: Mines and Quarries*, 96 and 678, and the derived descriptive statistics have been calculated from the latter source.

[b] *Ed.* – This total contains a rounding error.

[c] *Ed.* – In those calculations where a lower class limit of the bottom class and an upper class limit of the top class are needed, the following values have been used; for the American data, $0.25 and $4.49, and for the German data, 1.76 marks and 6.00 marks.

TABLE 7 Distributions of average weekly wages or wage rates of adults of sixteen years or more in the cigar-making industry of 1889 in Baden and in 1890 in the American South or the United States as a whole, by sex (per thousand)

MEN			
Baden		*The American South*	
Less than 6.00M	207	Less than $6.00 (25.20M)	232
6.00M–8.99M	285	$6.00–$9.99 (25.20M–41.96M)	304
9.00M–14.99M	429	$10.00–$14.99 (42.00M–62.96M)	391
15.00M or more	79	$15.00 (63.00M) or more	72
	1000		999[a]
Derived Descriptive Statistics			
Mean[b]	9.34M		$9.89 (41.54M)
Median	9.06M		$9.75 (40.95M)
Semi-interquartile Range	2.50M		$3.03 (12.73M)
Quartile Coefficient of Variation	0.218		0.316

WOMEN			
Baden		*The United States*	
Less than 4.00M	55	Less than $4.00 (16.80M)	56
4.00M–6.99M	397	$4.00–$5.99 (16.80M–25.16M)	437
7.00M–11.99M	472	$6.00–$8.99 (25.20M–37.76M)	472
12.00M or more	76	$9.00 (37.80M) or more	35
	1000		1000
Derived Descriptive Statistics			
Mean[b]	7.79M		$6.07 (25.94M)
Median	7.37M		$6.01 (25.24M)
Semi-interquartile Range	1.95M		$1.04 (4.37M)
Quartile Coefficient of Variation	0.225		0.171

Sources: For the Baden data see Note 19 of this Section. The American data are from Dewey, *Employees and Wages*, 410–11.

Notes

[a] *Ed.* – This total contains a rounding error.

[b] *Ed.* – In the calculation of these means the following values have been used for the lower class limit of the bottom class and the upper class limit of the top one: for the men of Baden, 2.00 marks and 19.99 marks; for the men of the American South, $3.50 and $22.99; for the women of Baden, 2.00 marks and 19.99 marks; and for the women in America as a whole, $1.50 and $10.49.

For workers in American bituminous coal-mining we have wage data from the Census Bulletin,[18] and for coal-miners in Germany (at least in western Germany) we have comparable data in the figures of the miners' association in Bochum. These provide the picture shown in Table 6, where both sets of data pertain to the year 1902.

In Table 6 I have intentionally arranged the total number of wage-earners in the two countries into approximately the same class intervals in order to make the picture clearer.

It is also possible to contrast comparable figures for the cigar-making industry. The German data are admittedly for the Grand Duchy of Baden,[19] where the wages of cigar-workers are the lowest in Germany. One may say that the average for the whole of Germany is 50 to 100 per cent higher.[20] For America I have therefore taken merely the figures that refer to the Southern states.[21] As before, I have formed the same class intervals as far as possible, and the results are shown in Table 7. The Baden data are for 1889 and the American ones for 1890, because this is closer to the date of the German figures than any more recent information.

TABLE 8   Distributions of average weekly wages in 1896 in five selected chemical plants in Baden (in percentages)

| | Plants | | | | |
	B	C	D	E	F
Less than 10.00M	7.67	0.44	1.09	0.00	1.37
10.00M–11.99M	4.51	4.85	1.09	1.62	0.68
12.00M–14.99M	8.42	19.38	13.04	7.26	10.22
15.00M–17.99M	19.10	32.60	27.18	29.03	13.02
18.00M–20.99M	26.47	27.31	34.78	34.67	23.29
21.00M–23.99M	19.40	10.57	15.21	21.77	25.34
24.00M or more	14.43	4.85	7.61	5.65	—
24.00M–26.99M	—	—	—	—	13.70
27.00M–29.99M	—	—	—	—	10.27
30.00M or more	—	—	—	—	2.05
	100.00	100.00	100.00	100.00	99.94[a]
Derived Descriptive Statistics					
Mean	18.82M	17.48M	19.00M	19.35M	21.00M
Median	19.16M	17.33M	18.65M	19.04M	21.16M
Semi-interquartile Range	3.34M	2.46M	2.37M	2.34M	3.15M
Quartile Coefficient of Variation	0.175	0.140	0.129	0.123	0.149

Note
[a] *Ed.* – The discrepancy between this total and 100.00 is found in the primary source of these data.

Also from the area of jurisdiction of the unforgotten Woerishoffer[22] come statistics on wage-distributions in five chemical plants.[23] The average weekly wages received per hundred workers in 1896 in each of the five plants are shown in Table 8.

The great bulk of workers (three-quarters to four-fifths) earn between 15.00 marks and 26.99 marks in Plant B (in fact, 74.59 per cent) and between 15.00 marks and 23.99 marks in Plants D and E (in fact, 77.17 per cent and 85.47 per cent respectively); in Plant F 72.60 per cent earn between 18.00 marks and 29.99 marks, and in Plant C 79.29 per cent earn between 12.00 marks and 20.99 marks. As far as I know, wages in the chemical plants of Baden are not especially low but are close to the German average. It will therefore be permissible to contrast them with wages in the American chemical industry, treating the latter as equivalent to the average for the United States. The weekly wages drawn per thousand male workers sixteen or more years old, as given in the Census Report, are shown in Table 9. (Wage data on categories of workers other than adult males are not provided.)

Table 9 shows that the earnings of the great bulk of these workers (in fact, 76.2 per cent) were between 31.50 and 52.46 marks.

TABLE 9 Distribution of average weekly wage rates in 1900 of adult male workers of sixteen years of more in the American chemical industry (per thousand)

Less than $7.50 (31.50M)	63
$7.50–$9.99 (31.50M–41.96M)	444
$10.00–$12.49 (42.00M–52.46M)	318
$12.50–$14.99 (52.50M–62.96M)	83
$15.00–$19.99 (63.00M–83.96M)	70
$20.00 (84.00M) or more	21
	———
	999[a]
Derived Descriptive Statistics	
Mean[b]	$10.63
	(44.65M)
Median	$9.97
	(41.87M)
Semi-interquartile Range	$1.78
	(7.48M)
Quartile Coefficient of Variation	0.174

Source: Dewey, *Employees and Wages*, 402–3.

Notes

a *Ed.* – This total contains a rounding error.

b *Ed.* – In the calculation of this mean $2.50 has been used for the lower class limit of the bottom class and $50.49 for the upper class limit of the top one.

Finally, I am going to contrast wages of workers in the woodworking industries with each other. In the case of Germany we possess valuable material for this category of worker in the form of the survey by the Woodworkers' Union, although only very gross features about wage conditions are portrayed.[24] The weekly wages of 67,151 male workers[25]

TABLE 10   Distributions of average weekly wages or wage rates of adult male workers in the woodworking industries in 1902 in Germany and in 1900 in the United States (in percentages)[a]

GERMANY	
Less than 20.01M	41.2
20.01M–25.00M	35.6
25.01M–30.00M	19.1
30.01M or more	4.1
	100.0
Derived Descriptive Statistics	
Mean	21.79M
Median	21.24M
Semi-interquartile Range	3.72M
Quartile Coefficient of Variation	0.177

UNITED STATES	
Less than $5.00 (21.00M)	3.2
$5.00–$7.49 (21.00M–31.46M)	11.4
$7.50–$11.99 (31.50M–50.36M)	46.5
$12.00–$23.99 (50.40M–100.76M)	38.3
$24.00 (100.80M) or more	0.8
	100.2[b]
Derived Descriptive Statistics	
Mean[c]	$13.35 (56.07M)
Median	$10.92 (45.86M)
Semi-interquartile Range	$3.93 (16.51M)
Quartile Coefficient of Variation	0.316

Notes

[a] *Ed.* – For the source of the German data see Note 24 of this Section. For further information about the source of the American data see Note 26 of this Section.

[b] *Ed.* – This total contains a rounding error.

[c] *Ed.* – In the calculation of this mean $1.50 has been used for the lower class limit of the bottom class and $66.99 for the upper class limit of the top one.

given in this source, in contrast with those earned by 38,387 similar workers in the United States, are given in Table 10.[26]

I am sure, however, that I can let the whole matter rest with these examples. However questionable from the standpoint of strict statistical method the individual sets of data (and particularly each comparison between German and American figures) may be, taken together I feel they give a full and correct picture that is unanimously attested to by figures coming from the most varied sources. On the basis of the preceding statistical material I believe that the following can be said with moderate certainty: monetary wages earned by workers in the United States are two to three times as high as in Germany.[27] They are certainly at least twice as high, for scarcely a single one of the preceding comparisons produced a lesser ratio. On the other hand there are numerous cases where the American wage amounts to three times the German one, while in some individual (albeit atypical) cases there is a fourfold difference – such as in the sugar industry, and in the cigar-making industry if we use Baden as the basis of comparison. Compare too the average wage given for the industrial association administering accident insurance in the tobacco industry; this is a third to a half of the American equivalent. Perhaps one can formulate judgement in the following terms. American wages (perhaps with the exception of those in the South) are 100 per cent higher than those in the best-paying regions of Germany (i.e., the west), and they are certainly 150 to 200 per cent higher than those in the regions of Germany with low wages (i.e., the east and parts of the south). The wages of miners are the best illustration of this.

However, it was not really the wages of American workers that we wanted to determine, but rather their living standard. To ascertain this we must now determine what in the way of goods the worker can acquire with his much higher wages and thus see whether the gap in living standards between American and German workers is as great as it is with regard to wages. This therefore becomes a question about the relative size of real incomes, and we intended first to try to deal with this by considering overall price levels.

3 The Cost of Living in America and Germany

Before going into the research on individual prices I shall make some observations of a general nature about the distinctive way that prices in America are determined, something that so often astonishes the non-specialist.

Like economic life as a whole, the determination of prices in the United States is particularly influenced by two forces: the continuing colonial character of the country and the highly developed state of capitalism, the latter being expressed pre-eminently in the advanced development of the technology of production and transportation.

In the first place, the colonial character of the country is responsible for the high price of labour, a fact that we have just established. On the other hand, to the same factor is also to be attributed the fact that all commodities and entertainments whose production is highly labour-intensive are expensive. This applies particularly to all types of personal service, and the wages of domestic servants are particularly high. Similar considerations apply to all services and entertainments that rely to a large extent on human labour (for example, cabs, theatres, but also elegant restaurants and first-class hotels in which a large staff is employed). Moreover, all goods that have to be traded or marketed by labour-intensive methods (for example, goods offered for sale in small quantities like milk, fruit, and so on) are expensive. The same is true of all goods in the manufacture of which a large amount of specially qualified labour is expended (i.e., all luxury items whose manufacture needs technical skill).

On the other hand, the colonial character of the country gives a cheap price to land, so that all commodities in which the price of the ground-rent amounts to a substantial proportion are relatively cheap. This applies to agricultural produce grown in bulk, and there is an inverse relationship between its price and the amount of human labour needed to produce and distribute it; but a further factor that also keeps the price of agricultural products low is the relatively high productivity of cultivated land. The overall cheap price of land is also seen – even if to a lesser degree – in the low ground-rent in cities, except when one is considering exceptional cases such as the island-city of New York. House prices are therefore low, at least for those houses where the very high cost of labour constitutes a small proportion of the price, although all large, elegant buildings require large amounts of labour in their construction.

In comparison, highly advanced technology means that industrial products made in bulk are cheap, especially when they are also sold through large-scale concerns.

What results from these few considerations is the following: life in America becomes more expensive as more personal services are required and the demand for luxury increases. A given domestic economic unit therefore finds life more expensive (relatively, of course) if it is at the comparatively high end of the income hierarchy. It is quite inadmissible to compare overall the value of the dollar with that of the mark, as it varies entirely according to respective living standards. A family with an income of $20,000 in New York will perhaps be unable to afford any more luxuries than a family with an income of 20,000 marks in Berlin. A New York family with $10,000 is perhaps equivalent to one in Berlin with 15,000 marks, and so on down the range of incomes until a point is reached where the dollar has the purchasing power of 3 and even 4 marks. As I note in anticipation of what follows, this is the case among the working population. The following enquiries should demonstrate this.

Housing.   I am beginning with housing, as it is the most important requirement. A well-known fact that should first of all be pointed out is the way in which the American worker in large cities and industrial areas meets his housing requirements: this has essential differences from that found among continental-European workers, particularly German ones. The German worker in such places usually lives in rented tenements, while his American peer lives correspondingly frequently in single-family or two-family dwellings. Apart from New York, Boston and Cincinnati, rented tenements are practically unknown in the large cities of America. Thus even the cities of Chicago and Philadelphia, each with over a million inhabitants, house their populations in dwellings of one or two storeys that hold for the greater part no more than two families, and three or four in exceptional cases. These dwellings derive their origin directly from the old log hut and even today they are still built of wood in the great majority of American cities. This method of building in separate units has undoubtedly had great significance in the formation of national character, and one should not reject out of hand the hypothesis that the slow development of collectivist orientations in America (and in England too) is connected with the fact that housing needs are met by building in individual housing units.

Now we want to know how much the American worker's housing costs him. On first inspecting the household budget of any arbitrarily chosen working-class family, one is tempted to answer: 'A lot, and more than that of the European worker.' Thus, it was the general opinion of those who took part in the Mosely Industrial Commission that the American worker has to spend more than does his English counterpart to cover his housing requirements, although I agree they added that this was true *only* as regards housing requirements.[28] I cannot decide whether their conclusion is correct, but I doubt it. In a comparison between the American and the German worker one's judgement undoubtedly has to be the reverse of this: housing costs the American worker less rather than more than it does his German counterpart. When I said that at first sight the reverse would seem to be true, as the men on Mosely's Commission maintain, this was connected with the fact that the much more bountiful manner in which housing requirements in America are satisfied is not being taken sufficiently into account.

To be sure, the American worker pays out much more than does, say, the German worker, frequently twice or three times the amount, but what the former receives in return is also correspondingly larger and more comfortable.[29] If, on the other hand, one reckons what it costs to cover approximately the same housing requirements – say a room – one finds that prices in America are on average lower than in Germany. I want to verify this with some figures that refer to large and medium-sized American cities and are extracted from the report entitled *The Tenement House Problem*.[30]

Baltimore (508,957 inhabitants). The norm is the single-family house with four to six rooms. Rent is \$7 to \$8 per month, or 353 to 403 marks a year, so that a room is let at 75.6 marks a year.

Boston (560,892 inhabitants). In 1902 a four-room tenement cost \$12.14 in rent a month and a six-room tenement \$19.30. This would correspond to an annual price per room of around 150 to 160 marks.[31]

Buffalo (352,387 inhabitants). Exact data are available on the rented tenements in which the Italians and Poles live. The former paid an average of \$5.30 a month for a dwelling with an average of 2.3 rooms, which is 116.14 marks annually per room. The latter paid \$3.11 for a dwelling with an average of 2.5 rooms, or 62.70 marks annually per room.

Cincinnati (325,902 inhabitants). The three-family and four-family house predominates. Monthly rent in the poorest houses is \$5 to \$6, or 250 to 300 marks a year. The number of rooms is not given. Even if we assume it to be only two, the yearly rent per room comes out at 125 to 150 marks.

Cleveland (381,768 inhabitants). The norm is the single-family house. Scarcely 5 per cent of all houses contain more than one family. In better two-family houses each dwelling costs \$10 to \$15 a month. We may here assume that there are four rooms per dwelling, so that the annual cost of each room would amount to 125 to 190 marks.

Denver (133,859 inhabitants).   The population lives in one-storey houses with three to six rooms that command a monthly rent of $4 to $12. With an average of four rooms, that would result in an annual price of 50 to 150 marks.

Detroit (285,704 inhabitants).   The norm is the single-family house. The average rent of the ordinary working man is $8 to $10 monthly for six well-situated rooms with running water in the kitchen; this is 400 to 500 marks yearly, so that one room would come out at 66.67 to 83.33 marks a year.

Nashville (80,865 inhabitants).   The norm is the single-family house. Monthly rent is $2 to $6. Assuming an average of three rooms, this is 35 to 100 marks annually per room.

New York.   All kinds of housing occur here, but the large rented tenement increasingly prevails. One should remember that the difficulty of accommodating this huge mass of approximately five million people on a given terrain can scarcely be equalled anywhere in the world. One would expect to conclude from this that the cost of housing would be enormous. However, it is not really so bad: a dwelling of four rooms costs $12 to $18 monthly in the thickly populated parts of the city. In the houses of the City and Suburban Homes Company, for example, which has houses on East 64th Street and which reflects as far as possible the rents paid in the neighbourhood, the following rates apply: a dwelling of two rooms costs $6.80 a month, one of three rooms $11.40 a month, and one of four rooms $14.60 a month. One may therefore put the monthly cost of a room in the working-class parts of New York at $3.50, which would come out as an average annual rental of 176 marks per room.

Philadelphia (1,293,697 inhabitants).   Just think – a million people housed in single-family houses! At a distance of thirty minutes from the city centre one pays $8 to $10 a month for a dwelling with four to six rooms. At a distance of not more than twenty-five minutes from the centre a new four-roomed house measuring fourteen feet by twenty-eight feet in area, with a heater in the cellar and a bathroom, costs $12 a month, and a precisely similar six-roomed house measuring sixteen feet by forty feet in area costs $16 a month. The annual cost per room therefore works out at 100 to 150 marks.

Rochester (162,608 inhabitants).   Most of the working population lives in detached dwellings with five to seven rooms let at $1.50 to $3.00 a week. The annual cost per room is therefore about 50 to 100 marks.

San Francisco (342,782 inhabitants).   Here there are small houses for one or two families. The monthly rent for four to five rooms is $13 to $15. One room costs 150 to 160 marks annually.

St. Paul (163,065 inhabitants). This city has mostly single-family houses. The normal worker's house is let at $3 to $4 a month; assuming a house to have a maximum of three rooms, a room costs 50 to 100 marks annually.

It will now suffice, I think, if I contrast these figures with the statistics that we have on housing conditions in large German cities. What we have were gathered largely through surveys in the larger German cities carried out in connection with the Census (the last one therefore being on 1 December 1900).[32]

According to this source, the average annual cost in marks on 1 December 1900 of a room with heating in rented dwellings without any additional industrial or trading utilisation and with one to four rooms with heating was as shown in Table 11.

One might now retort that German rooms are larger than American ones. (That would be right, but against this the latter have the incomparable advantage of a more free and airy condition.) Or one might retort that not all rooms counted in the American dwellings are heated – this may even be so, although we have no actual evidence for this. However, this cannot alter the carefully weighed judgement formulated by me on this matter: it certainly costs the American urban worker no more in strict cash terms to obtain the same housing requirements as those of his German counterpart, and in addition one can say with some certainty that in the main it costs him even less.

In order that what I have established should not be limited to larger cities, I am also going to say something about rents in the coal-mining areas, where there are no large cities. I am in a position to be able to do this thanks to the thorough research by Peter Roberts on the condition of workers in the anthracite regions of Pennsylvania.[33] Here housing conditions are especially bad and some of the workers are assigned to dwellings provided for them by the mining companies.[34] The following summaries given in Tables 12, 13 and 14 provide information about the rents paid there. Table 12 shows the distribution of houses rented out by the Philadelphia and Reading Coal and Iron Company, Table 13 that of those rented out by Coxe Bros. & Co. (unfortunately, there are no data on the number of rooms involved), and Table 14 gives information for some other companies. One can see that the average residential room costs $0.75 to $1.25 a month, or about 3 to 5 marks.

One can compare this with some statistics on living accommodation that are available for the industrial region of Upper Silesia.[35] These figures are clearly minima for German industrial areas, and furthermore they refer to the period at the beginning of the 1890s. Rents have certainly not gone down since then. From the large body of material presented in this research I have prepared Table 15.

The lowest rates in this table of 2.00 to 3.00 marks per room are from

TABLE 11   Average annual cost in marks on 1 December 1900 of a room with heating in rented dwellings containing from one to four such rooms in selected German cities

Cities	Number of rooms with heating				
	1		2	3	4
	Without all conveniences	*With all conveniences*			
Altona[a]	154	233	199	134	138
Breslau		152	126	174	195
Charlottenburg[b]		216	174	208	231
Dresden		221	179	176	193
Düsseldorf (on 3 December 1901)		122	112	103	103
Essen		90	83	84	96
Frankfurt an der Oder	79	89	92	105	115
Hamburg		214	152	141	158
Hanover		211	177	179	195
Leipzig	92	191	144	143	162
Lübeck	82	146	119	120	125
Magdeburg		154	126	138	145
Mannheim	113	186	118	142	159
Munich	231	340	149	172	190
Plauen[c] (on 12 October 1901)	79	179	158	158	155
Posen[d] [Poznań] – front-facing houses	112	152	139	168	182
Posen[d] [Poznań] – rear-facing houses	108	159	129	147	162
Strasbourg[e]	63	103	81	94	116

Source: Statistisches Jahrbuch Deutscher Städte, xi 89.

Notes

[a] *Ed.* – Altona was formerly an important seaport just to the west of Hamburg; since 1937 it has been part of the city of Hamburg.

[b] *Ed.* – Charlottenburg was formerly a residential area about five miles west of the centre of Berlin; in 1920 it became part of the city of Berlin and it is now in the British sector of West Berlin.

[c] *Ed.* – Plauen is now in the German Democratic Republic about sixty miles south of Leipzig.

[d] *Ed.* – Posen [Poznań], though now in Poland, was in the German Empire when Sombart was writing.

[e] *Ed.* – Strasbourg (in Alsace), though now in France, was in the German Empire when Sombart was writing.

TABLE 12 Distribution of houses rented out by the Philadelphia and Reading Coal and Iron Company in the Pennsylvania coalfields, by number of rooms and average monthly revenue from rent

Number of rooms in each house	Number of houses	Average monthly revenue from rent
2	6	$2.08 (8.74M)
3	469	$2.81 (11.80M)
4	1115	$3.78 (15.88M)
5	269	$4.58 (19.24M)
6	85	$5.07 (21.29M)
7–12	89	$8.11 (34.06M)

Source: Roberts, *Anthracite Coal Communities*, 127.

TABLE 13 Distribution of houses rented out by Coxe Bros. & Co. in the Pennsylvania coalfields, by monthly rent

Monthly rent	Number of houses	Monthly rent	Number of houses
$1.00 (4.20M)	4	$3.75 (15.75M)	20
$1.50 (6.30M)	29	$4.00 (16.80M)	348[a]
$2.00 (8.40M)	44	$4.50 (18.90M)	24
$2.75 (11.55M)	25	$4.60 (19.32M)	28
$3.00 (12.60M)	10	$4.75 (19.95M)	45
$3.25 (13.65M)	13	$5.00 (21.00M)	131
$3.50 (14.70M)	10	$5.50 (23.10M)	119

Source: Roberts, *Anthracite Coal Communities*, 126.

Note
[a] These are probably the four-roomed houses that are typical.

TABLE 14 Monthly rents of houses with different numbers of rooms rented out by six selected mining companies in the Pennsylvania coalfields

Company	Number of rooms in each dwelling	Monthly rent
A	4 and 5	$4.00 (16.80M) and $5.00 (21.00M)
B	5 and 6	$7.00 (29.40M) and $8.00 (33.60M)
C	4	$5.00 (21.00M)
D	2	$2.00 (8.40M) and $3.00 (12.60M)
E	Average of 5.8	Average of $5.40 (22.68M)
F	5	$4.00 (16.80M) to $8.00 (33.60M)

Source: Roberts, *Anthracite Coal Communities*, 128–9, 131.

villages located away from the centre. If one excludes these cases, one arrives at the conclusion that the average amount paid per month in rent for a residential room fluctuates at approximately the same level as in America. If one wants to reformulate the earlier judgement very conservatively, one might say that the miner in Pennsylvania pays 10 to 20 per cent more than was paid by his counterpart in Upper Silesia fifteen years ago for equivalent accommodation.

TABLE 15   Size and rent of dwellings of workers' families in about 1890 in selected areas of Upper Silesia

Area	Average number of residential rooms in the dwelling of a worker's family	Average monthly rent for the dwelling of a worker's family	
		In houses rented from the trade union	In other types of houses
Rural District:			
Beuthen [Bytom]	1 or 2	3.60M–7.50M	3.00M–8.00M
Districts:			
Gleiwitz [Gliwice]	1 or 2	3.00M–7.50M	2.00M–8.00M
Zabrze	1 or 2	5.25M–7.25M	2.50M–7.25M
Kattowitz [Katowice]	1 or 2	2.00M–7.50M	2.00M–9.50M
Towns:			
Gleiwitz [Gliwice]	2	7.25M	7.50M
Königshütte [Chorzów]	2	7.50M	6.50M
Kattowitz [Katowice]	2	5.50M	9.50M
Myslowitz [Mysłowice]	2	6.25M	5.75M
Beuthen [Bytom]	Not given	8.00M	8.00M

However, in addition to the outlays on housing, we must also reckon those for *lighting, heating and fittings*. We must now ask how prices for these items in Germany compare with those in the United States.

The main means of lighting, paraffin, is naturally much cheaper in the country where the oil wells are than it is in Germany. The export price in New York is about half of what the price is in Mannheim or Breslau.

Bituminous coal costs about as much in Germany as in America, something that is made clear by the comparison in Table 16.

According to my researches, *room-furnishings* are rather cheaper in the United States than they are in Germany. Of course, the differing quality of the furniture is particularly important in this respect. However, it can be demonstrated with some certainty that some standard items of furniture cost less in America than in Germany. All the German furniture-suppliers with whom I have dealt have unanimously acknowledged to me that it would be unthinkable to supply, for example, a five-piece suite for 100 marks or even only 160 marks, which is what American stores do.

In what follows I am reporting the most important results of my enquiries; at the same time I also want to express here my thanks to those people who have been so kind in helping me to collect the data.

For America I have compiled the *lowest* prices for the most popular items of furnishing from three of the largest furniture stores in New York – two department stores and another specialising in the furniture business – where workers reckon to buy their furniture and similar requirements.

TABLE 16 Average annual prices in marks per ton[a] of coal from 1900 to 1904 in the United States and in Germany

	UNITED STATES	
	Anthracite coal at Philadelphia	Bituminous coal at Baltimore
1900	14.57	10.50
1901	15.96	10.50
1902	18.90	10.50
1903	18.90	15.75
1904	18.90	9.45

	GERMANY					
	District of Breslau		District of Dortmund[b]		District of Saarbrücken[b]	
	Lower Silesian gas-coal, lump-coal and slack	Upper Silesian gas-coal and lump-coal	Broken-up lump-coal and coal for export	Coal for puddling[c] and house-coal	Steam-coal	House-coal
1900	17.10	11.00	13.60	9.90	11.90	11.40
1901	17.80	11.80	14.00	10.00	12.80	12.50
1902	16.50	11.70	13.30	9.30	12.00	11.40
1903	15.00	11.50	12.10	9.00	11.80	11.00
1904	15.00	11.30	11.80	9.00	12.10	11.20

Sources: The American data: *Statistical Abstract of the United States, 1904*, XXVIII, 460.
The German data: *Statistisches Jahrbuch für das Deutsche Reich, 1905*, XXVI, 211.

Notes

[a] *Ed.* – The American ton-measure is the short ton, which equals 2000 pounds avoirdupois or 907.20 kilograms. The German ton-measure is the metric ton, which equals 2204.62 pounds avoirdupois or 1000 kilograms.

[b] All these prices are those at the mine or pit-head. Those for the Saarbrücken district include loading costs.

[c] *Ed.* – Puddling is the process of making wrought iron from pig iron.

As in Germany, American workers generally buy their furniture on hire-purchase by monthly instalments.

By way of comparison I am going to contrast the American figures with the following German material:

1. Information given to me by Workers' Secretary[36] Neukirch in Breslau on the basis of his personal experiences (A. in Table 17); and

TABLE 17   The prices of various items of household furniture in New York and in Breslau[a]

	NEW YORK		
	I	II	III
Iron folding bed	$2.90 (12.18M)	$2.75 (11.55M)	$10.00 (42.00M)
Wooden folding bed	$13.98 (58.72M)	$13.50, $15.00 (56.70M, 63.00M)	$15.00 (63.00M)
Mattress	$1.98 (8.32M)	$1.95, $2.70 (8.19M, 11.34M)	$5.00 (21.00M)
Chair	$0.65 (2.73M)	$0.98 (4.12M)	$0.65 (2.73M)
Kitchen table	$1.10 (4.62M)	$1.50, $1.98 (6.30M, 8.32M)	$1.50 (6.30M)
Dining table	—	$4.98 (20.92M)	$7.50 (31.50M)
Five-piece suite	$17.50 (73.50M)	$24.00 (100.80M)	$40.00 (168.00M)
Three-piece suite	—	$13.48 (56.62M)	$30.00 (126.00M)
Upholstered couch	$6.98 (29.32M)	$9.98 (41.92M)	$12.00 (50.40M)
Iron couch	$4.50 (18.90M)	$6.50 (27.30M)	$4.50 (18.90M)
Iron bed	$2.48 (10.42M)	$2.25, $2.98 (9.45M, 12.52M)	$4.00 (16.80M)
Sewing machine	$12.98 (54.52M)	$12.98 (54.52M)	—
Ice-box	$4.98, $7.45 (20.92M, 31.29M)	$4.98, $7.35 (20.92M, 30.87M)	$7.75 (32.55M)
Lamp	$1.25, $1.65 (5.25M, 6.93M)	$1.35, $0.69 (5.67M, 2.90M)	—
Drawing-room lamp	$2.49 (10.46M)	$3.25 (13.65M)	$3.50 (14.70M)
Rug	$1.74, $2.15 (7.31M, 9.03M)	$0.59, $0.98 (2.48M, 4.12M)	—
Carpet (per yard)	$0.57, $0.69 (2.39M, 2.90M)	$0.59 (2.48M)	—
Painting	—	$0.59, $1.00 (2.48M, 4.20M)	$1.00, $2.00 (4.20M, 8.40M)

BRESLAU		
A.	Wardrobe	70M
	Ornamental cabinet	60M
	Table	20M
	Sofa	60M
	Six chairs	40M
	Kitchen cupboard	30M
	Mirror	50M
	Two beds	90M
B.	Wooden bed with mattress	54M
	Wooden bed without mattress	24M
	Chair	5M
	Kitchen table	6M
	Extendable dining table	35M
	Ordinary painted table	14M
	Three-piece suite	225M
	Five-piece suite	300M
	Sewing machine	120M
	Rug	12M
	Stair-carpeting (per metre)	2M
	Picture	6M to 12M
C.	Iron folding bed	7.50M to 8M
	Mattress (seaweed filling)	6M
	Mattress (fibrous filling)	10M
	Mattress (semi-fibrous filling)	35M
	Sofa-bed	60M to 70M
	Viennese chair with cane seat	3.50M
	Kitchen table	6.50M
	Dining table with oil-cloth cover and drawer	8M
	Pull-out table	18M
	Three-piece suite	180M to 200M
	Five-piece suite	260M
	Iron bed with webbing	7.50M
	Rug	15M

Note
ª *Ed.* – The sources of these data are given in the text.

2. The lowest prices in the two most important hire-purchase businesses in Breslau that have a working-class clientele; these are given in B. and C. in Table 17, and wherever possible I have compiled them after personal consultation concerning actual circumstances with representatives of the businesses specified.

A comparison between the American and German figures (given in Table 17) will confirm the correctness of the judgement that I expressed above.

Nutrition. Difficulties begin to accumulate here, especially if one wants to compare the living standards of different social strata. Conversion into pure quantities is considerably more difficult than with the issue of how housing requirements are met.

First of all, the nutritional habits of the American worker on the one hand and his continental-European counterpart, especially his German counterpart, on the other deviate extraordinary from each other. The American lives predominantly on meat, fruit, puddings and refined white bread, while the German eats potatoes, sausages and coarse rye bread. If one therefore contrasts prices in the two countries, one must always be aware of the fact that divergences in price have quite a different significance in each country, depending on the particular commodity to which they pertain. With the heavy meat content of the American's diet and the lesser amount of potatoes that he eats, it is less important to him whether potatoes are slightly higher or lower in price, while he has to care much more about the price of meat. With the German the situation is reversed. Of course, for a full evaluation of this matter one must consider the fact that foodstuffs maintain their absolute physiological value, whatever national peculiarities there may be in the eating habits of the people consuming them. Thus, one has to regard a price structure that results in or encourages the eating of meat as more beneficial to the common welfare than is true of the reverse situation where people are compelled to eat potatoes.

Even then, however, it is exceedingly hard to give anything like a reliable price even for just the same foodstuff, and it is twice as hard to compare prices in different countries with each other. This is principally because of the great variations in quality, which is differently determined from place to place and from country to country. One may think of meat prices, which vary in a ratio of one to three according to the quality of the cut. In America, in particular, there are especially large variations between the lowest and the highest qualities as far as most foodstuffs are concerned, and there are corresponding differences between the lowest and the highest price; the case of meat is an example of this. Of course, this benefits the less affluent sections of the population. Prices also fluctuate according to the time of year (look at eggs, for instance), and a final complication is that the methods of establishing, quoting and publishing prices are so entirely different that one loses all inclination to make large comparative studies of them. Instead, we shall have to be satisfied with approximate values that give us – very much at a distance and very roughly – a picture of actual circumstances. However, the sources that we have are sufficient for this purpose. The sources that I am using are:

1. For the United States, the *Eighteenth Annual Report of the Commissioner of Labor* already cited,[37] which (as I have stated at

length) contains one of the most important – perhaps *the* most important – collection of retail prices.

2.   For Germany:[38]

(*a*) the average prices of animal-derived foodstuffs published regularly for the Kingdom of Prussia in the *Zeitschrift des Königlichen Preußischen Statistischen Bureaus* [*Journal of the Royal Prussian Statistical Office*].[39]

(*b*) the retail prices from nineteen German cities that are assembled regularly in the *Statistisches Jahrbuch Deutscher Städte.*[40]

(*c*) the list of prices of the Breslau Co-operative Society.

Both because we can be concerned only with gross average prices and also because the German sources (*a*) and (*b*) above contain only these, I have extracted from the American report for comparative purposes the general table that has been distilled from the thousands and thousands of individual figures. This table quotes the average price of each commodity as ascertained from the price data in 2567 household budgets. My final conclusion, made on the basis both of studying the sources and of personal experience, is this: that the prices of the most important foodstuffs are by and large the same in the United States as in Germany. Meat is about the same price, many items (like potatoes and rice) are more expensive in America than in Germany, and on the other hand other items like flour and bacon are considerably cheaper. Thus, with the same amount of money the working-class family in America will be able to buy about the same quantity of foodstuffs as its counterpart in Germany. It may perhaps be said that the German working-class family has been merely obstinate in sticking to a diet consisting exclusively or predominantly of potatoes; but it certainly does not do so because it does not have to.

I think that the figures about to be given in Table 18 will confirm the correctness of my judgement. I start by noting that the figures for America and those for Germany from sources (*a*) and (*b*) pertain to 1901, but that for comparative purposes I have intentionally taken another year (February 1904) for source (*c*). The American statistical data, which are in pounds weight (1 pound avoirdupois is 0.45359 kilograms) and cents, have been converted by me into kilograms and pfennigs.[41] The figures in Table 18 give prices in pfennigs for 1 kilogram where nothing else is noted.

A good control on the correctness of the point being rather circuitously made here, *viz.*, that food is no more expensive for the American worker than for the German one, is provided by an inspection of the price-lists of the cheap restaurants that workers frequent. At the lowest level in the soup-kitchens, the so-called hash houses,[42] one finds menus whose prices are scarcely more than those prevailing in our German soup-kitchens. These are the ten-cent restaurants. Here one gets meat

TABLE 18   The retail prices of various items of food in the United States and in Germany (in pfennigs per kilogram unless otherwise stated)[a]

| | United States | Germany | | |
| | | (a) | (b) | (c) |
Item	(in 1901)	(in 1901)	(in 1901)	(in Feb 1904)
Best butter	227	227	179–260	272
Eggs (for 5 dozen)	414	388	300–582	—
Fresh beef	134	127	127–163 (Leg)	—
Fresh pork	114	138	133–200 (Leg, fat back)	—
Coffee	213	—	223–372 (Java, yellow, roasted)	176–400
Potatoes (per litre)	10	—	4.5–5.0[b]	—
Wheaten flour	23	—	25–46	36
Milk (per litre)[c]	26.67	—	—	—
Rice	76	—	—	40–56
Smoked bacon	116	164	140–203	168–190
Tea	463	—	—	400–600
Sugar	54	—	—	42–72

Notes

[a] *Ed.* – The sources of these data are given in the text or in notes on the text.

[b] *Ed.* – The price ranges in (b) all refer to the lowest and highest values to be found on average in the year in question in the larger cities of the German Empire. For most cities the data source gives the retail price of potatoes in terms of two-kilogram units, but for two cities (Hanover and Lübeck) prices are given in two-litre units, the respective prices being 9 and 10 pfennigs.

  One litre, as a unit of dry measure, is 0.0284 American bushels.

[c] In Breslau at the present time milk costs 18 to 20 pfennigs per litre; in other large cities it costs more.

with potatoes, bread and butter, and coffee, tea or milk, or else pork, veal or mutton chops, salted meat, fried sausage or three eggs, with the same extras, all for 10 cents, or 42 pfennigs.[43] The fifteen-cent restaurants are really quite good, and here the better-employed unmarried workers eat. In New York I myself have often 'dined' in taverns where the regular dinner (consisting of soup, meat, vegetables, potatoes, dessert, and a cup of tea, coffee, milk or cocoa) cost 25 cents, or just over 1 mark.

Clothing.   Here we lack any reliable information. No budget theorist has ever really come to grips with this difficult subject. Underpants and nightshirts are not featured in any official or semi-official price statistics. Of course, there is a good reason for this, since nowhere does a price

TABLE 19 The prices of various items of clothing worn in working-class families in New York[a]

Item	Men's Clothing
Hats	$1.00–$1.25–$2.00 (4.20M–5.25M–8.40M)
Underwear:	
each	$0.25–$0.50 (1.05M–2.10M)
a set (consisting of under-pants and vest [under-shirt])	$0.50–$1.00 (2.10M–4.20M)
Flannel working shirts	$1.25–$3.00 (5.25M–12.60M)
Coloured cotton shirts	$0.49–$1.00 (2.06M–4.20M)
Socks:	
a pair	$0.05–$0.16–$0.25 (0.21M–0.67M–1.05M)
two pairs (usually)	$0.25 (1.05M)
Handkerchiefs	$0.05 (0.21M)
Scarves	$0.10–$0.25 (0.42M–1.05M)
Suits	$7.50, $9.00, $12.00 (31.50M, 37.80M, 50.40M)
Overcoats	$11.00–$13.00 (46.20M–54.60M)
Shoes	$1.25–$5.00 (5.25M–21.00M)
Trousers	$1.00–$2.00 (4.20M–8.40M)
Rubber Wellington boots	$3.75 (15.75M)
Shorts	$0.25–$0.50 (1.05M–2.10M)
Sweaters	$0.75 (3.15M)
	Women's Clothing
Housecoats (of the sort worn when doing housework)	$0.49, $0.90, $1.50 (2.06M, 3.78M, 6.30M)
Underwear (each)	$0.25–$0.50 (1.05M–2.10M)
Stockings (a pair)	$0.07, $0.08–$0.25 (0.29M, 0.34M–1.05M)
Shoes	$1.00–$2.00 (4.20M–8.40M)
Slippers	$0.50 (2.10M)
Overcoat	$2.98 (12.52M)
Skirt	$2.00–$2.98 (8.40M–12.52M)
Petticoat	$0.25 (1.05M)
Gloves	$0.10, $0.15, $0.50 (0.42M, 0.63M, 2.10M)
Hats	$0.29–$2.00 (1.22M–8.40M)
Blouses	$0.49–$1.98 (2.06M–8.32M)
Black costume	$15.00 (63.00M)
Corsets	$0.50–$1.25 (2.10M–5.25M)
	Children's Clothes
Children aged 1–5	
Shoes	$0.50–$0.75 (2.10M–3.15M)
Shirts	$0.05 (0.21M)
Suits	$0.15, $0.18, $0.20 (0.63M, 0.76M, 0.84M)
Caps	$0.25 (1.05M)
Small vests [undershirts]	$0.10 (0.42M)

Girls aged 6–10
    Coat (or jacket) $1.00–$1.69 (4.20M–7.10M)
    Hats $0.25 (1.05M)
    Stockings $0.06–$0.10 (0.25M–0.42M)
    Dresses $0.98 (4.12M)
    Shoes $0.75, $1.00, $1.50 (3.15M, 4.20M, 6.30M)
Boys aged 6–10
    Trousers $0.25–$0.50 (1.05M–2.10M)
    Shirts $0.25 (1.05M)
    Overcoats $2.50 (10.50M)
    Sweaters $0.39 (1.64M)
    Blouses $0.25–$0.50 (1.05M–2.10M)
    Suits $1.50–$3.00 (6.30M–12.60M)
Girls aged 11–15
    Skirts $1.25 (5.25M)
    Underwear $0.10–$0.25 (0.42M–1.05M)
Boys aged 11–15
    Suits $5.00–$6.00 (21.00M–25.20M)
    Trousers $0.50–$1.50 (2.10M–6.30M)
    Hats $1.00 (4.20M)
    Overcoats $3.50 (14.70M)
    Caps $0.25 (1.05M)
    Shirts $0.49–$1.25 (2.06M–5.25M)
    Shoes $1.00 (4.20M)

Note
a *Ed.* – The source of these data is given in the text.

mean less than is the case with clothing. A 'suit', even if described still more precisely as being 'of blue cheviot twill', costs 30 marks, but also 300 marks; a 'pair of ladies' buttoned boots in calf' cost 8 marks, but also 40 marks; and so on. Even giving price-lists therefore has little value here. To be sure, if one wanted to quote the cheapest prices of German department stores, for example, one would include prices of a cheapness that one would hardly find in America. Thus, one shop that is especially known for its cheapness and is now represented in several large European cities offers the following: lounge suits for men 'made of fancy material, as well as of black or blue cheviot twill' for 13.50 marks, summer overcoats for men for 15 marks, as well as ready-made ladies' costumes 'lined in fancy materials' for 13.50 marks. The same firm sells men's elastic-sided pull-on boots 'in skived leather' for as little as 5.50 marks, as well as ladies' laced boots in horsehide for 5.50 marks. Furthermore, men's hats in black or coloured woollen felt are sold for 1.90 marks, men's shirts for 1.90 marks, and so on.

However, even if the cheapest articles of clothing cost more in the United States, the real reason for this is that nobody in America, including the worker, wants to buy such notorious trash.

TABLE 20 The prices of various items of clothing worn in working-class families in Breslau[a]

Item	Men's Clothing
Suit:	
on hire-purchase	50.00M–60.00M
cash	30.00M
Overall	20.00M
Boots	9.00M
Hat	4.00M
Underwear (a set)	3.50M
Flannel working shirt	2.50M
Coloured shirt	2.00M
Socks (a pair)	0.50M–0.60M
Coloured handkerchiefs	0.10M
Overcoat:	
on hire-purchase	50.00M
cash	30.00M
Sweater	2.50M–3.00M
	Women's Clothing
Gown	25.00M
Flannel petticoat	2.00M–3.00M
Stockings (a pair)	1.00M
Hats	4.00M–5.00M
Boots	7.00M
Blouse	3.00M, 6.00M, 8.00M

Note
[a] *Ed.* – The source of these data is given in the text.

If one compares items of approximately equal quality, one will find that footwear in America is rather cheaper than in Germany. I happen to know of no German shoe shop where one would find, for example, a pair of men's laced boots that were just as durable as a pair costing $2.50 to $3.00 (11 to 13 marks) in America. On the other hand, linen wear, suits, and the like, seem to be somewhat more expensive in America than in Germany. At any event the working-class family there pays out more for individual items of these.

The best comparative material for just clothing will always be what experts who are in contact with workers have collected on the basis of their own experience. For America I have figures compiled by Mrs Charles Husted More and kindly supplied to me by her. Mrs Husted More is a lady who has investigated – using the appropriate methodology – the standard of living of about 200 working-class families in the vicinity of Greenwich House, a settlement in New York whose head worker is the admirable Mrs Simkhovitch.[44] The figures are given in Table 19.

For some contrasting German data on the prices of articles of clothing that are typically worn by workers, I am indebted once again to Workers' Secretary Neukirch of Breslau, who kindly gave them to me. These are given in Table 20.

If one is willing to take as typical the data in Table 19 and Table 20 and to contrast America and Germany on the basis of these data, one will find that even clothing costs the American worker no more, or only infinitesimally more, than it does his German counterpart.

4 How the Worker Lives

Now if the American worker receives a money-wage which is twice or three times that received by his German counterpart, but the procurement of the same quantity of the necessary means of sustenance is not really any more expensive than in Germany, what form does the American's standard of living really take? In other words, what use does he make of his surplus income? Does he save more? Or does he fulfil his 'necessary' requirements of food, housing and clothing more extravagantly? Or does he spend more on luxuries? These are the three possibilities available to him.

As far as I can see and on the basis of what is revealed in the preceding material, he makes use of all three possibilities, perhaps most often of the second.

The housekeeping budgets now come into their own as the most important sources of relevant information. The task is to contrast approximately comparable budgets. For America we have the frequently quoted enquiry of the Washington Bureau of Labor (hereinafter cited as 'Washington'), which compiled its data from 25,440 workers' budgets. Supplementing and supporting this enquiry and able to provide a control on its results are the researches conducted in 1902 by the Massachusetts Bureau of Statistics of Labor (hereinafter cited as 'Massachusetts'), which cover 152 working-class families.[45] The average income of the families studied by the Washington Bureau was $749.50, that of the 2567 families for whom specially detailed data exist was $827.19, and finally, that of the 152 families from Massachusetts was $877.84.

Now we recollect that our comparisons of wage statistics led us to the conclusion that wages in the United States are twice or three times as high as in Germany. The equivalents of those American families whose household budgets we know about are therefore German working-class families with incomes of 1574 marks, 1737 marks and 1843 marks – that is if we assess the income of the American worker as only twice as much as that of the German one; if we assess the American worker's income as three times as high, the equivalents would be German working-class families with incomes of 1049 marks, 1158 marks and 1229 marks.[46]

Accordingly, it is not possible that the collections of German workers' budgets upon which I have drawn to make the comparison describe a relatively lower social stratum than do the American data-collections. With the second and third examples that I use rather the opposite is the case. The following, however, are what I take to be the most valuable of the more recent compilations – as well as being the most useful for the purposes of this study – and in passing I have already mentioned one or two of them.

1.   Max May, *Wie der Arbeiter lebt: [Zwanzig] Arbeiter-Haushaltungs-Rechnungen aus Stadt und Land; Gesammelt, im Auszug mitgetheilt und besprochen von Max May [How the Worker Lives: Housekeeping Accounts of [Twenty] Urban and Rural Workers; Assembled, Abridged and Discussed by Max May]* (Berlin, 1897) – hereinafter cited as 'May'. The incomes vary between 647 and 2019 marks, the overall average income in 1219 marks, and the average of the workers in large cities fluctuates between 1445 and 1957 marks.[47]

2.   Adolf Braun, *Haushaltungs-Rechnungen Nürnberger Arbeiter: Ein Beitrag zur Aufhellung der Lebensverhältnisse des Nürnberger Proletariats; Bearbeitet im Arbeiter-Sekretariate Nürnberg [Housekeeping Accounts of Nuremberg Workers: A Contribution to the Clarification of the Living Conditions of the Nuremberg Working Class; Compiled in the Office of the Nuremberg Workers' Secretary]* (Nuremberg, 1901) – hereinafter cited as 'Nuremberg'.[48] The enquiry is based on forty-four workers' household budgets, which have the following income figures.[49]

Less than 1000M	2
1000M–1499M	20
1500M–1749M	12
1750M–1999M	7
2000M or more	3
	—
	44

3.   Fuchs, *Verhältnisse der Industriearbeiter in 17 Landgemeinden bei Karlsruhe* – hereinafter cited as 'Karlsruhe'. The money-income of the fourteen workers' households examined varies between 1060 and 2285 marks. The average is 1762 marks.

4. Berlin, Statistisches Amt, *Berliner Statistik herausgegeben vom Statistischen Amt der Stadt Berlin: 3. Heft; Lohnermittelungen und Haushaltrechnungen der minder bemittelten Bevölkerung* [*Berlins*] *im Jahre 1903* (Bearbeiter: Professor Dr E. Hirschberg) [*Berlin Statistics Published by the Statistical Office of the City of Berlin: Part 3; Findings on Wages and Household Accounts of the Less Well-off Population* [*of Berlin*] *in 1903* (Compiler: Professor Dr E. Hirschberg)] (Berlin, 1904) – hereinafter cited as 'Berlin'. This is based on 908 households, whose total average income amounted to 1751 marks. In 221 cases income lay between 1201 and 1500 marks, in 303 cases it was between 1501 and 1800 marks, and in 169 cases between 1801 and 2100 marks. Thus, 693 cases had incomes between 1201 and 2100 marks.[50]

Let us first consider how income and expenditure are related to each other in the budgets that are to be compared here and what prospect there is of saving in each case.[51]

May: Of twenty families five save an average of 92 marks each.

Nuremberg: Thirty families have an average surplus of 121 marks each, and fourteen have a deficit of 109 marks each.[52]

Berlin: 399 households have an average surplus of 53 marks each; 464 have a deficit of 79 marks each.

Massachusetts: In the cases of ninety-six families income exceeds expenditure – by an average of $87 (365M); in nine cases income and expenditure are equal; and forty-seven cases wind up with an average deficit of $77 (323M) each, although it should be noted that two deficits alone among the latter total $710.85 (2985.57M) between them.

Washington: 12,816 families have an average surplus of $120.84 (508M) each, 4117 have an average deficit of $65.58 (275M), and the other 8507 families balance their income and expenditure.

The Americans are therefore in a somewhat more favourable position, but they are a very long way short of what one might expect. The number of families who save something from their annual income is really no greater than in Germany (a half as opposed to four-ninths in Berlin, if one is willing to accept that the other proportions are rather chancy because of the small numbers of cases involved). Thus, even the American worker spends everything that he earns – and more – just as frequently as the German one. Accordingly, he must live considerably better than the German worker, and there can be no doubt that he does so.

I have said already that the American worker spends his much higher income in satisfying more amply his 'necessary' requirements in life. In other words, he is better housed, he dresses better and he eats better than his German colleague.

I have already commented so far as is necessary upon the different characteristics of housing conditions in America and Germany. It may be accepted that the American worker's dwelling has an average of four rooms, whereas that of the German worker does not average even two. The 908 Berlin households, who most certainly represented a rather above-average group, had dwellings with around 1.4 rooms on average, while among the 25,440 American families the ones living in rented houses had an average number of 4.67 rooms and those with their own houses had an average number of as much as 5.12 rooms. However, interior domestic fittings are also incomparably more comfortable in America than in Germany. The better workers' dwellings in America give the impression throughout of the dwelling of a member of the German middle class. They are generously furnished with good-quality beds, comfortable chairs, carpets, and so on. The difference does not appear as obvious if we consider the initial outlay on furniture. According to reliable information, the American urban worker spends around $100 to $150 (420M to 630M) for a first set of furnishings, while the German pays 300 to 400 marks. On the other hand, there are very large differences between the amounts in the household budget that are allowed for the replacement, repair, and so on, of furniture. In the German budgets these are mostly ridiculously low in comparison with the corresponding sums in the American ones. It therefore seems as if the American worker, as does the German middle class, acquires his furnishings in stages, while the German worker must content himself with initial acquisitions and with such repairs as are absolutely urgent.

The forty-four[53] Nuremberg families taken together spent only 635.36 marks on furniture and room-furnishings (which is 1.07 per cent of their total expenditures); they spent 169.33 marks (0.29 per cent of total expenditure) on kitchen-fittings, so that their average expenditure for house and kitchen was 20 to 21 marks. The 908 Berlin families each spent about 20 marks on furniture, house-moving, and so on (1.2 per cent of total expenditure); the Karlsruhe families spent 23 marks (1.3 per cent) each, and May's families 18 marks each. On the other hand, the workers in Massachusetts spent $22.94 (96.35M) each (2.71 per cent of expenditure) on these things and the 2567 families in the large Federal inquiry spent $26.32 (110.54M) each (3.42 per cent of expenditure). The American families therefore spend five to six times the amount that the German ones do for the replacement and maintenance of their domestic furnishings and fittings, and for this they undoubtedly achieve an extra increment in terms of real comfort.

We can assess best how eating habits in Germany and the United States differ if we know the quantities of food consumed, and then we can compare and contrast in kind the consumption of the two countries. The large American enquiry contains useful and relevant information on this, and of the German studies, two – those for Karlsruhe and Nuremberg[54] – have figures that are at least partly comparable.

One should note that the size of the families is almost exactly the same in each case: 5.31 in America, 5.36 in Karlsruhe and 5 in Nuremberg. I have converted the American measures (bushels, quarts, pounds avoirdupois, loaves) into kilograms in order to make them comparable with the German figures. No comparable figures could be obtained for the foodstuffs against which there are gaps.

The amounts consumed annually by the average working-class family are shown in Table 21. According to this, the American worker eats almost three times as much meat, three times as much flour and four times as much sugar as his German counterpart. (The high consumption of flour, eggs and sugar suggests a substantial indulgence in pies and puddings.)

However, because Table 21 does not include one range of important foodstuffs, it fails to show the full gap between the two sets of eating habits. Expenditure on vegetables in the American families amounted to $18.85, or about 79 marks, while among the Berlin families it was 23 marks,[55] among the Nuremberg families 15 marks and among the Karlsruhe ones 9 marks. Expenditure on fruit (which has an importance in the American household that is unknown in Germany) was $16.52, or about 70 marks, in the American families, while among those of Berlin, Karlsruhe and Nuremberg it was 13 marks, 7 marks and 8 to 9 marks respectively.

As a control I am now going to group together the amounts of money which the various enquiries state are spent for the most important foodstuffs and which should be compared with the data on prices given in Table 18 if they are to be evaluated correctly. In Table 22 are the various yearly expenditures in marks on selected foodstuffs.

To sum up: in his eating habits as in other things the American worker is much closer to the better sections of the German middle class than to the German wage-labouring class. He does not merely eat, but dines.

It is perhaps the American worker's clothing that shows most clearly that with regard to his standard of living he is much better classified with the German bourgeoisie than with the German working class. This attracts the attention of anyone who comes to America for the first time. Kolb gives the following impressionistic picture:[56]

There [in the bicycle factory] many even wore starched shirts; the collars were unbuttoned during work; and the cuffs – which were always solidly sewn – were rolled back to the elbow. Then, when the factory whistle blew and people stripped off their overalls, they hardly looked like workers at all. Large numbers rode home on their bikes. Many rode off wearing elegant hats, yellow laced boots and fashionably coloured gloves, looking as splendid as anyone. These are unskilled manual workers earning $1.25 a day.

TABLE 21   Average amounts of selected foodstuffs consumed annually by working-class families in the United States, around Karlsruhe and in Nuremberg

Items	Units	In the United States	Around Karlsruhe	In Nuremberg
Black rye bread	kilograms	} 114.6	582	—
White bread	,,		132	—
Meat[a]	,,	384.8	112	95.2[b]
Potatoes	,,	379.1	647	268.3
Flour	,,	308.8	91	42.3[c]
Butter	,,	53.1	20	5.3
Other fats[d]	,,	38.3	32	22.6
Cheese	,,	7.3	12	—
Milk	litres	335.5	737	—
Eggs	number	1022	612	—
Sugar	kilograms	121.8	31	—
Rice	,,	11.4	—	5.6

Notes
[a] This means meat and sausage together for Germany, and fresh and salted meat, fish and poultry together for the United States.
[b] This is without sausage.
[c] *Ed.* – This is incorrectly given as 55 in Sombart's original text. See Braun, *Haushaltungs-Rechnungen Nürnberger Arbeiter*, pp. XVIII–XXXI, for the data from which the figure is calculated.
[d] This includes dripping and salad oils for Germany and means lard for the United States.

And what about the female workers, the 'ladies', as they are generally called? Their clothing, especially that of the young girls, is often quite elegant. In more than one factory I have seen the female employees in light-coloured blouses, of white silk even, and they almost always wear a hat on their way to the factory. 'White kid gloves were *en règle*', reports Mrs van Vorst about a social attended by some female employees, and she describes as follows the attire of the ladies in the restaurant where they lunch – note that this is on work days in the midday break during factory hours:

They came in groups – a rustling frou-frou announced silk under-fittings [just imagine!]; feathers, garlands of flowers, masses of trimming weighed down their broad-brimmed picture hats, fancy veils, kid gloves, silver side-bags, embroidered blouses and elaborate belt buckles completed the detail of their showy costumes, the whole worn with the air of a manikin.[57]

TABLE 22 Average annual amounts in marks spent on selected foodstuffs as reported for particular samples of working-class families in the United States and in Germany

	Meat (including sausage, salted meat, and fish such as herrings, etc.)	Bread	Milk	Eggs
The 2567 Washington families	464	52	90	71
The Massachusetts families	606	—	131	—
May's families	161	128	79	—
The Nuremberg families[a]	233	139[b]	73	26
The Karlsruhe families	145	134	34	13
The Berlin families	426[c]	136	73	37

Notes

[a] *Ed.* – In calculating all the figures in this row Sombart incorrectly assumed that amounts of total expenditure on specific items given in his source cover all forty-four families. In fact, they cover only forty-one. The figures given in this table have been recalculated using the correct divisor.

[b] *Ed.* – Although Sombart does not say so, this figure contains an annual amount of about 4 marks per family spent on cake.

[c] *Ed.* – Sombart's original text states this as 270 marks, but there was no way in which the latter figure could be reconciled with recalculations from the data source. In fact, the entry in this cell is the sum of results derived from a series of convoluted recalculations of data given in the source. Strangely, Sombart seems to have forgotten to include the 154 marks spent on meat when he summed the components of this entry; instead, he included only the approximately 253 marks spent on bacon and sausage and the 18 marks spent on herrings and other fish.

The next question is whether the extravagance of this clothing can be expressed in numerical terms so that it can be compared with that in other countries. Peter Roberts, despite the fact that he looks on the modern 'luxury' of the working population with a censorious and fault-finding eye, none the less gives some very interesting information on this issue of expenditure on clothing in his research on the condition of Pennsylvania miners.[58] While the newly arrived 'Sclav' woman manages her clothing requirements with $25 a year, the average American woman needs $50 to $60, and some need up to $100 and $150. Of the men he reports as follows: the 'Hun' spends $5 for a suit, the 'Pole' $10, and the 'Lett' $15. The Anglo-Saxon pays $15 to $25. Many wear tailor-made suits. They never go without collar and tie, cuffs and white shirt, studs, buttons, and a gold watch and chain, and seldom without a gold ring. They pay $2 to $3 for a pair of shoes and about the same price for a hat. They never buy in a second-hand clothing store. Everyone has a comfortable overcoat for cold weather; many have two, one for spring and autumn and the other for winter. In contrast to the recently arrived immigrants, as well as to the older indigenous generation, young Americans change their clothing extremely frequently. If a suit is somewhat worn, it is discarded. Last year's hat is not worn any more this year. Collars and ties are changed according to the dictates of fashion. Even for linen and underwear a lot is paid. The average young man of native birth – married or single – would need $40 to $50 for clothing. This information is confirmed in the figures of our household budgets. In all of them expenditure on clothing is high in absolute terms, and even in relative ones in relation to income, and it is considerably higher than in Germany.

The 2567 Washington families have the following average yearly expenditure:[59]

For the husband's clothing:	142 marks	(4.39 per cent of total expenditure)
For the wife's clothing:	109 marks	(3.39 per cent of total expenditure)
For the children's clothing:	202 marks	(6.26 per cent of total expenditure)
Total	453 marks	(14.04 per cent of total expenditure)

The Massachusetts families spend a yearly average on clothes of 456 marks (12.81 per cent of total expenditure).

Mrs Charles Husted More, the lady already mentioned, came to a similar conclusion – that in American working-class families expenditure on clothing amounts on average to 12 per cent of income.

On the other hand, the average annual expenditures on clothes of the contrasting German families are as follows:

May's families:	163 marks	(13.72 per cent of total expenditure)
The Karlsruhe families:	218 marks	(12.54 per cent of total expenditure)
The Nuremberg families:	129 marks	(8.34 per cent of total expenditure)
The Berlin families:	143 marks	(8.11 per cent of total expenditure)

It may be accepted that the last two figures are closer to the truth than are the first two. The reporter himself explains the high expenditure on clothing on the part of the Karlsruhe families by the greater need for footwear – due to the longer distances to and from their places of work. It is not clear why May's families expend so much more for clothing than do those of Nuremberg and Berlin. In view of the small numbers of cases looked at, it could be a matter of chance. In any case, on the basis of the figures submitted one can say that the

TABLE 23   Average comparative expenditure patterns as reported for particular samples of working-class families in the United States and in Germany

Households	Food	Housing (including heating and lighting)	Clothing	Percentage remaining for all other expenditure
Percentages of total expenditure spent on:				
United States				
11,156 'normal families'	43.13	23.81	12.95	20.11
2567 specially examined families	42.54	19.78	14.04	23.64
The Massachusetts families	49.01	18.11	12.81	20.07
Germany				
The Karlsruhe families	34.79[a]	11.0[b] (8.17)	12.54	41.67 (44.50)
The Berlin families	48.07[c]	20.31	8.11	23.51
May's families[d]	48.16	17.59[e]	13.40	20.85
The Nuremberg families	42.00[f]	18.56	8.34	31.10

Notes

[a] *Ed.* – Sombart's entry for this cell in the original text is 47.1 per cent. However, such a figure *includes* expenditure on alcoholic drinks; Sombart's soon-to-be-revealed purpose is to argue that the German working-class family squanders so much of its 'free' income on liquor that ultimately it has a smaller proportion of such income to spend on other luxuries than its American counterpart. To include expenditure on alcohol both within that for food and that which is 'free' for luxuries is highly misleading and an appropriate correction has been made by the Editor. This correction has some substantial effects on one or two of Sombart's later inferences from his German studies. However, it should be remembered that the Karlsruhe families differ from those in the other German studies in that they are rural and so able to grow a substantial part of their food themselves.

[b] The low amount is explained by the fact that it refers to rural workers. [The figure of 11.0 per cent is that given in the original text as the proportion of expenditure spent on housing by the Karlsruhe families, but recalculations of the data on the subject in the primary source could not replicate this result. The figure of 8.17 per cent shown in parentheses below Sombart's entry is the Editor's estimation of the correct value. This comprises 3.05 per cent of expenditure on rent, 0.98 per cent on upkeep of the home and 4.14 per cent on wood, coal and lighting. Even if Sombart had included expenditures on household items (1.32 per cent) and on soap and other cleaning materials (1.09 per cent) – as is possible, even if scarcely defensible in view of the nomenclature of this item – the entry would still have been only 10.58 per cent. If the entry under housing is set at 8.17 per cent, the figure for the Karlsruhe data in the extreme right-hand column of the table becomes 44.50 per cent, as is also shown in parentheses. – *Ed.*]

[c] This excludes alcoholic drinks consumed at home. [Sombart's entry for this cell in the original text is 47.34 per cent, but an examination of his source showed that it should be 48.07 per cent; an appropriate correction has therefore been made in the

American worker spends in absolute terms three times as much for clothing as does the German one, and in relative terms the former spends half as much again as the latter.

The American worker's custom of satisfying his requirements for housing, food and clothing in so abundant a manner naturally means that his 'free' income as a percentage of his total income is no higher than is the case with his German colleague, despite the fact that the former's total income is so much higher. On the contrary, the German worker comes out with a rather more favourable proportion. Even if chance factors may have played some spurious role and even if the different methods of compiling the budgets may have introduced some discrepancies, the results of our enquiries cannot none the less be rejected totally out of hand, certainly not those results that concern the division of expenditure into the major categories. According to our findings as set out in Table 23, after meeting his requirements for housing, food and clothing, the income remaining for the American is nearer a fifth of the original amount (in two cases) than it is to a quarter (which is not quite attained in one case), while the German is very likely to have over a quarter (close to three-tenths)[60] left over for 'sundries'. The figures are given in Table 23.[61]

What does the German worker do with the surplus that remains after his 'necessary' expenditure has been laid out – a surplus that is (relatively) so much greater than what remains to the American worker? Does he spend more on education? Or on amusements? On clubs? On taxes? On the doctor? No, not any of these. What he 'saves' after his expenditure on housing, clothing and food is squandered on drink.

---

extreme right-hand entry for this set of data and this affects very slightly the validity of the inference Sombart makes from these data in the text. – *Ed.*]

d These percentages are of total income, which for all families together is a trifle greater than total expenditure. [It is a mystery why Sombart used total income rather than expenditure as the base for May's families; the respective percentages of total expenditure for these families are: 49.32; 18.01; 13.72; and 18.95. – *Ed.*]

e *Ed.* – Sombart's entry for this cell in the original text is 14.50 per cent, but it proved impossible to replicate that figure using data from the primary source. Expenditure on housing among May's families, as a proportion of income, is 12.57 per cent and that on heating and lighting is 5.02 per cent – totalling 17.59 per cent overall. The entry for this row in the extreme right-hand column of the table is therefore reduced significantly to 20.85 per cent, making the percentage of 'free' income in May's families very similar to that in the American studies and thereby affecting the validity of the inference that Sombart draws in the text from this set of data. Of course, if the figure of 18.95 per cent – this being the percentage of total *expenditure* on items other than food, housing, and clothing given in Note d, above – is substituted, May's study becomes even less favourable to the point Sombart wants to make. However, it should be mentioned that the lack of a systematic accounting in this study of expenditure on alcoholic drinks admits the possibility that some part of the expenditure on 'food' was in fact on alcoholic drinks.

f This excludes all alcoholic drinks.

The entire difference – and more – between the 'free' income of the American worker and that of the German one is absorbed by expenditure on alcoholic drinks!

The fact that the American worker is apparently less given to alcohol than is his German colleague has often been alluded to in recent years.[62] I am in a position to confirm the correctness of this observation with statistics.

Exactly half of the 2567 American working-class families that were specially examined were total abstainers. Altogether only 50.72 per cent had any expenditure on alcoholic drinks. Even among those who indulged in the consumption of alcohol, expenditure for 'intoxicating liquors' – the technical term for alcoholic drinks in the statistics – fluctuated within modest limits. These families spent a yearly average of $24.53 (103.03M). (The native-born ones lay out an average expenditure of $22.28 (93.58M) and the foreign-born ones an average of $27.39 (115.04M); the maximum was reached by the Scots with $33.63 (141.25M) – and by the Germans with $33.50 (140.70M).) The amount of $24.53 is 3.19 per cent of total expenditure. If, however, one calculates the expenditure on alcoholic drinks made by those families that drank as a fraction of the total expenditure of all families, there results an average budgetary debit due to this item of $12.44 (52.25M), or 1.62 per cent. (The budgets of the Massachusetts families unfortunately contain no separate data on this expenditure.)

If one is to appreciate adequately how the German figures contrast with this, one must remember that alcoholic beverages, particularly beer, are considerably more expensive in the United States than in Germany. The usual draught measure of locally brewed beer will contain from about 0.2 to 0.5 litres and generally costs 5 cents, or about 20 pfennigs. For the same amount of money the German receives *at least* double the quantity of beer, and in southern Germany probably three times as much. Of course, American beer might be brewed with a somewhat stronger alcoholic content than particularly the south German kind. Having said that, I can give the figures from the German budgetary studies. (May contains no separate data for alcoholic drinks.)

The Berlin families are relatively sober. They spend a yearly average of 117 marks on beer and brandy, which amounts to 6.61 per cent of their total expenditure. Nevertheless, they drink four to five times as much as the Americans.

However, the alcoholic consumption in the south German families is enormously large. The Karlsruhe families spend an average of 214 marks on alcoholic beverages, which is more than a quarter of the costs of their housekeeping and 12.31 per cent of their total expenditure.[63] We are also told what quantities are represented by this amount of money; the average family consumes 769 litres of beer, 138 litres of wine and six litres of brandy. Cheers!

In the budgets of the Nuremberg families the item for expenditure on alcoholic drinks is somewhat less. Even so, such families spend an average of 143 marks on such drinks, which is equal to 9.63 per cent of total expenditure, of which 9.21 per cent goes on beer alone. In view of the cheap price of beer in the beer-brewing city of Nuremberg, the amount consumed here will not fall far behind that of the Karlsruhe families. Thus, the German working-class family spends three to four times as much on alcoholic beverages as the American one; it therefore drinks perhaps six to ten times as much as the American one, and this item debits its budget at least by the extra amount that the Americans spent for housing, food and clothing. It is probable that after deducting expenditure on alcoholic beverages the amount of income that remains to the worker to be spent as he fancies amounts to a larger percentage in America than it does in Germany. For our families the amounts would be as follows:

In the United States (the 2567 specially
    examined families):   22.02 per cent
In Karlsruhe: 29.36 (32.19) per cent[64]
In Berlin: 16.90 per cent
In Nuremberg: 21.47 per cent

The extra that the American gains in this way is used partly for religious and charitable purposes (1.30 per cent) and partly for purchases for the home (3.42 per cent), while the same amounts that remain over for 'sundries' are distributed fairly uniformly, both in Germany and America, between the same items of expenditure. Approximately equal amounts are spent on amusements, taxes, books and newspapers, the doctor and the pharmacist, insurance (which is private in America and a State concern in Germany), memberships of organisations, and so on.

5 Standard of Living and Ideology

It would be precarious to wish to show in detail the effect that a standard of living as different as that of the American worker has upon social perception. I must leave it to specialists in dietetics in particular to uncover the connections that exist between the anti-Socialist mentality of the American worker and his predominantly meat-and-puddings diet or his abstemiousness towards alcohol. Abstinence fanatics who are favourable to capitalism will be ready to discover close connections between the poison of alcohol and the poison of Socialism. However, we shall let that be.

This much is certain: the American worker lives in comfortable circumstances. On the whole, he is not familiar with oppressively impoverished housing conditions. He is not forced out of his home into the tavern, because his home is not like the 'room' of the worker in the large cities of continental Europe. Instead he can indulge fully in sentiments of the most acute selfishness – of the sort that is cultivated by comfortable domesticity. He is well fed and is not acquainted with the discomforts that must necessarily result in the long run from the mixing of potatoes and alcohol. He dresses like a gentleman and she like a lady, and so he does not even outwardly become aware of the gap that separates him from the ruling class. It is no wonder if, in such a situation, any dissatisfaction with the 'existing social order' finds difficulty in establishing itself in the mind of the worker, particularly if his endurable – indeed, comfortable – standard of living seems permanently assured; and up to the present time he has been able to be quite certain of that. We ought never to forget the continuous progress that 'economic prosperity' in the United States has made, apart from short interruptions, in the last two generations, during which time one would have thought that Socialism could not have failed to take root. Evidently this prosperity was not in spite of capitalism but because of it.

A glance at the summary figures in the statistics is sufficient to dispel any doubt about the reality of this prosperity; indeed, the sparrows and every business advisor sing it from the rooftops. The following statistics apply to manufacturing, trade and transportation:[65]

Year	Number of wage labourers	Amount of wages paid	Average wage
1850	957,059	$236,755,464	$247
1870	2,053,996	$775,584,343	$378
1890	4,251,535	$1,891,209,696	$445

To the extent that the economic situation of the average labourer improved and to the extent that the increasing affluence in his standard of living gave him the opportunity to experience the temptations of materialist depravity, he had to learn to like the economic system that shaped his lot for him; he had to learn slowly to adapt his mentality to the distinctive mechanism of a capitalist economy, and finally he had even to fall to the spell that is irresistibly exerted on almost everyone by the speed of change and the growing force of measurable size in this amazing period of time. An input of patriotism, impinging as it did upon the proud consciousness that the United States led all other nations on the path of (capitalist) progress, established the cast of his business-oriented mentality and made him into the sober, calculating businessman without ideals whom we know today. All Socialist utopias came to nothing on roast beef and apple pie.

However, yet another set of different factors had to operate for the benefit of the worker before he could take full and hearty pleasure in these beautiful things. What I mean is that his style of living had to be not only materialistically ideal but it also had to be lived through in a situation of social ease. The following pages should explain this further.

SECTION THREE

The Social Position of the Worker

1 The Democratic Style of Public Life in America

It is not only in his position *vis-à-vis* the material world (that is, in his material standard of living) that the American worker is so much more favoured than his European counterpart. In his relations to people and to social institutions, and in his position in and to society – in short, in what I call his social position – the American is also better-off than he would be in the contrasting European situation. For him 'Liberty' and 'Equality' (not only in the formal political sense but also in the economic and social sense) are not empty ideas and vague dreams, as they are for the European working class; for the most part they are realities. The American's better social position is largely the result of his political position and his economic situation – of a radical-democratic system of government and of a comfortable standard of living. Both these are to be found within a colonising population with no history, which basically consisted, and still does consist, wholly of immigrants; a population in which there are no feudal institutions, except in some Southern slave states.

Unfortunately, it is not possible to determine the nature of this social position of the worker as exactly as was the case with his political and economic situation, either with the help of sections of the law or of numbers. Demonstration has to rest partly on intuitions, it has to be satisfied with the assessment of symptoms, and it should not underestimate details; yet it will still remain incomplete overall. The general impression must then replace what exact proof cannot demonstrate.

Anyone who has ever observed, even only fleetingly, male and female American workers as they carry on their life outside the factory or the workshop, has noticed at first sight that they are a different breed of people from German workers. We saw earlier how smartly and frequently elegantly clothed the workers are, especially the female ones, as they go on their way to work. On the street they are like members of the middle class and they act as working gentlemen and working ladies. In the external appearance of the American worker there is not the stigma of being the class apart that almost all European workers have about them. In his appearance, in his demeanour, and in the manner of his conversation, the American worker also contrasts strongly with the European one. He carries his head high, walks with a lissom stride, and is as open and cheerful in his expression as any member of the middle class. There is nothing oppressed or submissive about him. He mixes with everyone – in reality and not only in theory – as an equal. The trade-union leader taking part in a ceremonial banquet moves with the same self-assurance on the dance floor as would any aristocrat in Germany. However, he also wears a finely fitting dress suit, patent-leather boots and elegant clothes of the latest fashion, and so, even in his appearance, nobody can distinguish him from the President of the Republic.

The bowing and scraping before the 'upper classes', which produces such an unpleasant impression in Europe, is completely unknown. It does not occur to a waiter, or to a street-car conductor, or to a police-man, to behave differently when he is confronted by an ordinary worker than he would if he had the Governor of Pennsylvania in front of him. That produces a spirit of self-respect, both in the person who behaves in this way, and in the one to whom the behaviour is directed if he belongs to the poorer population.

The whole of public life has a more democratic style. The worker is not being reminded at every turn that he belongs to a 'lower' class. Indicative of this is the one class of carriage on all railways (which just lately is beginning to be done away with because of the advent of Pullman cars).

Snobbery about personal status is also less common in the United States than in Germany in particular. It is not what one is and still less what one's parents were that decides one's prestige, but what one accomplishes, and for that reason the very word 'work' in its abstract form is made into an honorary title. Thus, even the worker is treated respectfully, although – or rather because – he is only a worker. It is therefore natural that he feels differently from his counterpart in a country where a person only begins to be considered a person when he is, if not a baron, then a reserve officer, a doctor, or a person on proba-tion for a profession.

Because of the democratic system of government, universal educa-tion, and the higher standard of living of the worker, there is genuinely a lesser social distance between the individual strata of the population, and – due to the effect of the customs and perceptions described – this distance becomes even smaller in the consciousness of the various classes than it really is.

2 Employer and Worker

This stress on equality of rights, to which social and public life in the United States is geared, is even to be found inside capitalist businesses. Even here the employer does not confront the worker as the Lord who demands obedience, which was and is the usual case in old Europe with its feudal traditions. From the beginning a purely business standpoint became the prevailing rule in the bargaining of wage agreements. There was no question of the worker having first to engage in long conflict with the employer for the equality between them to be formally recognised. The American woman was treated with great tenderness because she was scarce; similarly, the employer took the trouble to behave towards the labour force, which was not originally available in the quantity he wanted, in a polite and accommodating manner that found strong support in the democratic atmosphere of the country. Today even English workers are still astonished at the respectful tone that employers and foremen in the United States adopt towards the worker, and they are astonished at the licence given to the American worker even in his workplace; he is 'freed from what one may call vexatious supervision'. They are surprised that he can take a day or two off, that he can go out to smoke a cigar – indeed, that he smokes while working – and that there is even an automatic cigar-vending machine for his use in the factory.[1] It is also a characteristic of American manufacturers that they fail to put into effect even the simplest protective measures in their plants and that they are not in the least bit concerned that the set-up of the place of work be good when objectively assessed. (Quite frequently places of work are overcrowded and have similar deficiencies.) On the other hand, they are most eager to provide anything that could be perceived subjectively by the worker as an amenity; in other words, they take care of 'comfort': bathtubs, showers, lockers, temperature control in the workrooms, which are cooled by fans in the summer and are preheated in the winter. This arrangement, which is found fairly generally in American factories, was a special source of wonder to the English workers on the Mosely Commission. 'Imagine the response of an English manufacturer who was asked to take such measures for the well-being of his staff,' says the ironfounder, Mr Maddison,[2] and all the others are 'impressed by the exceptional organisation done to ensure the comfort and well-being of the staff'.

These are certainly all trivialities, but the saying that 'small gifts preserve friendship' is applicable even here. Later I shall try to show that – when the matter is considered objectively – the worker in the United States is more exploited by capitalism than in any other country in the world, that in no other country is he so lacerated in the harness of capitalism or has to work himself so quickly to death as in America. However, this is irrelevant if one is engaged in explaining what working-class sentiments consist of. To account for their character all that is important is what individuals perceive as being pleasure or pain and what they assess as being valuable or worthless. It is one of the most brilliant feats of diplomatic artifice that the American employer (in just the same manner as the business-oriented politician) has realised how to keep the worker in a good mood despite all actual exploitation, and that the latter is a long way from achieving consciousness of his real position. This generosity in small matters has contributed substantially to the present situation.

However, there is yet another matter that has a similar effect; this is that the worker has been psychologically influenced into thinking that he was not an enemy of the capitalist system but even a promoter of it. American employers realised perfectly how to interest the worker in the success of the business in order to identify his interests to some extent with those of the capitalists. This is done not so much by profit-sharing (although this also occurs in all varieties in the United States) as by a system of small measures that are mutually reinforcing and that, when taken together, achieve miraculous results. Firstly, it is said in praise of all American employers (for example, the people on the Mosely Commission may again be cited) that they do not seek to reduce the extra high earnings that the worker occasionally obtains from an agreed piece rate by cutting the rates per unit, as the European employer usually does. When this liberal practice is followed, the worker remains in a constant fever of excitement about his work and earnings and he is kept in a good mood by the possibility of *very* high gains.

A second generally practised custom of the American employer is to interest the worker directly in technical progress by accepting with great alacrity every suggestion for an improvement of the machinery and so on, and, if it is introduced and proves its usefulness, letting the worker profit directly or indirectly from it. The worker therefore comes very quickly to perceive the organisation into which he is incorporated to be his own firm in which he shares the ups and downs. This custom of accepting suggestions and complaints from the workers and of always examining them seriously is found in all branches of American industry: in concerns using blast-furnace processes and in shipbuilding, in the manufacture of knives and in spinning, in leather processes and in bookbinding, in the manufacture of paper and in the chemical or optical industry.[3] In most factories there is a so-called 'suggestion box', which is a container into which the workers cast their suggestions and proposals. The system in the renowned model factories of the National Cash Register Company at Dayton, Ohio, is – like all such arrangements – particularly advanced. Here enclosed writing-desks stand in every department of the factory and next to these desks a board is fixed with the words 'Complaints and Suggestions' on it. Every worker is free to write his complaints about defective tools, machines or work processes and his suggestions for improvements, along with his name, on the strip of paper that covers the surface of the desk. After this he can tear off and keep the top strip of paper – there are two of them, one on top of the other – and by means of a handle he can roll the bottom copy into the inside of the desk, where the strip winds itself on to a roll. The rolls that have been written on are periodically retrieved and the suggestions are examined. Twice a year honorary diplomas and cash prizes are distributed for noteworthy suggestions. The amount of the prizes is determined by the value of the innovation. Every year the firm gives away a few thousand marks for this purpose. All male and female employees – over 2000 people – are invited to a session where prizes are distributed, and the festive activity takes place amid music and speeches. In 1897 4000 suggestions had poured in, of which 1078 were acted on. In 1898 there were 2500 more and in 1901 2000, of which a third were wholly or partly introduced into the firm.

Finally, the capitalists seeks to buy off the worker by granting him a proportion of their profits. The method of doing this is by offering stock on advantageous terms. In certain circumstances the capitalists thereby kill two birds with one stone. Firstly, they draw the worker into the hurly-burly of running the business and arouse in him the base instincts both of acquisitiveness and of morbid excitement in speculation, thus binding him to the system of production that they champion. Secondly, however, they dispose of their inferior stock, averting an impending fall in prices and perhaps at the same time influencing the stock market momentarily in such a way as to secure extra pickings for themselves.

This system has been used on a large scale by the Steel Trust. In 1903 the company first spent $2,000,000 of its profits from the previous year in buying up 25,000 of its preference shares. These were offered to the 168,000 employees at a rate of $82.50 each, payable within three years.

In order that the workers should be induced to hang on to their stock, an extra dividend of $5.00 annually per share was promised in the event that the stock remained for more than five years in the possession of the person who first acquired it. The offer met with general approval and 48,983 shares were acquired by employees of the company. Shortly after this there followed a fall in prices – although the purpose behind this piece of charity had been to retard or avoid just such a fall. The U.S. Steel Corporation's preference shares fell to

$50.00 each. The company then produced a new trick. In order to pacify the workers but at the same time to prevent a further decline in the price (which would have come about if the workers had disposed of their stock), the company pledged itself to buy back at a rate of $82.50 a share the stock being held by the workers, in case the latter should hold on to them until 1908! As early as December of the same year (1903) the Corporation made a new offer to the workers – under conditions similar to the first one – except that the price of the preference shares was fixed at $55.00 each. Again, 10,248 employees entered into the proposition and altogether they acquired 32,519 shares. Since meanwhile the shares had risen again to $82.00 each, the workers received a benefit from their purchase this time.[4]

The result – at least temporarily – of a policy of this sort is clear: 'Partners in the great enterprise, the multitude of petty shareholders are led more and more to consider economic questions from the employers' standpoint.'[5] 'The chances of collision . . . will disappear . . . when their differences are merged in a sense of common ownership . . .'[6] Above all, the worker becomes steeped in the capitalist mentality:

> The present ambition of the higher wage earner seems to incline more to the pecuniary rewards of his work than to the work itself. Doubtless this tendency is due in no slight degree to the fact that the wage earner is brought into constant and immediate contact with the money-making class. He sees that the value of the industry is measured chiefly by its profits. Sometimes the profits are flaunted in his face. At all times the thing most in evidence to him is money.[7]

3 The Worker's Escape into Freedom

However enticing the temptations that capitalism uses to approach the worker may now be and however much these may affect the weaker souls, one may none the less doubt whether what capitalism was able to offer the worker would alone have been sufficient to turn almost all sections of the working class into the peaceable citizens that they are, unless the worker had been prevailed upon from another angle to reconcile himself to the existing economic system, or at least not to adopt a hostile attitude towards it. Even American capitalism puts tight fetters on the individual, even American capitalism cannot deny that it holds its workers in a condition of slavery, and even American capitalism has had periods of stagnation with all their destructive consequences for the worker (such as unemployment, pressure on wages, and so on). In time a confrontational mentality would most certainly have developed in America, at least among the best of the working class, if escape from the orbit of the capitalist economy, or at least from the restricted confines of wage labour, had not stood open to so many groups of workers: to the robust, to those upon whom the chains were beginning to press, to the rebellious, to those among the workers who were adventurous, and to those who were dissatisfied or refractory.

In saying this I am alluding to the characteristic of the American economy that has come to have the very greatest importance in accounting for how the proletarian psyche has evolved. One must accept that there is a grain of truth in all the nonsense spoken by the Carnegies and those parroting them who want to lull the 'boorish rabble' to sleep by telling them miraculous stories about themselves or others who began as newsboys and finished as multimillionaires. The prospects of moving out of his class were undoubtedly greater for the worker in America than for his counterpart in old Europe. The newness of the society, its democratic character, the smaller gap between the employing class and the workers, the colonial vigour of many of its immigrants, Anglo-Saxon determination of purpose, and many other things, all worked together to let a far from insignificant number of ordinary workers ascend the rungs of the ladder of the capitalist hierarchy to the top or almost to the top.[8] Their much larger savings (as compared with the situation in Europe) enabled others in their turn to set themselves up in such petty-bourgeois livelihoods as shopkeepers or saloon-keepers.

However, another goal beckoned to the great majority of dissatisfied wage labourers. In the course of the past century hundreds of thousands and millions actually sought and attained this goal, and it brought them emancipation from the oppression of capitalism, emancipation in the fullest sense of the word: their goal was a free homestead in the unsettled West.

I fully believe that the fact supplying the principal reason for the characteristic peaceable mood of the American worker is that many men with sound limbs and no capital or hardly any were able to turn themselves into independent farmers almost as they wished by colonising free land.[9]

This is not the place to sketch the story of the settlement legislation and of the actual settlement of the vast country, or even to give merely its basic features.[10] It is sufficient for our purposes to establish the following points.

Through the Homestead Act from 1863 onwards[11] any person who is over twenty-one years old and is a citizen, or expresses his intention of becoming one, receives the right to take possession of eighty acres of public land (1 acre is 0.4 of a hectare) if these acres lie within railway land grants, or 160 acres if they are located elsewhere. The only condition is that he declares on oath that he intends to occupy and cultivate the property fully and exclusively for his own use and intends to bestow no direct or indirect benefit on anyone else in so doing. Nothing except an insignificant fee has to be paid for permission to do this. Under certain easily fulfilled conditions the settler is recognised as having proprietary right to this homestead after five years.

It is a universally known fact that during the last half century millions of people have settled as farmers in the United States, and there is no need to produce any proofs of this. It is only to evoke the right conception of the size of this movement that I quote the number of farms enumerated in the respective Census years. These are:

1850	1,449,073	1880	4,008,907
1860	2,044,077	1890	4,564,641
1870	2,659,985	1900	5,737,372

All these are new farms being formed on virgin soil, for the area of improved land increased almost parallel with the number of farms in the same years. In acres the areas were:

1850	113,032,614	1880	284,771,042
1860	163,110,720	1890	357,616,755
1870	188,921,099	1900	414,498,487

This means that an area with twice the expanse of the German Empire became cultivated for the first time in the two decades from 1870 to 1890![12]

However, it is the Americans themselves who have comprised the largest proportion of this new settlement. In other words, settling free land in the West is just as much the goal of the inhabitants of American states that send their 'surplus population' out there as it is of the foreign immigrant; it may be more so. Internal migration in the United States occurs on a greater scale than in any other country, and its character is very different from that of internal migration in European countries. Over here it is essentially the stronger pull of the cities and industrial regions *vis-à-vis* the predominantly rural districts that mobilises the population. At the moment a similar pull exists in the United States, especially in the East, and it is becoming stronger year by year. However, alongside this urban migration and far surpassing it in strength is an opposing movement from the more densely settled, more industrial areas into the sparsely populated regions with free land.

A glance at the figures with which the Census presents us in superabundant profusion shows that these are human migrations on the largest scale.[13]

In 1900 13,511,728 or 20.7 per cent of those born in America were living outside the state of their birth and 6,165,097 of those were living outside the 'division' of their birth – divisions being conventionally defined combinations of states: North Atlantic States, South Atlantic States, North Central States, South Central States, and Western States.[14] Those six million had therefore migrated some great distance. As may be imagined, most of them had in fact migrated from the Eastern States into the Central and Western States: the latter had received around five of the six million. Let us single out some of the states with more fully developed industry and see how much of their surplus population they had disposed of up to 1900 by sending them into other, more rural divisions of the country:

Massachusetts	115,532
Rhode Island	12,942
Connecticut	44,597
New York	806,553
New Jersey	76,346
Pennsylvania	707,344
Ohio	362,475
Illinois	303,318
	2,429,107

During one generation, therefore, two-and-a-half million people have been attracted to freedom from these eight states alone. That is about a fifth to a quarter of the entire number of American-born inhabitants of these states!

However, other data are needed to show that most of this migration is connected with the evolution of capitalism and that most of it represents an escape from the nexus of capitalist organisation of the sort that I have described. These other data are the numbers of homesteads distributed according to individual years. We can clearly follow how their number advances rapidly in times of economic depression, but without the explanation for this being an increase in immigration. This therefore means that during these years it is the 'industrial reserve army' that flows out of the industrial areas into the open country and settles there. This is especially true of the earlier periods when settlement was even easier. For example, the number of acres that were sold as a result of the Homestead Act and (since 1875)[15] of the Timber Culture Act rises from 2,698,770 in 1877 to 6,288,779 and 8,026,685 in the succeeding two years,[16] in which the industrial crisis reached its peak, while immigration in 1878 was less than at any time since 1862.[17] The economic depression then lasted all through the 1880s. Immigration consequently sank by a half – from 669,000 and 789,000 in 1881 and 1882[18] to 395,000 and 334,000 in 1885 and 1886. None the less, the number of acres sold rose from seven to eight million at the beginning of the 1880s to over twelve million in the second half of the 1880s.[19] In the middle of the 1880s the crisis in the American working class became critical due to the continuing depression. In Chicago and other cities anarchism raised its head. The following of the Knights of Labor, which originally had a strong Socialist orientation, increased between 1883 and 1886 from 52,000 to 703,000, only to sink to almost half this figure in 1888.[20] The force of the storm was broken. In ever increasing numbers the revolt-prone surplus population began to leave for the free land in the West.[21]

However, if one is explaining the development of the proletarian psyche, the significance of the fact that American capitalism evolved in a country with vast areas of free land is in no way exhausted merely by stating the number of settlers who have escaped from capitalist bondage over the years. Instead, it has to be borne in mind that the mere knowledge that he *could* become a free farmer at any time could not but make the American worker feel secure and content, a state of mind that is unknown to his European counterpart. One tolerates any oppressive situation more easily if one lives under the illusion of being able to withdraw from it if really forced to.

It is obvious that this is why the position of the working class to the problems of the future shape of the economy was bound to develop in a highly idiosyncratic manner. The possibility of being able to opt for capitalism or not transforms every incipient opposition to that economic system from an active to a passive form, and it takes away the thrust of any agitation against capitalism.

In the following words Henry George has splendidly described how far the American's cheerful and frank character, his inner contentment, his harmony with the world as a whole and with the social world in particular, are all intimately bound up with the existence of free, unsettled land:

> This public domain – the vast extent of land yet to be reduced to private possession, the enormous common to which the faces of the energetic were always turned, has been the great fact that, since the days when the first settlements began to fringe the Atlantic Coast, has formed our national character and colored our national thought. It is not that we have eschewed a titled aristocracy and abolished primogeniture; that we elect all our officers from School Directors up to President; that our laws run in the name of the people, instead of in the name of a prince; that the State knows no religion, and our judges wear no wigs – that we have been exempted from the ills that Fourth of July orators used to point to as characteristic of the effete despotisms of the Old World. The general intelligence, the general comfort, the active invention, the power of adaptation and assimilation, the free independent spirit, the energy and hopefulness that have marked our people, are not causes, but results – they have sprung from unfenced land. This public domain has been the transmuting force which has turned the thriftless, unambitious European peasant into the self-reliant Western farmer; it has given a consciousness of freedom even to the dweller in crowded cities, and has been a well-spring of hope even to those who have never thought of taking refuge upon it. The child of the people, as he grows to manhood in Europe, finds all the best seats at the banquet of life marked 'taken', and must struggle with his fellows for the crumbs that fall, without one chance in a thousand of forcing or sneaking his way to a seat. In America, whatever his condition, there has always been the consciousness that the public domain lay behind him; and the knowledge of this fact, acting and reacting, has penetrated our whole national life, giving to it generosity and independence, elasticity and ambition. All that we are proud of in the American character; all that makes our conditions and institutions better than those of older countries, we may trace to the fact that land has been cheap in the United States, because new soil has been open to the emigrant.[22]

These are roughly the reasons why there is [no][23] Socialism in the United States. However, my present opinion is as follows: *all the factors that till now have prevented the development of Socialism in the United States are about to disappear or to be converted into their opposite, with the result that in the next generation Socialism in America will very probably experience the greatest possible expansion of its appeal.*

However, to prove this requires a thorough analysis of the whole state of American political and social life. I hope to be able to provide this at some time in the future.

Abbreviations of Journal Titles

ASS   *Archiv für Sozialwissenschaft und Sozialpolitik [Works in Social Science and Social Policy]*

MLB   *Massachusetts Labor Bulletin*

QPASA *Quarterly Publications of the American Statistical Association*

ZVSV   *Zeitschrift für Volkswirtschaft, Sozialpolitik und Verwaltung [Journal of Political Economy, Social Policy and Administration]*

Notes

For the purposes of notation the Editor's Introductory Essay and the translation of Sombart's text have been regarded a separate entities. Thus references common to both entities that are given in full when they first appear in the Introductory Essay are likewise given in full when they first appear in the translation.

PREFACE TO THE ORIGINAL GERMAN EDITION

1 *Ed.* – The studies appeared under the general title, *Studien zur Entwicklungsgeschichte des nordamerikanischen Proletariats* [Studies in the Historical Development of the North American Proletariat], in three separate parts. On pages 210–36 was *I: Einleitung* [I: Introduction] corresponding to the Introduction of the present work. On pages 308–46 was *II: Die politische Stellung des Arbeiters* [II: The Political Position of the Worker] corresponding to Section One of the present work. On pages 556–611 were *III: Die Lebenshaltung des Arbeiters in den Vereinigten Staaten* [III: The Standard of Living of the Worker in the United States] and *IV: Die soziale Stellung des Arbeiters* [IV: The Social Position of the Worker] corresponding respectively to Section Two and Section Three of the present work.

2 *Ed.* – This is not quite the truth. Abbreviated versions of the Introduction and Section One of the present work did appear in the *International Socialist Review* shortly after they were published in the *Archiv für Sozialwissenschaft und Sozialpolitik*. They had been translated into English by A. M. Simons, the editor of the *Review*. In Volume 6, Number 3 (Sep 1905), 129–136, there appeared parts of the Introduction of the present work under the title, 'Study of the Historical Development and Evolution of the American Proletariat'. In Volume 6, Number 5 (Nov 1905), 293–301, were pieces of the first part of Section One of the present work under the general title, 'The Historical Development of the American Proletarian', and subtitled 'The Political Position of the Worker'. In Volume 6, Number 6 (Dec 1905), 358–367, was the remainder of Section One entitled 'Studies in the History and Development of the North American Proletariat'. However, Section Two of the present work, in which Sombart argued that American capitalism had been successful enough to buy off the radicalism of American workers, clearly offended the leaders of American Socialism, and no further translation appeared in the *Review*. Instead, in Volume 7, Number 7 (Jan 1907), 420–5, there appeared a vitriolic review of *Why is there no Socialism in the United States?* that had been translated from *Vorwärts* [*Forward*], the newspaper of the German Social Democratic Party, of 9 October 1906; in the review Sombart comes in for some harsh substantive and *ad hominem* criticism. At the bottom of the final page of this review is the following footnote by the editor of the *Review*: 'The first chapters of the work reviewed above containing the

valuable statistical portions appeared in the *International Socialist Review*. When we came to the nonsense on the condition of the American worker we stopped further publication. As Sombart has used the fact of such publication as an endorsement of his work, we publish the above to make this explanation – Editor.' Even this is not fully true, however, since most of the statistical material used by Sombart is included in the sections of his work that the *Review* chose not to publish.

3 *Ed.* – This reference is to Sombart's *Sozialismus und soziale Bewegung*, 5th ed. (Jena, 1905). The sixth edition of this work appeared in German in 1908 and was then translated into English by M. Epstein as *Socialism and the Social Movement* (London, 1909).

4 *Ed.* – Breslau is the German name for the city now in Poland that is called Wrocław. In 1906, of course, it was in Germany. From 1890 to 1906 Sombart was Extraordinary Professor of Economics at the University of Breslau. When denied promotion to a regular professorship at Breslau, largely for political reasons, he became Professor of Political Economy at the Berlin Handelshochschule [Commercial University].

FOREWORD

1 Cf. Walter Dean Burnham, *Critical Elections and the Mainsprings of American Politics* (New York, 1970).

2 Leon Samson, *Toward a United Front: A Philosophy for American Workers* (New York, 1933).

3 Stephan Thernstrom, 'Socialism and Social Mobility', in *Failure of a Dream?: Essays in the History of American Socialism*, ed. John H. M. Laslett and Seymour Martin Lipset (Garden City, 1974) pp. 509–27; Lipset's 'Comment', in ibid., pp. 528–46; Thernstrom's 'Reply' to this, in ibid., pp. 547–52.

4 Adolph Sturmthal, 'Comment 1 [on an excerpt from Sombart's *Why is there no Socialism in the United States?*]', in ibid., pp. 610–11.

5 Michael Harrington, *Socialism* (New York, 1972).

EDITOR'S INTRODUCTORY ESSAY

1 *Failure of a Dream?: Essays in the History of American Socialism*, ed. John H. M. Laslett and Seymour Martin Lipset (Garden City, 1974), contains a comprehensive review of the reasons to which the failure of American Socialism has been attributed, and the reader is referred to this for a fuller presentation of the current issues in this subject.

That book does contain a small translated excerpt from *Why is there no Socialism in the United States?*, but the parts chosen are from the end of the book, where Sombart is presenting his material on the effects of affluence on the working-class psyche and where he argues that the democratic character of social life in America had repressed radical tendencies. None of Sombart's arguments about the effects of the American political system is contained in the excerpt reproduced. In addition, the present translation incorporates editorial corrections of some of Sombart's data, which have been reproduced in their original incorrect form in *Failure of a Dream?*.

2 For example, Henry F. Bedford's *Socialism and the Workers of Massachusetts 1886–1912* (Amherst, 1966) documents how the Socialist Party in that state failed quite quickly to live up to its dramatic early promise. John

H. M. Laslett, *Labor and the Left: A Study of Socialist and Radical Influences in the American Labor Movement, 1881–1924* (New York, 1970) contains a series of locally oriented studies.

3 Arthur Mitzman, *Sociology and Estrangement: Three Sociologists of Imperial Germany* (New York, 1973) 133–264.

4 See the articles on Werner Sombart by Georg Weippart in *Handwörterbuch der Sozialwissenschaften* [*Concise Dictionary of the Social Sciences*], ed. Erwin v. Beckerath *et al.* (Stuttgart, Tübingen and Göttingen, 1956) IX 298–305, and by Jürgen Kuczynski in *International Encyclopedia of the Social Sciences*, ed. David L. Sills (New York, 1968) XV 57–9.

5 Mitzman, *Sociology and Estrangement*, 264.

6 Ibid., 227.

7 Tom Bottomore, 'Class structure and social consciousness' in *Aspects of History and Class Consciousness*, ed. István Mészáros (London, 1971) p. 58.

8 Karl Marx, *Essential Writings of Karl Marx*, selected by David Caute (New York, 1970) 197.

9 V. I. Lenin, *What is to be Done?*, translated by S. V. and Patricia Utechin (Oxford, 1963 ed.) esp. 61–118.

10 For example, Frederick Engels, 'Socialism: Utopian and Scientific', in Karl Marx and Frederick Engels, *Selected Works in Two Volumes* (Moscow, 1962) II 116.

11 See, for example, his discussion of German national character in Werner Sombart, *Socialism and the Social Movement*, translated from the sixth (enlarged) German edition by M. Epstein (London, 1909) 171.

12 Ralph Miliband, *Parliamentary Socialism: A Study in the Politics of Labour*, 2nd ed. (London, 1973).

13 David Coates, *The Labour Party and the Struggle for Socialism* (Cambridge, 1975).

14 See E. J. Hobsbawm, 'Labour Traditions', in his *Labouring Men: Studies in the History of Labour* (Garden City, 1967 ed.) 441, for an example of militance combined with political moderation in the case of workers in the small Sheffield metal crafts.

15 Tony Lane, *The Union Makes Us Strong: The British Working Class, Its Trade Unionism and Politics* (London, 1974).

16 Comments on the more detailed aspects of some of Sombart's arguments appear in the Notes to the text added by the Editor. These comments are intended to evaluate Sombart's evidence or to assess the particular argument of his in the light of subsequent research and debate on the subject.

17 Daniel Bell, 'The Failure of American Socialism: The Tension of Ethics and Politics', in his *The End of Ideology: On the Exhaustion of Political Ideas in the Fifties*, new, revised ed. (New York, 1962) 275–98.

18 Joseph A. Schumpeter, *Capitalism, Socialism and Democracy*, 3rd ed. (New York, 1962 ed.) 331.

19 David M. Potter, *People of Plenty: Economic Abundance and the American Character* (Chicago, 1954) e.g., 118–19.

20 Seymour Martin Lipset, *The First New Nation: The United States in Historical and Comparative Perspective* (London, 1964) esp. 170–204.

21 T. H. Marshall, *Citizenship and Social Class; and Other Essays* (Cambridge, 1950) 1–85.

22 Reinhard Bendix, *Nation-Building and Citizenship: Studies of our Changing Social Order* (New York, 1964) 55–104.

23 Guenther Roth, *The Social Democrats in Imperial Germany: A Study in Working-Class Isolation and National Integration* (Totowa, 1963).

24 Robert McKensie and Allan Silver, *Angels in Marble: Working-Class Conservatives in Urban England* (London, 1968).

25 Norman Thomas, 'Pluralism and Political Parties', in *Failure of a Dream?*, pp. 654–60.

26 Richard Hofstadter, *The Age of Reform: From Bryan to F.D.R.* (New York, 1955) 97–8.

27 The view put forward by Ira Kipnis in his *The American Socialist Movement, 1897–1912* (New York, 1952) that Socialism failed in America because the Socialist Party was taken over by right-wing leaders ready to jettison the really Socialist planks of the Party's platform in an effort to win votes at any price would be consistent with this analysis of the role of third parties in America. James Weinstein, in his *The Decline of Socialism in America, 1912–1925* (New York, 1969 ed.) 109–10, also reports a sentiment expressed by Walter Lippmann in 1913 that the Socialists should include in their programme only measures that could not be stolen by Progressives.

28 C. A. R. Crosland, *Can Labour Win?*, Fabian Tract 324 (London, 1960) 4, 11–13. D. E. Butler and Richard Rose, in *The British General Election of 1959* (London, 1960) 2, 15–16, provide a version of the *embourgeoisement* thesis that is somewhat more refined than the simple assertion that prosperous working-class voters tend to support working-class political parties less merely because of ownership of consumer luxuries. Butler and Rose regard affluent workers with middle-class standards of living as being socially marginal between the working and middle classes and hence less likely to support a working-class-based political party. A further classic presentation of the *embourgeoisement* thesis, although it lacks an explicit consideration of voting behaviour, is Ferdynand Zweig, *The Worker in an Affluent Society: Family Life and Industry* (London, 1961) 133–8, 205–12.

29 John H. Goldthorpe *et al.*, *The Affluent Worker: Political Attitudes and Behaviour* (Cambridge, 1968).

30 Richard F. Hamilton, *Class and Politics in the United States* (New York, 1972) esp. 188–238.

31 Ralf Dahrendorf, *Class and Class Conflict in Industrial Society* (Stanford, 1959) 57.

32 Seymour Martin Lipset and Reinhard Bendix, *Social Mobility in Industrial Society* (Berkeley, 1959) 12.

33 See, for example, D. Lockwood, 'Sources of Variation in Working Class Images of Society', in *The Sociological Review*, New Series, XIII–XIV (1965–1966) 249–67, esp. 251.

34 Karl Marx, 'The Eighteenth Brumaire of Louis Bonaparte', in *Selected Works*, I, 255.

35 Frederick J. Turner, 'The Significance of the Frontier in American History', in *Annual Report of the American Historical Association for the Year 1893*, 199–227. Somewhat more overt references to the safety-valve effect, or at least to the democratising effect, of the frontier are contained in

Turner's *The Frontier in American History* (New York, 1947 ed.) e.g., 211–15, 277, 307 and 320.

Turner's 1893 essay won approbation in some surprising circles; it was reprinted in its entirety in the *International Socialist Review*, VI (1905–6) 321–46. An editorial by A. M. Simons (ibid., 369) describes the essay as 'the greatest contribution yet made in the application of the materialistic interpretation of history to American conditions'. Turner himself had little sympathy for Socialism: 'It would be a grave misfortune if these people so rich in experience, in self-confidence and aspiration, in creative genius, should turn to some Old World discipline of socialism or plutocracy, or despotic rule, whether by class or by dictator,' he said in 1914 (Turner, *The Frontier*, 307).

The most comprehensive account of the Populist movement, which is still generally respected by historians although it was first published in 1931, accepted (but not without subsequent criticism) that Populism was a response to the closing of the frontier; see John D. Hicks, *The Populist Revolt: A History of the Farmers' Alliance and the People's Party* (Lincoln, Nebr., 1961 ed.) 95.

36 *Vorwärts*, Review of Werner Sombart's *Warum gibt es in den Vereinigten Staaten keinen Sozialismus?* (9 Oct 1906).

37 See his comments on the two books, Mrs John van Vorst and Marie van Vorst, *The Woman Who Toils: Being the Experiences of Two Gentlewomen as Factory Girls* (New York, 1903) and Alfred Kolb, *Als Arbeiter in Amerika: Unter deutsch-amerikanischen Großstadtproletariern* [*As a Worker in America: Among German-American Workers in Large Cities*] (Berlin, 1904), in his literature review, „Quellen und Literatur zum Studium der Arbeiterfrage und des Sozialismus in den Vereinigten Staaten von Amerika (1902–1904)" ['Sources and Literature in the Study of the Worker Question and Socialism in the United States of America (1902–1904)'], in *Archiv für Sozialwissenschaft und Sozialpolitik*, XX (1905) 683.

38 Robert Hunter, *Poverty* (New York, 1904). This has been reprinted and re-issued as *Poverty: Social Conscience in the Progressive Era*, ed. Peter d'A. Jones (New York, 1965).

39 The inconsistency is also noted in the *Vorwärts* review cited in Note 36, above.

40 H. G. Wells, *The Future in America: A Search After Realities* (London, 1906) 144. An analysis of the views of various European observers on the American working class at the turn of the century is contained in Robert W. Smuts, *European Impressions of the American Worker* (New York, 1953). Smuts discusses, *inter alia*, the inability of Europeans to understand the apparent paradox of strikes by well-off workers.

41 Otto L. Bettmann, *The Good Old Days – They Were Terrible!* (New York, 1974) 190.

42 Karl Marx and Frederick Engels, 'Manifesto of the Communist Party', in *Selected Works*, I 45.

43 Karl Marx, 'Wage Labour and Capital', in *Selected Works* I 93–4; Marx is here discussing 'the most favourable case', when wages go up.

44 Frederick Engels, 'Preface to *The Condition of the Working Class in England*', in *Selected Works*, II 417. Engels also used the affluence-thesis to

account for the slow growth of American Socialism; see his letter on 2 December 1893 to Friedrich A. Sorge in *Karl Marx and Friedrich Engels: Basic Writings on Politics and Philosophy*, ed. Lewis S. Feuer (London, 1969) p. 496.

45 Sombart, *Socialism and the Social Movement*, 152–3.

46 E. J. Hobsbawm, 'The Labour Aristocracy in Nineteenth-Century Britain', in his *Labouring Men*, 356; Hobsbawm suggests here that the twentieth-century experience may be that all workers, not merely the aristocracy of labour in the nineteenth-century sense, may benefit from the imperialism or monopoly capitalism of their country.

47 Peter Roberts, *The New Immigration: A Study of the Industrial and Social Life of Southeastern Europeans in America* (New York, 1912) Table XIX, 372.

48 Gerald Rosenblum's recent book, *Immigrant Workers: Their Impact on American Labor Radicalism* (New York, 1973), develops the view that American immigrants repressed the development of an indigenous radical movement. Rosenblum's thesis has been strongly attacked by John C. Leggett in a review appearing in *Contemporary Sociology: A Journal of Reviews*, IV (1975) 27–9. Leggett's critique, doubtless derived from one of the major themes in Weinstein's *The Decline of Socialism in America, 1912–1925*, is essentially that Rosenblum fails to take account of the persecution that immigrants faced in America if they resorted to radicalism. This, however, is to bring the period of crucial interest forward by at least twenty years. Although the persecution of the Red Scare period after the First World War was directed heavily against immigrants and may have turned them away from radicalism, it does not explain their limited proclivity to Social Democracy in the crucial period around the turn of the century.

49 Friedrich Engels, 'The Labour Movement in the United States', in *Basic Writings*, pp. 532–3.

50 Weinstein, *Decline of Socialism*, 173–6.

51 Alejandro Portes, 'Political Primitivism, Differential Socialization, and Lower-Class Leftist Radicalism', in *American Sociological Review*, XXXVI (1971) 820–35.

52 William L. Riordon, *Plunkitt of Tammany Hall* (New York, 1963 ed.) 25–8. Incidentally, it may be worth noting Plunkitt's views on the sources of Socialism in America – failure of the entry examination into the 'cussed civil service'; see ibid., 12.

53 Oscar Handlin, *The Uprooted: The Epic Story of the Great Migrations That Made the American People* (New York, 1951) 211.

54 Ibid., 218.

55 Wells, *Future in America*, 179.

56 The classic account of the perpetuation of a particular ethnic culture is contained in Louis Wirth's *The Ghetto* (Chicago, 1928), particularly the discussion of Russian Jews who arrived after 1882; see 179–261 *passim*.

57 Roberts, *New Immigration*, 106.

58 Selig Perlman, in his *A History of Trade Unionism in the United States* (New York, 1950 ed.) 285–6, attributes the lack of a labour party in America partly to the supposed futility of seeking power in a federal system of government; 'labor would have to fight not on one front, but on forty-nine different

fronts'. This particular argument is not entirely convincing, since the various agrarian movements of the later nineteenth century wanted political power, although some of their objectives might have been achieved equally well by trying a tactic like withholding produce from the market, such as is currently attempted in America by the National Farmers Organization.

In other respects, parts of Perlman's analysis of the various political attitudes of the American worker that were inimical to the development of Socialism are rather similar to Sombart's.

59 Hofstadter (*Age of Reform*, 97) was perhaps the most succinct in describing the historical fate of third parties in America: 'Third parties are like bees: once they have stung, they die.'

60 This is a point made at various places by Seymour Martin Lipset and Stein Rokkan in the editors' introductory essay, 'Cleavage Structures, Party Systems and Voter Alignments: An Introduction', in *Party Systems and Voter Alignments: Cross-National Perspectives* (New York, 1967) pp. 1–64. Their essay also mentions various factors inhibiting the rise of working-class movements that find their equivalents in Sombart's analysis; for example, early enfranchisement, high mobility, and a federal system of government.

61 See, for example, Angus Campbell, Philip E. Converse, Warren E. Miller and Donald E. Stokes, *The American Voter* (New York, 1960) 168–265, and Philip E. Converse, 'The Nature of Belief Systems in Mass Publics' in *Ideology and Discontent*, ed. David E. Apter (New York, 1964) pp. 206–61; both these deal with the American electorate of the 1950s. For the British electorate of the early 1960s, see David Butler and Donald Stokes, *Political Change in Britain: Forces Shaping Electoral Choice* (New York, 1969) 173–214.

62 Converse's model of political socialisation is stated clearly in Philip E. Converse, 'Of Time and Partisan Stability', in *Comparative Political Studies* II (1969) 139–71.

63 Walter Dean Burnham, for example, has written about the decline in the twentieth century in the consistency of party commitment since its days of high stability in the nineteenth century; see his 'The End of American Party Politics', in *Trans-action*, VII (1969) 17–19, and his *Critical Elections and the Mainsprings of American Politics* (New York, 1970), Table 3.6, 52, for relevant data on Pennsylvania.

64 George Wallace's American Independent Party of 1968 appealed disproportionately to the young for precisely this reason; see Philip E. Converse, Warren E. Miller, Jerrold G. Rusk and Arthur C. Wolfe, 'Continuity and Change in American Politics: Parties and Issues in the 1968 Election', in *American Political Science Review*, LXII (1969) 1103–4. There is also reason to believe that support for the Nazi party during the Weimar Republic was disproportionately young.

65 Realignment towards a rising third party is less likely when the two major parties are in equipoise; Pinard, for example, has advanced the view that the rise of third parties is encouraged by situations of one-party domination; see Maurice Pinard, *The Rise of a Third Party: A Study in Crisis Politics* (Englewood Cliffs, 1971) 36–71.

66 A genealogy of German political parties between 1871 and the present day is presented in Derek W. Urwin, 'Germany: Continuity and Change in

Electoral Politics', in *Electoral Behavior: A Comparative Handbook*, ed. Richard Rose (New York, 1974), Figure 2, 129. This figure clearly shows the complicated pattern of fusion and fission in German nineteenth-century politics, although the Social Democrats are incorrectly titled for the period between 1875 and 1891.

67 For a standard history of the Party under the Socialist Law, see Vernon L. Lidtke, *The Outlawed Party: Social Democracy in Germany, 1878–1890* (Princeton, 1966); Lidtke's account tends to emphasise the more mundane and prosaic aspects of this period. For an account that glorifies its 'heroic' side more, see Institut für Marxismus-Leninismus beim Zentralkomitee der SED, *Geschichte der Deutschen Arbeiterbewegung: Kapitel III; Periode von 1871 bis zum Ausgang des 19. Jahrhunderts* [*History of the German Workers' Movement: Chapter III; Period from 1871 to the End of the Nineteenth Century*] (Berlin, 1966) 56–121.

68 See not only Robert Michels, *Political Parties: A Sociological Study of the Oligarchical Tendencies of Modern Democracy*, translated by Eden and Cedar Paul (New York, 1966 ed.) but also Mitzman's account of the frustration of the young Michels at the docility of the German working class, whom the latter regarded as having been narcoticised by parliamentarianism (*Sociology and Estrangement*, 295).

69 For example, Lidtke, *Outlawed Party*, 320–32. The standard account of the split in the Party between reformists and revolutionaries in Carl E. Schorske, *German Social Democracy, 1905–1917: The Development of the Great Schism* (New York, 1955).

70 Lane, *The Union*, 86–9.

71 E. J. Hobsbawm, 'Dr. Marx and the Victorian Critics', in his *Labouring Men*, 284. Robert Hunter, the author of *Poverty*, had noted the comparative lack of Socialist strength in London in 1899 and 1903 and was surprised by the evidence of it in 1906. In fact, Keir Hardie had apparently advised him to move out into the provinces to see Socialist activity; see Robert Hunter, 'First Impressions of Socialism Abroad: No. 4; The Congress of the British Labour Party', in *International Socialist Review*, VII (1906–7) 513–27. This picture was not entirely accurate, and Hardie's judgement was doubtless affected by the limited success of the Independent Labour Party in London, where the Social Democratic Federation was the predominant left-wing force at this time.

72 J. H. Rosney, 'Socialism in London', in *Harper's New Monthly Magazine*, LXXVI (1887) 405–19. This author also makes some interesting comments on the existence of Socialism in a cross-national comparative context; neither the 'iron regime of Germany' nor the 'liberty of America' seemed to check the growth of Socialism, he remarked, but till about 1877 England appeared to have 'escaped the contagion'. He also calls England the 'most refractory country in Europe for Socialism' (see ibid., 405).

73 Francis A. Walker, 'Socialism', in *Scribner's Magazine*, 1 (1887) 113.

74 Robert Roberts, *The Classic Slum: Salford Life in the First Quarter of the Century* (Harmondsworth, 1973 ed.) 167.

75 Hobsbawm, 'Labour Traditions', 447.

76 E. J. Hobsbawm, *Primitive Rebels: Studies in Archaic Forms of Social Movement in the Nineteenth and Twentieth Centuries* (New York, 1963) 118.

77 Robert Moore, *Pit-Men, Preachers & Politics: The Effects of Methodism in a Durham Mining Community* (Cambridge, 1974) 182–90.

78 Robert Roberts (*Classic Slum*, 168) writes: 'Apathy, docility, deference: our village as a whole displayed just those qualities which, sixty years before, Karl Marx had noted, stamped the poor industrial workers – qualities which convinced him that the English proletarian would never revolt of his own accord.' For an example of similar sentiments by Engels, see his 'Special Introduction to the English Edition of 1892 of "Socialism: Utopian and Scientific"', in *Selected Works*, II 112–13.

79 See, for example, Michels, *Political Parties*, 85–97.

80 Sombart, *Socialism and the Social Movement*, 171.

81 For one view that the First World War was decisive in accounting for the growth of the Labour Party, see Roy Douglas, 'Labour in Decline, 1910–1914', in *Essays in Anti-Labour History: Responses to the Rise of Labour in Britain*, ed. Kenneth D. Brown (London, 1974) pp. 105–25.

82 Roberts, *Classic Slum*, 179–81.

83 Chamberlain has recently put forward the argument that much of the Labour Party's growth after the First World War came from voters who were either *de facto* or *de iure* disfranchised before the passage of the 1918 Representation of the People Act, rather than from Liberal converts. There is undoubtedly some merit in this view, but it in no way invalidates the point being made about the need for some sort of crisis to induce realignment towards a rising third party; without the crisis these newly enfranchised voters would probably merely have followed the path trodden by existing voters into the Conservative or Liberal Parties. See Chris Chamberlain, 'The growth of support for the Labour Party in Britain', in *British Journal of Sociology*, XXIV (1973) 474–98.

84 V. O. Key, Jr., put the term 'critical election' into political-science vocabulary in order to describe a particular type of election where voters were unusually deeply concerned, where the extent of political involvement was relatively quite high, and where the decisive results of the voting revealed a sharp alteration of the pre-existing cleavage within the electorate. The Presidential election of 1896 was just such an election, although in the New England states that Key examined the Republican gains were among all population groups; see V. O. Key, Jr., 'A Theory of Critical Elections', in *Journal of Politics*, XVII (1955) 3–18.

85 A good systematic summary of the issues in this debate is contained in Michael Paul Rogin, *The Intellectuals and McCarthy: The Radical Specter* (Cambridge, Mass., 1967) 168–91.

86 For evidence in the case of Texas, see Roscoe C. Martin, *The People's Party in Texas: A Study in Third Party Politics* (The University of Texas Bulletin No. 3308: 22 February 1933; Bureau of Research in the Social Sciences, Study No. 4) 72–88.

87 Besides his Presidential candidacies, William Jennings Bryan is probably best known as the man who in 1925 prosecuted and secured the conviction of John Scopes, a Tennessee schoolteacher, for teaching about evolution.

88 David Burner's book, *The Politics of Provincialism: The Democratic Party in Transition, 1918–1932* (New York, 1968), describes the process

whereby power in the organised Democratic Party was wrested from the rural and fundamentalist power-holders.

89   Samuel P. Hays, *The Response to Industrialism: 1885–1914* (Chicago, 1957) 46–7.

90   See, for example, Paul Kleppner, *The Cross of Culture: A Social Analysis of Midwestern Politics, 1850–1900* (New York, 1970) 289–90.

91   Norman Pollack, in his *The Populist Response to Industrial America: Midwestern Populist Thought* (Cambridge, Mass., 1962) 63–5, even argues that the Populists reached out a hand in fraternal sympathy to the American labour movement, but that this hand was rebuffed by the conservative labour leaders of the time.

92   Marc Karson, 'Catholic Anti-Socialism' in *Failure of a Dream?*, pp. 164–80.

93   For the case of Texas see Martin, *People's Party in Texas*, 72. For Oklahoma and Louisiana see David A. Shannon, *The Socialist Party of America: A History* (Chicago, 1967 ed.) 35–7. In addition to these three states, Weinstein also mentions Alabama and Missouri; see Weinstein, *Decline of Socialism*, 16.

94   Ibid., 106–7.

95   In April 1918 there was a special election for the United States Senate in Wisconsin, and the Socialist candidate, Victor Berger, won 26 per cent of the state-wide vote, a fourfold increase over the normal Socialist vote in Wisconsin; see ibid., 167–9.

96   Charles W. Furgeson, for example, in *Confusion of Tongues*, as quoted in Robert Coughlan, 'Konclave in Kokomo', in *The Aspirin Age, 1919–1941*, ed. Isabel Leighton (New York, 1949) pp. 111–12.

97   A standard history of this episode, which included the illegal deportation of thousands of foreign-born radicals, is Robert K. Murray, *Red Scare: A Study in National Hysteria, 1919–1920* (New York, 1964 ed.).

98   For evidence of middle-class contribution to the early growth of the 1920s Ku Klux Klan, see Seymour Martin Lipset and Earl Raab, *The Politics of Unreason: Right-Wing Extremism in America, 1790–1970* (New York, 1970) 125.

99   John Higham, *Strangers in the Land: Patterns of American Nativism, 1860–1925* 2nd ed. (New York, 1970 ed.) 264–99.

100   One piece of evidence for this is given in C. T. Husbands, *The Campaign Organizations and Patterns of Popular Support of George C. Wallace in Wisconsin and Indiana in 1964 and 1968* (unpublished doctoral dissertation, Department of Sociology, University of Chicago, 1972) 393–4.

INTRODUCTION

1   *Ed.* – In 1906 the German Empire extended from Alsace-Lorraine in the west to East Prussia in the east and included a large part of what is now Poland. The Empire then comprised 208,830 square miles.

2   *Ed.* – Max Weber's essay, *Die protestantische Ethik und der Geist des Kapitalismus*, a later version of which was translated into English by Talcott Parsons as *The Protestant Ethic and the Spirit of Capitalism*, new ed. (New York, 1958), was first published in the *Archiv für Sozialwissenschaft und Sozialpolitik*, XX–XXI (1904–5). The present work of Sombart's also first appeared in Volume XXI of the same journal; see Preface to the Original

German Edition, p. vii. Max Weber and Werner Sombart were both associated with the *Archiv* in editorial capacities.

3 *Ed.* – The figure given actually covers accidents in the three years from 1
July 1897 to 30 June 1900. Sombart has apparently taken his reference to the
account in the New York *Evening Post* from John Graham Brooks, *The
Social Unrest: Studies in Labor and Socialist Movements* (New York, 1903)
210. See also, for example, U.S. Department of Commerce, Bureau of the
Census, *Historical Statistics of the United States: From Colonial Times to
1957* (Washington, D.C., 1960) 437. The same *Evening Post* reference has
been used recently in Otto L. Bettmann, *The Good Old Days – They Were
Terrible!* (New York, 1974) 71.

4 The figures used in the standardisation calculations are those of Philippovich. [In the several volumes and editions of his major work, *Grundriß der
Politischen Oekonomie* [*Outline of Political Economy*], the economist Eugen
von Philippovich (1858–1917) sometimes uses data on changes in the length of
railway track in different countries as a measure of the growth of productive
capital. These are the data to which Sombart is referring here. Philippovich's
work apparently contains nothing on railway accidents *per se* or on the number of passengers carried.

The Editor has some misgivings about the total accuracy of the American
data. It is unclear why Sombart explicitly says 1903 as being the year to
which these data refer, for till 1916 the Statistical Reports of the Interstate
Commerce Commission, which are the primary sources for American railway-
accident data, reported for years ending 30 June. In the year ending 30 June
1903 9840 people were reported as having been killed on American railways;
see, for example, *Historical Statistics*, 437. (In the following twelve months
the figure was 10,046, and Sombart's figure of 11,006 cannot be located in
any of the standard sources.)

In calculating the accident rate per length of track, Sombart has apparently
used length-of-track data referring to 1902, or, if referring to some other
year, an arithmetic error or misprint occurs in his text. There were 202,472
miles (325,821 kilometres) of 'first' railway track owned by railway companies in the continental United States in 1902 (ibid., 429). However, the
same source gives the figure of 1903 as 207,977 miles (334,711 kilometres).

In calculating the accident rate per million passengers carried Sombart has
apparently used as his base the number of passengers carried in the year ending
30 June 1900, which was 576,831,000; however, the figure for the number
carried in the year ending 30 June 1903 is 694,892,000 (ibid., 430).

Therefore the recalculated rates of deaths for the year ending 30 June 1903
are 2.94 per hundred kilometres and 14.2 per million passengers carried. – *Ed.*]

5 United States, Fifty-eighth Congress, House of Representatives, *Forty-
second Annual Report of the Comptroller of the Currency, 1904* (Washington,
D.C., 1904) 1 51–2.

6 Ibid., 1 42.

7 *Ed.* – For the years 1890 and 1900 there are slight discrepancies between
the figures that Sombart has given in his text and those in the Census source
that he must have consulted. For 1890 the figure should be $6,525,156,486,
and for 1900 it should be $9,835,086,909; the latter figure includes information
on eighty-five governmental establishments in the District of Columbia, so

that comparisons with the figures of earlier Censuses are possible, and it excludes data on Hawaii (which became a Territory of the United States in 1900). See United States Census Office, *Census Reports, Twelfth Census of the United States Taken in the Year 1900*, VII, Manufacturers, Part I, United States by Industries (Washington, D.C., 1902) Table I, p. xlvii.

8   *Ed.* – Sombart's reference is to *Capital*, Vol. II, Part VIII, Chapter 32, 'Historical Tendency of Capitalistic Accumulation'. See, for example, Karl Marx, *Capital: A Critical Analysis of Capitalist Production* (London, 1938) 786–9.

9   John Moody, *The Truth About the Trusts: A Description and Analysis of the American Trust Movement* (New York, 1904). This book is very useful because it compiles some extremely valuable material from such primary sources as prospectuses, business reports, balance sheets, and so on. [The book was reprinted and re-issued in 1968 – *Ed.*]

10   *Ed.* – The exchange rate at the time Sombart was writing was 4.20 marks for 1 American dollar.

11   James Bryce, *The American Commonwealth*, 2nd ed. (London, 1889), 2 vols, II 531.

12   *Ed.* – Sombart has taken the American data from United States Census Office, *Occupations at the Twelfth Census* (Washington, D.C., 1904), Table XXI, p. lxxxvi.

Sombart's data on the occupational distributions between different sectors of the German economy cannot be reconciled fully with those given in official sources. The most recent data available to Sombart when he was writing would have pertained to 1895. According to German Empire, Kaiserliches Statistisches Amt, *Statistisches Jahrbuch für das Deutsche Reich, 1904* [*Statistical Yearbook for the German Empire, 1904*], XXV (Berlin, 1904) 13, 36.19 (not 36.12) per cent of the employed population in 1895 were principally engaged in agriculture, horticulture, animal-breeding, forestry or fishing, while 10.21 (not 11.39) per cent were engaged in trade and transportation (including the running of inns and public houses).

13   *Ed.* – The verbal distinction in German is between *Stadt* and *Groß-stadt*. Since 1887 official international statistical practice had recognised several categories of city according to the criterion of size. Sombart's use of the word *Stadt* embraces all categories, but a *Großstadt* necessarily had more than 100,000 inhabitants.

14   All numerical data for which no special source is named are taken from the Census. [Sombart has clearly taken some of his data on American urbanisation from United States Census Office, *Twelfth Census*, I, Population, Part I, Table XXIX, p. lxxxiii.

However, some of his figures do not totally agree with those given in other standard sources, and in one respect Sombart is seriously misleading because he has failed to realise that a new Census definition of 'urban' was introduced into some of the analyses of the 1900 Census. 'In the reports of 1880, 1890, and 1900 Censuses, the urban population was variously defined as the population living in places of 4000 inhabitants or more, or 8000 inhabitants or more. The first publication in which the population of places having 2500 inhabitants or more was officially designated as urban was the *Supplementary Analysis of the Twelfth Census (1900)*.' (*Historical Statistics*, 2.)

United States, Department of Commerce and Labor, *Statistical Abstract of the United States, 1911*, XXXIV (Washington, D.C., 1912) 54, says that the urban population in 1900, namely 'that residing in cities and other incorporated places of 2,500 inhabitants or more, including New England towns of that population', was 40.5 (not 41.2) per cent of the whole, and, if the Eastern states that Sombart mentions correspond to the New England and Middle Atlantic geographic divisions, their rural population in 1900 was 30.9 (not 31.8) per cent.

The so-called change in the urban population from 29.2 to 41.2 (or perhaps 40.5) per cent confuses two definitions of the urban population; the first incorporates the 8000 minimum and the second the 2500 minimum. Between 1890 and 1900 the percentage of the population living in places of 8000 or more changed from 29.2 to 33.1 per cent (*Twelfth Census*, I, Table XXIX, p. lxxxiii). In the same period the percentage living in places of 2500 or more changed from 36.1 to 40.5 per cent (*Statistical Abstract, 1911*, 54). All these figures pertain to all states and territories in the contiguous continental United States. – *Ed.*]

15 See Charles B. Spahr, *An Essay on the Present Distribution of Wealth in the United States* (New York, 1896) 56, as well as Brooks, *Social Unrest*, 163, and Robert Hunter, *Poverty* (New York, 1904) 21–7, 44. [The 1900 edition of Spahr's book was reprinted and re-issued in 1970. Hunter's book has also been reprinted and re-issued as *Poverty: Social Conscience in the Progressive Era*, ed. Peter d'A. Jones (New York, 1965). – *Ed.*]

16 *Ed.* – This is $60,000,000,000. An American or continental billion equals a thousand millions.

17 *Ed.* – Sombart is referring to Newport, Rhode Island. Baiae was a luxury watering-place in the imperial Roman period situated near Cumae on the Bay of Naples. It was a favourite of the poet, Horace. Only ruins of the Roman establishment now remain.

18 Of course, a working-class city like Berlin or Vienna is totally out of place in discussions of businesses of this kind.

19 It lacks the broad theoretical sweep that has made Engels's book a landmark in the development of the social sciences. [Florence Kelley's review to which Sombart refers appeared in *American Journal of Sociology*, X (1905) 555–6. Florence Kelley (1859–1932) had been General Secretary of the National Consumers' League since 1899 and was an Associate Editor of *Charities*. She had translated Engels's *The Condition of the Working Class in England* into English. – *Ed.*]

20 This figure is based on official research by the New York State Board of Charities. There are probably many cases of duplication. Otherwise it really would be dreadful.

21 *Ed.* – Potter's Field is an American term for a burial ground for paupers or unknown persons, so called after a burial place for strangers in Jerusalem. The Gospel According to St Matthew, Chapter 27, Verse 7, states: 'And they [the chief priests] took counsel, and bought with them [the thirty pieces of silver accepted and subsequently returned by Judas Iscariot] the potter's field, to bury strangers in.'

An idea of what being buried in Potter's Field in New York meant at the turn of the century can be gained from the fate of one of the heroine's lovers in Theodore Dreiser's novel, *Sister Carrie*, which was first published in 1900: 'A slow black boat setting forth from the pier at Twenty-seventh Street upon its weekly errand bore, with many others, his nameless body to the Potter's Field.'

22 *Ed.* – The preceding remarks are almost certainly directed against Hugo Münsterberg, author of *The Americans*, translated by Edwin B. Holt (New York, 1904); this book, originally written in German, was widely read in the period when Sombart was writing. Münsterberg argues that American political life is characterised by 'the spirit of self-direction', economic life by 'the spirit of self-initiative' intellectual life by 'the spirit of self-perfection', and social life by 'the spirit of self-assertion'.

23 *Ed.* – These are references to the financial district of London and Berlin respectively.

24 *Ed.* – Sombart is referring to Georg Simmel's *Philosophie des Geldes* [*Philosophy of Money*] (Leipzig, 1900). See also Simmel's 'The Metropolis and Mental Life', in *Cities and Society: The Revised Reader in Urban Sociology*, ed. Paul K. Hatt and Albert J. Reiss, Jr. (New York, 1957) pp. 635–46.

25 In *Our Benevolent Feudalism* (New York, 1902) 159–60, W. J. Ghent writes: 'With all ranks and conditions Success becomes the great god; and as though there were not already priests and votaries enough for his proper worship, a special class of publications has recently arisen, which serve as his vowed and consecrated ministers. These teach to the devout but unsophisticated followers of the great god the particular means best adapted to win his grace; how his frown may be averted; or, if his anger is kindled, by what penances and other rites he is to be propitiated. They chant the praises and recite the life-incidents of those who have been most conspicuously blessed and to all the rest of mankind they shout, "Follow our counsel, and some day you shall be even like unto these." '

26 *Ed.* – This seems to be a reference to Amendment XIV of the Constitution, which forbids states to 'abridge the privileges or immunities of citizens of the United States'.

27 We would never let some of these things happen in our so-called autocratically governed Germany. One thinks of the legal impediment in the U.S.A. to the partaking of alcohol.

28 For example, the free supply of all educational materials to all children in the New York public-school system.

29 This is even more true of the Romance-speaking countries and of England than it is of Germany. In Germany, as I have tried to show elsewhere, conditions analogous to those in America predominate in this respect, even though they grew from quite different roots.

30 Nobody has recognised this more clearly than James Bryce; see *American Commonwealth*, II 534–5, 540. I cannot stop myself from reproducing the appropriate passages because, when Bryce sees such things, they are expressed as clear as day.

> In the United States a much larger part of the population, including professional men as well as business men, seem conversant with the subject, and there are times when the whole community, not merely city people but also store keepers in country towns, even farmers, even domestic servants, interest themselves actively in share speculations. ... In many country towns there are small offices, commonly called 'bucket shops', to which

farmers and tradesmen resort to effect their purchases and sales in the great stock markets of New York.... But go where you will in the Union, ...you feel bonds, stocks and shares in the atmosphere all around you. *Te viente die* – they begin the day with the newspaper at breakfast: they end it with the chat over the nocturnal cigar.... The habit of speculation is now a part of their character, and it increases that constitutional excitability and high nervous tension of which they are proud.

31 *Ed.* – Sombart has taken these data from Morris Hillquit, *History of Socialism in the United States* (New York, 1903); they are to be found on p. 309 of the 5th edition of the book, published in 1910.

32 *Ed.* – Many of the vote-totals given by Sombart at various places throughout the book invariably differ slightly from those given in several modern standard sources, such as, for example, *The New York Times Encyclopedic Almanac, 1971* (New York, 1970) 140–3. The size of these discrepancies is always inconsequential.

33 *Ed.* – The year 1878 saw the passage of the so-called Socialist Law, which made propaganda activities by the Sozialistische Arbeiterpartei Deutschlands [Socialist Workers' Party of Germany] illegal until 1890. In the Reichstag elections of 30 July 1878 the Party polled 437,100 votes, nearly 8 per cent of the total number cast nationally. (Sozialistische Arbeiterpartei Deutschlands was the official name of German Social Democracy from 1875 to 1891, when it became the Sozialdemokratische Partei Deutschlands [Social Democratic Party of Germany].)

34 *Ed.* – When Sombart was writing this work, the Freisinnige Vereinigung was a liberal-left group in German politics; it was formed when the Deutschfreisinnige Partei [German Liberal Party] split in two in 1893 after an internal difference on military policy, the other party emerging from the split being the Freisinnige Volkspartei [Liberal People's Party]. In the Reichstag elections of 16 June 1903 the Freisinnige Vereinigung received 243,200 votes, 2.6 per cent of the total vote.

By 1906 the Anti-Semites had evolved into basically two groups, the Christlichsoziale Partei [Christian Social Party] and the Wirtschaftliche Vereinigung [Economic Alliance]. The former was the parent anti-Semitic party in German politics, having been founded in 1878, while the latter was an amalgamation of various political groups that had originally split from the Christlichsoziale Partei in 1889 and 1890, had united and divided from each other during the 1890s, only to unite with other small groups into the Wirtschaftliche Vereinigung in 1903. In the 1903 elections the Anti-Semites received 244,500 votes altogether, 2.6 per cent of the total vote.

At the same election the Sozialdemokratische Partei Deutschlands received 3,010,800 votes, 31.7 per cent of the total cast.

35 *Ed.* – Several editorial comments upon the data in Table 1 are in order. One or two of the declines from previously higher vote-totals, e.g., in Chicago and New York, are clearly due, at least in part, to the usual decline in turnout in off-year elections. The decline in the absolute size of the Socialist vote in Texas between 1902 and 1904 is due largely to the fact that the state restricted suffrage by adopting a poll tax by constitutional amendment in 1902, which would have substantially influenced turnout for the first time in 1904. However, there had been a steady decline in turnout in Texas elections since

the Populist peak of 1896; see V. O. Key, Jr., *Southern Politics in State and Nation* (New York, 1949) 534–5. In a later passage Sombart discusses the case of Colorado between 1902 and 1904.

The Southern states of Alabama and Texas still produced far from negligible support for the People's Party, even in the period under review. In the South there was a certain mutual substitutability between the People's Party and the Socialist Party, and this worked to the disadvantage of the latter in the period being considered. In 1900 the People's Party's Presidential candidacy won 2.6 per cent of the vote in Alabama and 5.1 per cent in Texas; in 1904 the respective percentages were 4.6 and 3.4 per cent.

36 *Ed.* – Sombart clearly assumes some kind of rank-ordered scale of trade-union radicalism. Least radical are the 'old English pure trade-unionists' with their *manchesterlich* principles, who abhor State intervention and State Socialism. Somewhat more radical is the pragmatic or instrumental trade-unionism of most American trade unions (and also of the 'older English unions', Sombart says later (Introduction, Note 51) – very confusingly in view of his other characterisation of earlier English unionism). At the radical end of the scale are those trade unions that are trying in some way to promote Socialism.

Subsequent historical scholarship casts probable doubt on the accuracy of some of Sombart's classifying. His inconsistency regarding the older English trade unions has been noted. The attribution to the older English trade-unionists of an adherence to *manchesterlich* principles stems from the classic work of Sydney and Beatrice Webb, *The History of Trade Unionism, 1666–1890* (London, 1894). However, this view has been under revision since at least 1937. The seminal articles on the subject are G. D. H. Cole, 'Some Notes on British Trade Unionism in the Third Quarter of the Nineteenth Century', in *International Review for Social History*, II, Leiden, (1937) 1–23, and R. V. Clements, 'British Trade Unions and Popular Political Economy, 1850–1875', in *Economic History Review*, 2nd Series, XIV (1961) 93–104; see also A. E. Musson, *British Trade Unions, 1800–1875* (London, 1972) 54.

37 This is the representative body of the great mass of American trade unions and is led by the conservative Mr Gompers; up to nine-tenths of its Executive Council is made up of anti-Socialist trade-union leaders. [Samuel Gompers (1850–1924) was President of the American Federation of Labor from its formal founding in 1886 to his death, with the exception of 1895, when he was defeated for the Presidency. – *Ed.*]

38 The political programme was accepted in this form at the annual convention of the American Federation of Labor in 1894; the eighth and ninth planks were accepted unanimously. At the next year's convention a resolution was then passed which stated that the Federation has no political programme as such, since what had been proposed on an advisory basis in the previous year had admittedly been accepted in all its individual points, but not as a whole. The Federation had therefore established only 'legislative demands'. This alters nothing as far as we are concerned.

39 Those knowing the worker's psyche well speak of an 'air of contentment and enthusiastic cheerfulness'; this phrase was written by Professor William G. Sumner and is quoted in Ghent, *Our Benevolent Feudalism*, 122–3. [Actually, Ghent's precise quotation from Summer is: 'An "air of contentment

and enthusiastic cheerfulness . . . characterizes our *society* [Editor's emphasis]," writes Professor William G. Sumner, of Yale, in a recent number of *The Independent*.' Moreover, Ghent himself was highly critical of Sumner's description; see *Our Benevolent Feudalism*, 174. Kipnis describes Ghent as a member of the Center faction of the Socialist Party in the latter years of the Party's history; see Ira Kipnis, *The American Socialist Movement, 1897–1912* (New York, 1952) 204. – *Ed.*]

40 *Ed.* – This phrase is from the Sermon on the Mount; it is to be found in The Gospel According to St Matthew, Chapter 5, Verse 13.

41 Bryce, *American Commonwealth*, II 334.

42 John Mitchell, *Organized Labor: Its Problems, Purposes and Ideals and the Present and Future of American Wage Earners* (Philadelphia, 1903) 219. [John Mitchell (1870–1919) was President of the United Mine Workers of America from 1898 until his forced retirement at the hands of miners of bituminous coal in 1907. – *Ed.*]

43 See William Jewett Tucker (President of Dartmouth College, Hanover, New Hampshire), 'Labor and Education', in *Massachusetts Labor Bulletin*, No. 33 (Sep 1904) 237–42.

44 Mitchell, *Organized Labor*, 415.

45 From a speech by the young Secretary-Treasurer of the Minnesota Federation of Labor, W. E. McEwen, entitled 'The Future Relations of Labor and Capital', in *Public Policy, Employers and Employes: Full Text of the Addresses Before the National Convention of Employers and Employes, with Portraits of the Authors, Held at Minneapolis, Minnesota, September 22–25, 1902* (Chicago, 1903) 247–56. [William Edward McEwen (1874–1933) was Secretary-Treasurer of the Minnesota State Federation of Labor from 1896 to his voluntary resignation in 1914. During most of his period as Secretary-Treasurer he was also editor of *The Labor World*, which was published in Duluth, Minnesota, and he took up full-time duties as its editor after his resignation. He served as Postmaster in Duluth from 1904 to 1908. – *Ed.*]

The reader can find a thorough assessment and exact statement of all the relevant literature in a review that I have given as „Quellen und Literatur zum Studium der Arbeiterfrage und des Sozialismus in den Vereinigten Staaten von America (1902–1904)" ['Sources and Literature in the Study of the Worker Question and Socialism in the United States of America (1902–1904)'], in *Archiv für Sozialwissenschaft und Sozialpolitik*, XX (1905), 633–703.

46 Edward J. Gainor, 'The Government as Employer', in *Public Policy, Employers and Employes*, 100–5. [Edward J. Gainor (1870–1947) was elected to the Executive Committee of the National Association of Letter Carriers in 1901, was elected National Vice-president of the Association in 1905, became President in 1914 and remained in this position till 1941. He was Eighth Vice-President of the American Federation of Labor from 1934 and 1943. – *Ed.*]

47 *Ed.* – The Knights of Labor were first organised as a secret society in Philadelphia in 1869 under the title of the Noble Order of Knights of Labor. The society's membership increased during the 1870s, and its officers made public its existence in 1878. A series of reverses in 1886 led to a rapid loss of membership, partly by desertion into the ranks of the newly formed American

Federation of Labor. The Knights were led by Terence V. Powderly from 1879 to 1893.

48 *Ed.* – The American Labor Union assumed this title in 1902 when the Western Labor Union, a confederation of trade unions in the Rocky Mountain states and territories that had been founded in 1898, was persuaded by Eugene V. Debs to seek national support and therefore altered its name for this purpose. The American Labor Union recognised the political role of the Socialist Party, and in 1905 it also had delegates present at the founding meeting of the Industrial Workers of the World.

49 *Ed.* – The Socialist Trade and Labor Alliance was founded by De Leon in opposition to the American Federation of Labor and, more particularly, to the Knights of Labor, which De Leon and his supporters had previously joined in an attempt to capture its leadership. The Alliance began after De Leon's formal secession from the Knights of Labor, and it was an auxiliary to his political base, the Socialist Labor Party. By 1898 the Alliance had effectively failed and in 1905 its remnants merged with the Industrial Workers of the World.

Daniel De Leon (1852–1914) was born in Curaçao, was a lecturer in Latin-American diplomacy at Columbia University from 1883 to 1885, and joined the Socialist Labor Party in 1890. He was a part of its leadership from 1891 till his death.

50 This is true, even if their strength is not reflected in the composition of the Federation's Executive Council.

51 Or, perhaps it would be better to speak of a specifically Anglo-Saxon spirit, for, as far as I can see, the bulk of American unions are essentially indistinguishable in their behaviour from the older English unions.

52 Numerous unions levy high entry fees, which amount to as much as $50 (210M); this is the sum levied on foreigners and others by the Granite Cutters' International Association of America and the American Flint Glass Workers' Union. Most unions limit the number of apprentices. [The first statement is apparently a serious misrepresentation by Sombart. The constitution of the Granite Cutters' International Association of America that was in force in 1906 states:

> Sec. 62. The initiation fee for apprentices presenting themselves at the first regular meeting of the branch after the expiration of their term of apprenticeship, shall be $3. If application is not made as herein stated, they shall be governed by the following section.
>
> Sec. 63. The initiation fee for all others shall be as follows: For an applicant who has served his apprenticeship in North America, but who has never worked in the vicinity of any branches or districts, shall be $10. Applicants from countries outside of our jurisdiction who present a good standing card or certificate paid up to within three months of application, showing membership in an organization of our craft, shall pay $10. Applicants other than those covered by the above provisions of this section, shall pay $25.... Applicants who have worked in opposition to our Association, to be admitted to membership for $50, excepting that in extreme cases the fee to be $75.00.

Monthly dues to this Association in 1906 were $1.00 per month.

Similarly, in Article XVII of the constitution of the American Flint Glass Workers' Union, as revised and adopted by the Union's thirty-second session in 1909, it is stated:

Sec. 2. A foreigner applying for admission to membership shall be given a trial at work, and must prove his qualifications for membership before being admitted.

Sec. 3. If a foreigner proves his eligibility and presents a union card from an old country organization, he shall be admitted to membership without his name being submitted to the trade and his initiation fee shall be three dollars.

Sec. 4. If a foreigner applying for admission does not hold a union card, his name shall be submitted to the trade, and he shall pay an initiation fee of ten dollars.

The only mention of $50.00 is as a fine to be levied on individual branches who misrepresent the number of votes cast at their meetings. The same Article states:

Sec. 7. That any Local casting more votes than those present at the meeting, and voting, shall be fined $50.00 and their votes shall not be counted.

It did not prove possible to consult the version of the Constitution actually in effect at the slightly earlier time to which Sombart is referring, but it seems highly improbable that any reductions of initiation fees of the size that would necessarily be involved here were introduced in the 1909 version. – *Ed.*]

53 In America today jurisdictional or demarcation disputes between individual unions actually form the major subject of interest in trade-union circles. In the time of the guilds the individual guilds probably quarrelled with each other much less than do individual trade unions today, since technical innovations were not so frequent in that peaceful period.

54 *Ed.* – Although Sombart does not say so, this quotation is from Tucker, in *MLB*, No. 33, 239. Sombart has already called this writer a 'more conservative social legislator'. In its context the statement reads more as the author's belief in what the trade unions should see as their major task in order to assist workers to upward social mobility rather than as a description of what is necessarily the reality.

55 *Ed.* – The Gesellschaft für Soziale Reform was founded in 1901 as the German section of the International Association for Labor Legislation. It was dedicated to promoting the interests of the 'socially endangered and economically weak classes'. Its published reports and findings did have some influence on German social policy, especially before 1914.

56 The National Civic Federation (N.C.F.) was founded for the purposes of bringing employers and workers into personal contact, in order thereby to moderate their differences and, in particular, of intervening as a mediator in strikes. The Executive Committee consists of three parts: there are fifteen employers; there are fifteen non-partisan members drawn 'from the public'; however, over half are out-and-out capitalists, and in this section belong, among others, Andrew Carnegie, Grover Cleveland, Oscar S. Straus, the Seligman bankers, and James Speyer: finally, there are sixteen workers' representatives, among whom Samuel Gompers and John Mitchell are foremost.

The official organ of the N.C.F. engages in the particular sport of reproducing in every issue the photographs of some renowned trade-union leaders next to those of the big employers. [The National Civic Federation grew out of conferences on arbitration and conciliation held in Chicago in 1900 under the auspices of the Chicago Civic Federation. It assumed the title of National Civic Federation in 1901. Andrew Carnegie (1835–1919) was a millionaire steel magnate; Grover Cleveland (1837–1908) was twenty-second and twenty-fourth President of the United States and from 1905 had been majority stockholder in a life insurance company; Oscar S. Straus (1850–1926) was a lawyer who was ex-Minister to Turkey and had been a member of the Court of Arbitration at The Hague since 1902; only one of several Seligman bankers was, in fact, a member of the Federation's Executive Committee – he was Isaac N. Seligman (1856–1917) of the bankers, J. & W. Seligman & Co.; and James Speyer (1861–1941) was also a banker.

In fact, a few years after Sombart wrote these words the National Civic Federation became a serious source of contention within the American Federation of Labor between its conservative leadership and their radical opponents. The Civic Federation had the support of the majority of the leaders of labour, but in 1910 the Socialists in John Mitchell's union, the United Mine Workers, forced him to decide which of the two he wanted to belong to. Mitchell chose his union and resigned as head of the Trade Agreements Department of the National Civic Federation. At the American Federation of Labor's 1911 Convention Socialist delegates fought hard to force a severance of ties between the union movement and the Civic Federation; although their motion was defeated by 11,851 votes to 4924, their 29 per cent of this vote shows that Socialists became a far from insignificant minority within the American Federation of Labor. (See Philip Taft, *The A. F. of L. in the Time of Gompers* (New York, 1970) 225–32, and for the standard history of the National Civic Federation see Marguerite Green, *The National Civic Federation and the American Labor Movement, 1900–1925* (Washington, D.C., 1956).) – *Ed.*]

57 *Ed.* – This Latin sentence was not used by Sombart fortuitously. It had been used by Marx, without '*Europa*', in his preface to the first German edition of *Capital*, when he was trying to convince his German readers of the relevance to them of his book, despite the fact that most of his examples were English ones:

> However, in case the German reader should self-righteously shrug his shoulders at the conditions of English industrial and agricultural workers or should solace himself by believing optimistically that things are not nearly as bad in Germany, I must call out to him: *De te fabula narratur!*

See Karl Marx and Friedrich Engels, *Werke [Works]* (Berlin, 1964) XXIII 12.

SECTION ONE

1 *Ed.* – Although it is not always realised now, at the end of the nineteenth century Australia was widely admired by the European left as a society moving towards a model social and economic democracy; see, for example, Robin Gollan, *Radical and Working Class Politics: A Study of Eastern Australia, 1850–1910* (Melbourne, 1960).

2 To my knowledge no special research into the origin of the American proletariat exists.

3 The official immigration statistics have recently been well treated by Dr H. Schwegel, the Austrian Vice-Consul in Chicago; see his „Die Einwarderung in die Vereinigten Staaten von Amerika: mit besonderer Rücksicht auf die österreichisch-ungarische Auswanderung" ['Immigration into the United States of America: With Special Consideration of Emigration from Austria-Hungary'], in *Zeitschrift für Volkswirtschaft, Sozialpolitik und Verwaltung* [*Journal of Political Economy, Social Policy and Administration*], Vienna, XIII (1904) 161–207.

4 Ibid., Table XIV, 179.

5 United States Census Office, *Occupations at the Twelfth Census*, Table LXXIII, p. cxciii.

6 Schwegel, in *ZVSV* XIII, Table III, 165. [The percentages actually refer to the period from 1821 to 1903, and not to the whole of the nineteenth century. – *Ed.*]

7 *Ed.* – Sombart's attribution to German settlers in America of a lack of Socialist inclination should be modified somewhat in order to obtain an accurate picture. German migration to America during the nineteenth century was a complex process and the migrants represented a variety of political and religious dispositions; see Carl Wittke, *The Germans in America: A Student's Guide to Localized History* (New York, 1967) 6–9. However, the Socialist propensities of the Germans who settled in Milwaukee are well known; see Thomas W. Gavett, *Development of the Labor Movement in Milwaukee* (Madison, 1965) 27–8 and *passim*. On the other hand, Alfred Kolb, in his *Als Arbeiter in Amerika: Unter deutsch-amerikanischen Großstadtproletariern* [*As a Worker in America: Among German-American Workers in Large Cities*] (Berlin, 1904) 43–4, distinguishes between the political orientations of German settlers in Milwaukee and of those in Chicago. The former, comprising about three-quarters of the population, were ready to embrace Socialist attitudes, but the former, comprising a quarter of the population, were not anxious to be seen as German and were not noticeably Socialist; local organisation politicians regarded them as 'vote fodder'.

8 The following exposition makes absolutely no claim to shed new light either on political conditions in the United States or on the particular party politics characteristic of the country. Instead, the description is based entirely on the copious material that is brought together and partly analysed in the voluminous literature. What I bring to it that is new is merely the viewpoint from which I am classifying the known facts. This viewpoint is given in the question that is stated as the starting point of this entire exercise. From the tremendously large literature I single out the following more recent works as being sufficient for a general orientation. The standard work of Bryce, *American Commonwealth*, first published in 1888 and since printed in many thousands of copies, is naturally foremost, as it is concerned with a general overview of public life in the United States. A sort of continuation and extension of Bryce's book is represented in the work of M. Ostrogorski, *Democracy and the Organization of Political Parties*, translated from the French by Frederick Clark (London, 1902), 2 vols, which Bryce himself has furnished with an introduction. The second volume of this important work deals with

America. In it can be found material for the study of American party politics that is as copious as any researcher can wish for – the volume runs to 793 octavo-sized pages. As regards the technique of party organisation, scarcely anything can be added to Ostrogorski's book. Of course, even Ostrogorski does not offer us a history of the party system in the U.S.A. To my mind there is nothing that does this at the moment. Quite inadequate, being purely a superficial chronological rendering, despite its proud title, is the book by James H. Hopkins, *A History of Political Parties in the United States; Being an Account of the Political Parties since the Foundation of the Government; Together with a Consideration of the Conditions Attending Their Formation and Development; With a Reprint of the Several Party Platforms* (New York, 1900). Notwithstanding its inadequacies, the book is still of use, firstly because of the reproduction of the complete party programmes mentioned in the title, and secondly because of the statistical data on the votes received by the parties from their very beginnings. A separate little book is that of John Jay Chapman, *Government and Democracy; And Other Essays* (London, 1898), which appeared in America under the title, *Causes and Consequences* (New York, 1898). The great work of H. von Holst, *Verfassung und Demokratie der Vereinigten Staaten von Amerika* (Düsseldorf, 1873; Berlin, 1878–91), 5 vols continuing, has very little connection with the purposes being pursued in this study, since for the present it describes the situation only as far as the Civil War and it devotes only slight attention to those problems that are the focus of our interests. According to the plan of that gigantic work, only Part Three should 'discuss present political and socio-political conditions' – the existing five volumes do not even conclude Part One, though as an interim the author has published a short summary entitled *Das Staatsrecht der Vereinigten Staaten von Amerika* [*The Constitutional Law of the United States of America*]. This appeared in the series, *Handbuch des Oeffentlichen Rechts: Das Staatsrecht der außerdeutschen Staaten* [*Manual of Public Law: The Constitutional Law of Non-German States*], 4th volume, 1st half-volume, 3rd part (Freiburg i. B., 1885). [Von Holst's larger work was published in English as *The Constitutional and Political History of the United States*, translated by John J. Lalor *et al.* (Chicago, 1876–92), 8 vols. – *Ed.*]

From the French literature, which has always bestowed a special interest on the internal political conditions of the United States since de Tocqueville's masterpiece, the work of Claudio Jannet, among the more recent writings, is useful. This appeared first in 1875 as *Les États-Unis Contemporains, ou Les Moeurs, Les Institutions et Les Idées Depuis La Guerre de La Sécession* [*The Contemporary United States, Or Customs, Institutions and Ideas Since the War of Secession*] (Paris, 1875), and in 1893 it was published with the title, *Die Vereinigten Staaten Nordamerikas* (sic) *in der Gegenwart: Sitten, Institutionen und Ideen seit dem Sezessionskriege* (Freiburg i. B., 1893), having been translated, newly revised and considerably extended by Walter Kämpfe. Of course, the book has to be used with care because of the radical-catholic standpoint of its authors. Further rich material is contained in the large work of Auguste Carlier, *La République Américaine, États-Unis: Institutions de L'Union, Institutions d'État, Régime Municipal, Système Judiciaire, Condition Sociale des Indiens: Avec une Carte de la Formation Politique et Territoriale des États-Unis* [*The American Republic, the United States: Institutions of the Union, Institutions of State, Municipal Government, the Judicial System, Social Condition of the Indians: With a Map of the Political and Territorial Development of the United States*] (Paris, 1890), 4 vols.

9 *Ed.* – Sombart has drawn this information from Bryce, *American Commonwealth*, 1 484. In fact, twenty-five of the thirty-eight American states existing at the beginning of 1889 elected their superior judges directly; by the time of publication of Volume 1 of the 3rd edition of Bryce's book in 1893, thirty-one out of forty-four states then existing were electing their superior judges in this way.

10 *Ed.* – This listing and some of the subsequent comment upon it were translated by Sombart virtually verbatim from the version that appeared in ibid., 11 86–8.

11 *Ed.* – Sombart leaves most of the official political titles in English in his original text. He explains the reasoning for this as follows: 'I am quoting the specifically American (or English) offices by their designation in English and am not attempting to put them into German, which would often be very longwinded. For what the overview is supposed to demonstrate it is sufficient that the reader merely be aware of the existence of each of the categories of officials to be elected.'

12 Most of the American states are larger than Bavaria, Baden and Wurtemberg put together. Some are equal in area to the Kingdom of Prussia or even to the German Empire itself.

13 *Ed.* – Sombart has summarised most of this description from that given in ibid., 11 78–85, esp. 80–1.

14 *Ed.* – While, as Bryce makes clear, public participation in these primaries was indeed low, Sombart's statement is not true without qualification. Bryce says: 'Every voter belonging to the party in the local area for which the primary is held, is presumably entitled to appear and vote in it'; ibid., 11 83. He does, however, go on to describe how certain legitimate voters may *de facto* be prevented by party leaders from exercising their right to vote because of their presumed intractable independence of the leadership.

15 *Ed.* – Sombart has taken the listing of conventions almost exactly from Bryce; see ibid., 11 81. However, his mention of a ward convention in the larger cities is not in Bryce's original list, although Sombart was right to add it.

Bryce's descriptions of geographical electoral units, in common with those of others writing at the same time, are sometimes misleading. In one place (11 86) Bryce uses the term 'election district' very generally to cover 'every local area or constituency which chooses a person for any office'. However, in New York, for example, this specific term is usually used to describe the smallest geographical electoral unit, a usage that Bryce himself follows in another place (11 138). Bryce also implies in his account that the smallest geographical electoral unit is usually called a 'ward' when not called an 'election district'. This is true of many smaller and medium-sized cities, but in the larger cities where 'ward' has a meaning, it is not the smallest electoral unit, this latter usually being called a 'precinct', a term that is analogous to the New York election district. Although the word 'precinct' has had this meaning in American politics since about 1865, it is used nowhere in Bryce's account. When Sombart talks of a ward convention in the larger cities, he therefore means the convention of delegates elected for this purpose in precinct primaries.

For a general account of these matters see, for example, William Anderson, Clara Penniman and Edward W. Weidner, *Government in the Fifty States* (New York, 1960) 159–60.

16 *Ed.* – Sombart's original text quotes these phrases in English parenthetically to the German. The term 'wire-pullers' was in quite general vogue in both England and the United States to describe organisation politicians, and it is much used by Ostrogorski; see *Democracy*, I 352 *et seq.*, for a discussion of wire-pulling in English caucuses, and II 42, 49, for example, for the American context.

17 Bryce, *American Commonwealth*, II 142.

18 See Eltweed Pomeroy, 'Why I Do Not Join the Socialist Party', in *International Socialist Review*, II (1901–2) 647. [The details that Sombart gives pertain to the New York mayoralty election of 1901. Eltweed Pomeroy (born 1860) had been President of the National Direct Legislation League since 1896. He was a reformer of the American Fabian type who refused to join the Socialist Party, preferring to devote his energies to proselytizing for direct legislation by the initiative and referendum. – *Ed.*]

19 *Ed.* – This was the Presidential campaign of 1896. See ibid., 647, where the author says that he is quoting the figure of $5,000,000 from an article in the *Literary Digest*.

20 In this respect large amounts are always involved. In New York, for example, there were 2100 corporations in the middle of the 1890s with a combined capital of $2,000,000. Most are pledged to the party in power and pay their 'price of the peace', which amounts to up to $50,000 from each one; see Joseph Bishop, 'The Price of the Peace', in *The Century*, XLVIII (1894).

21 Bryce, *American Commonwealth*, II 112–13. Bryce continues: 'As a tenant had in the days of feudalism to make occasional money payments to his lord in addition to the military service he rendered, so now the American vassal must render his aids in money as well as give knightly service at the primaries, in the canvass, at the polls. His liabilities are indeed heavier than those of the feudal tenant, for the latter could relieve himself from duty in the field by the payment of scutage, while under the Machine a money payment never discharges from the obligation to serve in the army of "workers".'

22 Thus [in 1887 – *Ed.*], the Democratic Ring in New York City asked for $25,000 for nomination to the office of Comptroller and $5000 for nomination as State Senator. The salary of the Comptroller is $10,000 annually for three years, and that of a State Senator is $1500 annually for two years. See ibid., II 113.

23 See Frederick W. Whitridge, 'Assessments, Political', in *Cyclopaedia of Political Science, Political Economy, and of the Political History of the United States*, ed. John J. Lalor (Chicago, 1882) I 154; Bryce, *American Commonwealth*, II 113, 139–42; and Ostrogorski, *Democracy*, II 147–8, 425.

24 See the excellent descriptions in Ostrogorski, *Democracy*, II 367–440, esp. 376–81.

25 'Spoils', in this usage, was first coined by Senator Marcy in the 1820s. [Actually, Bryce reports that Marcy used the word in a speech in the Senate in 1832; Marcy was referring to the situation in New York and was himself an

associate of Martin Van Buren; see Bryce, *American Commonwealth*, II 126. However, the use of the word may in fact slightly predate 1832 and be attributable to another speaker. *The New English Dictionary on Historical Principles* (Oxford, 1919) IX: Part I, 649, confers the first recorded use of 'spoils' (in the plural) on J. S. Johnson in 1830: 'The country is treated as a conquered province, and the offices distributed among the victors, as the spoils of war' (*Congressional Debates*, 2 April 1830, 299). However, the use of 'spoil' (in the singular) to convey the same idea dates from the eighteenth century – *Ed.*]

26 The Spoils System in the U.S.A. today is no longer unrestricted. The so-called Civil Service Reform, whose purpose is the filling of offices according to the qualification of the candidate (as furnished by passing an examination) or according to length of service, achieved its first success with the law of 1883. According to this, at least some Federal offices are supposed to be filled in the designated manner; these constitute the 'classified service', a category whose coverage is determined by the Presidents. In reality, only a minor number of Federal posts have been withdrawn from the Spoils System in this way. As far as I know, only two states, New York and Massachusetts, have so far caught on to the idea of Civil Service Reform. Likewise, only a few cities (among the large ones are Chicago, New Orleans, San Francisco, and Philadelphia) have introduced the merit system; however, many, such as Philadelphia, have done this only on paper, although in others, such as Chicago, the reform of the appointment process is said to have made great progress; see United States Civil Service Commission, *Reports of the United States Civil Service Commission* (Washington, D.C., 1884 onward). For all that, there have obviously been till now only first steps towards the elimination of the Spoils System. These have been able to reduce only minimally the significance that the system portrayed in the text has for American party life. Yet there can be no doubt that a more extensive Civil Service Reform would have a decisive influence on the whole process of public life, especially on the position of the major parties. [The 1883 law to which Sombart refers is the so-called Pendleton Act, which, says Bryce, 'instituted a board of civil service commissioners (to be named by the President), directing them to apply a system of competitive examinations to a considerable number of offices in the departments at Washington, and a smaller number in other parts of the country'; see Bryce, *American Commonwealth*, II 133. – *Ed.*]

27 *Ed.* – Karl Legien (1861–1920) had been head of the General Commission of the German Trade Unions since its foundation in 1890. He opposed a militant political role for the German trade-union movement in favour of the co-operation of workers and employers on the basis of equality. From 1893 to 1898 and from 1903 onward he was a Social Democratic member of the Reichstag. Legien's reformism gave him an ideological resemblance to Samuel Gompers, his American counterpart. See Carl E. Schorske, *German Social Democracy, 1905–1917: The Development of the Great Schism* (New York, 1955) *passim*, esp. 8–16.

28 *Ed.* – Carroll Davidson Wright (1840–1909) was chief of the Massachusetts Bureau of Statistics of Labor from 1873 to 1888, and he was first Commissioner of the Federal Bureau of Labor from 1885 to 1905; the Bureau of Labor became the Bureau of Labor Statistics in 1913. In fact, Wright was not

succeeded at this post by the President of the American Federation of Labor, Samuel Gompers, but by Charles P. Neill, formerly a professor of political economy at Catholic University in Washington; see Ewan Clague, *The Bureau of Labor Statistics* (New York, 1968) 3, 13.

29 *Ed.* – Sombart called Mitchell 'victorious' because he was the dominant union leader in a successful strike of Pennsylvania anthracite miners in 1902. In fact, Mitchell did not receive the Under-Secretaryship of State that Sombart mentions.

Hermann Sachse (1862–1942) was President of the Verband Deutscher Bergarbeiter [German Miners' Union] from 1902 to 1919 and a Social Democratic member of the Reichstag from 1898 to 1918. The Verband Deutscher Bergarbeiter was a Social Democratic trade union, and like Legien, Sachse was a leading exponent of reformism; he was one of numerous Social Democratic deputies who signed a declaration in 1911 against Rosa Luxemburg's earlier call for the use of the general strike as a political weapon.

Otto Hué (1868–1922) was editor of the *Deutsche Bergarbeiterzeitung* [*German Miners' Newspaper*], organ of the Verband Deutscher Bergarbeiter, and he was a Social Democratic member of the Reichstag from 1903 to 1911. As editor of the miners' union's newspaper, Hué was considered almost *de facto* leader of the Verband. Hué was a leading trade-union reformist, like Legien and Sachse, and in 1900 he had published *Neutrale oder parteiische Gewerkschaften?* [*Neutral or Partisan Trade Unions?*], in which he had advocated partisan neutrality by the trade unions towards the Social Democratic Party. His was a brand of instrumental trade-unionism intended to alleviate the workers' immediate problems, and he was ready to work with Christian workers' associations to achieve this end.

30 *Ed.* – Sombart's source for this information is Brooks, *Social Unrest*, 3, although Brooks is less definitively quantitative than Sombart implies: 'I can count from memory thirteen men in Massachusetts, who were in their time and place leaders, who now occupy positions in politics or in business. A friend ... tells me that in Chicago he knows of more than thirty men, formerly at the front of their respective unions, who now hold political office in that city.'

31 The perennial exception is Switzerland, to which considerations similar to those for the United States apply.

32 *Ed.* – Arthur Stadthagen (1857–1917) was a Social Democratic member of the Reichstag and was among the more radical elements in the leadership of the Party during the period of the 'great schism' at the beginning of this century; see Schorske, *German Social Democracy*, 221, 266. Robert Michels, in *Political Parties: A Sociological Study of the Oligarchical Tendencies of Modern Democracy*, translated by Eden and Cedar Paul (New York, 1966 ed.) 298, describes him as an ex-barrister in the camp of the 'revolutionaries' of the Party.

33 *Ed.* – Hermann Ernst Christian Tessendorf (1831–95) was State Prosecutor at the Berlin City Court from 1873 to 1879 and became notorious for the persecution of Socialist sympathisers. For one such incident see Vernon L. Lidtke, *The Outlawed Party: Social Democracy in Germany, 1878–1890* (Princeton, 1966) 85–6.

34 *Ed.* – The Löbtau Judgement was handed down on 3 February 1899. The Dresden Assize Court sentenced nine workers from Löbtau, a suburb of Dres-

den, to a total of fifty-three years' penal servitude, eight years' imprisonment and seventy years' loss of civil rights for a series of trifling offences. On 6 February the Social Democratic group in the Reichstag called on sympathisers for financial support for the workers' dependents, and by 19 March 88,136.43 marks had been collected.

35 *Ed.* – Sombart is referring to the strikes at Cripple Creek (Teller County) and San Juan (Telluride County) in 1903 and 1904; for a fuller account see Philip Taft and Philip Ross, 'American Labor Violence: Its Causes, Character, and Outcome', in *Violence in America: Historical and Comparative Perspectives*, ed. Hugh Davis Graham and Ted Robert Gurr (New York, 1969) 307–9.

36 *Ed.* – The full story is more complicated than Sombart's description. The Democratic candidate, A. Adams, was inaugurated as Governor on 10 January 1905, but his election was judged by the Republicans to have been corrupted by alleged irregularities in Denver and elsewhere. The Republican legislature investigated the election and declared Peabody to have been elected, but only on condition that he gave them a written promise to resign in twenty-four hours. He was declared elected on 16 March 1905 and resigned on 17 March, when the Lieutenant-Governor Jesse F. M'Donald, a Republican, became Governor.

37 *Ed.* – Ludwig Thoma (1867–1921) was known at the time Sombart was writing as a satirical poet and author, having been editor of the satirical political weekly, *Simplicissimus*, since 1899. His major targets tended to be bourgeois narrow-mindedness and affected morality.

38 Bryce, *American Commonwealth*, II 48, writes: 'They are gregarious, each man more disposed to go with the multitude and do as they do than to take a line of his own.'

39 Ostrogorski, *Democracy*, II 591.

40 *Ed.* – Sombart is somewhat cavalier in his dismissal of the Anti-Masonic Party. In its heyday in the early 1830s it elected various state Governors and numerous State Representatives; although it had disappeared formally after a few years, it actually allied with the National Republicans in opposition to the Jacksonian Democrats, an alliance producing the Whig Party. See Seymour Martin Lipset and Earl Raab, *The Politics of Unreason: Right-Wing Extremism in America, 1790–1970* (New York, 1970) 39–47.

41 *Ed.* – Native Americans is in fact the generic title of a group of various nativist and Protestant parties and associations in the 1830s and 1840s. The Native Americans of New York formed the formal party, called the American Republican Party, in 1843; see ibid., 49–50.

42 The name 'Know-Nothings' refers to the fact that the members of the party, a sort of half-secret order, had to answer all questions concerning their organisation, etc. by saying, 'I know nothing'.

43 *Ed.* – These figures give the Know-Nothings 21.6 per cent of the 1856 Presidential vote.

44 *Ed.* – The rise of the American Party was assisted in part by the collapse of the Whigs. Although the changed historical circumstances of the late 1850s contributed to the American Party's decline, much of its support went to the new Republican Party; see ibid., 59–61.

45 *Ed.* – Henry George (1839–97) proposed in his principal work, *Progress*

and Poverty, which was finished in 1879, that all land should be made common property over time by a single annual tax to its full rental value. In 1886 he was candidate of the Union Labor Party for Mayor of New York, being supported by the Socialists; however, in 1887 he was repudiated by the latter when he explicitly favoured his single-tax prescriptions to orthodox Socialism. Towards the end of his life he argued vigorously for absolute free trade.

46　*Ed.* – The Deutsche Fortschrittspartei [German Progress Party] was formed in 1861 from the amalgamation of various liberal groups and radical democrats of 1848. The Nationalliberale Partei [National Liberal Party] formed after a split from the Fortschrittspartei in 1866, and then the latter was in turn part of an amalgamation into the Deutschfreisinnige Partei in 1884, when this was formed with the help of a group favouring free trade who had seceded from the National Liberals in the late 1870s. See also Note 48 of this Section, below.

The Freisinnige Volkspartei was one product of the bifurcation of the Deutschfreisinnige Partei in 1893; the other was the Freisinnige Vereinigung.

47　*Ed.* – Sombart's original text says 'Balaam's ass', but this is clearly a mistake. Balaam's ass was a highly decisive animal, its claim to fame being that it verbally rebuked its master for beating it; see The Book of Numbers, Chapter 22, verses 21–33. On the other hand, Buridan's Ass (named from the French scholastic philosopher, Jean Buridan, who lived from around 1300 to some time after 1358) refers to a particular sophism which says that, if a hungry ass is placed exactly between two bundles of hay of equal size and attractiveness, it must starve as there is nothing to determine its will towards either bundle. According to *Chambers's Encyclopaedia*, new ed. (London, 1950) ii 691–2, the sophism is wrongly ascribed to Buridan: 'The celebrated sophism known to the schoolmen under the name of Buridan's Ass . . . occurs nowhere in Buridan's books and was no doubt due to some opponent who wished to cast ridicule upon his determinism. . . . This hypothetical case is however found in Aristotle, *De Caelo*, and in Dante, *Paradiso*, book 4.'

48　*Ed.* – The Nationalliberale Partei, the circumstances of whose origins were given in Note 46 of this Section, above, had particular strength among the upper-middle class, particularly in Hanover, Hesse and Baden; in the Reichstag in the early 1870s the Party vigorously supported various economic-reform policies of Bismarck that were designed to facilitate the transition to a large, united German empire – hence the Party's centralism referred to by Sombart. The Party also pushed for greater power for the Reichstag.

The Old Conservatives, however, representing the interests of the Junker class, initially believed that Bismarck's imperial policy was a betrayal of his (and their) class in favour of the bourgeoisie, and the Conservatives were deeply suspicious of Bismarck's imperial designs – hence their particularism. However, by 1876, under pressure of capitalist development, the Old Conservatives had abandoned their opposition to Bismarck and to the Reich, and when in that year the Deutschkonservative Partei [German Conservative Party] became the new party of the Old Conservatives, its programme was submitted to Bismarck beforehand for his approval.

The National Liberals were split and seriously weakened by internal disagreements during the change from free-trade to protectionist policies in the later years of Bismarck's régime. Then, from 1887 to 1890 the National Liberals joined the Conservatives in the so-called *Kartell* that controlled the Reichstag and enabled Bismarck to pass his military policy.

In 1878 the Conservatives and the National Liberals had both supported passage of the Socialist Law, although the latter had done so only after a change of policy during the immediately preceding election campaign. In the 1890s both parties also wanted further repressive laws against Socialists.

Sombart's 'long, long, ago' therefore refers to the period before 1876 at the latest; by that date the class interests of the German upper-middle class and the Junkers were in many respects identical.

For further details see, for example, William Carr, *A History of Germany, 1815–1945* (London, 1969) 121–97 *passim*.

49 *Ed.* – This general statement is seriously to be doubted. Doubts about a universal German propensity for the Republicans in the late nineteenth century have been current since systematic research began on the subject. An early contribution to the debate is Joseph Schafer, 'Who Elected Lincoln?', in *American Historical Review*, XLVII (1941) 51–63. Schafer found that in Wisconsin German Catholics and the Irish were solidly opposed to Lincoln; a few German Lutherans and Forty-eighters did vote for Lincoln, but by no means all.

More recent research by Kleppner supports these findings. (See Paul Kleppner, *The Cross of Culture: A Social Analysis of Midwestern Politics, 1850–1900* (New York, 1970).) Kleppner shows that in the period from the 1850s to the 1890s Irish Catholics in the Midwest were almost unanimously Democratic, but German Catholics were only slightly less so. A majority of German Lutherans and German Reformed Church members were also Democratic. Among German voters only Sectarians were more Republican than Democratic. Moreover, Irish Protestants were strongly Republican (ibid., 70).

The Bryan candidacy of 1896 did disrupt these patterns somewhat and there was a shift among Catholics generally and among German Lutherans away from the Democratic Party, but this desertion was by no means total (ibid., 322–33).

50 At a procession in Baltimore in 1840 the supporters of Harrison carried banners with the inscriptions: 'Tippecanoe [Harrison's nickname given to him in memory of his victory over the Indians at Tippecanoe – *Ed.*] and no reduction of wages'; 'W. H. Harrison, the poor man's friend'; and 'We will teach the palace slaves to respect the log cabin'; see Ostrogorski, *Democracy*, II 75.

51 Pasquale Villari has also written: 'When a true divergence of interests and of principles is lacking and the parties still exist, they necessarily become personal and they fight only about power. Political corruption is then inevitable.' [Pasquale Villari (1826–1917) was an Italian historian and conservative politician. – *Ed.*]

52 See the figures in Hopkins, *History of Political Parties*, *passim*.

53 In any case I feel that attempts of this sort have always been unsuccessful till now and must necessarily be so.

54 *Ed.* – See Note 49 of this Section, above,

55 See Algernon Lee, *Labor Politics and Socialist Politics*, 3rd ed. (New

York, 1903), and John Spargo, *Shall the Unions Go Into Politics?* (New York, 1903).

56   *Ed.* – This appeared as Extra Number of *American Federationist*, IX: 1½ (15 Jan 1902) and was written by George H. Shibley. The system described began in about 1896 in Winnetka – then (as now) an affluent village about sixteen miles north of Chicago with (at that time) about 1800 inhabitants, many of them wealthy businessmen. The effect of the system as originally practised was that the village's Board of Trustees were obliged by popular pressure to refer all important measures to a direct ballot of voters; see ibid., 50–1.

57   Extra Number of *American Federationist*, XI: 7A (15 July 1904).

58   The questionnaires were reprinted along with the comments that are to be found in ibid.

59   This applies only to the issue being discussed here.

60   See also von Holst, *Verfassung und Demokratie*, I (1873), in the chapter entitled „Die Kanonisierung der Verfassung und ihr wahrer Charakter" ['The Worship of the Constitution, and Its Real Character']. [This is Chapter II of von Holst, *Constitutional and Political History* (Chicago, 1889) I 64–79. – *Ed.*]

61   We saw above that the working class is now asking for even greater rights for the population in the form of the initiative and the referendum. However, these rights are really only something being demanded as a consequence of the existing Constitution and not in opposition to it.

62   See, for example, von Holst, *Das Staatsrecht der Vereinigten Staaten von Amerika*, 142–4, 157.

63   *Ed.* – *Doléances* were formal complaints made to the States-General during the French Revolution.

SECTION TWO

1   *Ed.* – In this Section Sombart presents a considerable amount of data that were taken from a large variety of primary sources, either directly or after some necessary manipulation and recalculation. Where the original sources were accessible, as was true in almost every case, the figures given by Sombart have been checked by the Editor. This process revealed innumerable certain or probable errors – most of these were small, but some were quite substantial and of a size sufficient to affect the validity of inferences drawn by Sombart from the relevant figures. It would have been excessively tedious for the reader if an editorial note had commented on every single case where a correction seemed called for, and so the following practices have been adopted.

    Those errors that the Editor judged to be small and about whose incorrectness he was fully certain have been corrected in the text and tables without any editorial notation. Errors judged to be substantial, where the Editor was similarly certain of their incorrectness, have been amended in the text and tables; an editorial note explains the particular circumstances and implications, and also gives the figures in Sombart's original text.

    In certain cases the nature of the data-presentation in the primary source prevented the conclusive establishment of an error in Sombart's text, but the Editor none the less found it impossible to reconcile his own calculation of the datum in question with the figure given by Sombart. In such cases the Editor was disposed to assume an error by Sombart. Where errors of this character were considered small, Sombart's original figures have been left unaltered and no editorial comment has been made. Where, however, they seemed substantial – especially if the validity of some inference made from them was affected – Sombart's original figures have been used, but an editorial note draws attention to the probable errors and provides what are considered the correct figures.

One or two of Sombart's primary sources contained many arithmetic and similar errors, a fact often apparently not realised by the author, or at least not commented upon. Such sources receive additional editorial comment of their own, the content of such comment depending upon the particular issues raised by the errors in the primary source and upon Sombart's application of the data.

In this Section Sombart presents numerous examples of income-distributions, to which the following comments apply. Many of the class intervals of the data reproduced in Sombart's text do not form mutually exclusive classes or contain other small anomalies. Sometimes, though not usually, this is a mistake that is also to be found in the primary source. All such mistakes have been corrected – where possible according to the correct version given in the primary source.

Derived descriptive statistics of the income-distributions have been calculated and added by the Editor in order to provide substantiation of certain arguments in his Introductory Essay and also to assist the reader in assessing Sombart's argument. These calculations, however, have not necessarily been made on the basis of the class intervals given by Sombart, although of course it is these intervals that are reproduced in the translation. Some of the primary sources contain the ungrouped data, while others use class intervals that are smaller than those formed by Sombart. All calculations have been executed on data in their most undifferentiated available form – usually with the smaller class intervals of the primary source but sometimes with the completely ungrouped data. In the cases of some distributions the primary source also provides an 'average' value (that is, a mean) which Sombart does not quote in his text. In such circumstances this average has been inserted as the value for the mean because it can usually be said to have been calculated by the author of the primary source from the ungrouped data. Where necessary and appropriate, assumptions about the lower class limits of bottom classes and upper class limits of top classes have been stated in editorial notes.

In choosing statistics to show dispersion, the standard deviation and dimensionless measures derived from it are not used because of the pronounced skewness of some of the income-distributions. The semi-interquartile range and the quartile coefficient of variation are used instead. The semi-interquartile range is half the absolute difference between the first and third quartiles of a distribution. The quartile coefficient of variation is the absolute difference between the first and third quartiles divided by the sum of the first and third quartiles; it is a dimensionless measure of dispersion, meaning that its value is independent of the units in which the distribution was originally measured.

In some places in the text and in some tables giving American data, Sombart quotes figures in dollars without their equivalents in marks. Where necessary, conversions to marks have been added by the Editor, calculating on the basis of 1 American dollar being 4.20 marks. The reader is expected to make the appropriate comparisons in terms of marks. Conversions of marks into American dollars are not provided.

2 This is the only method by which absolute statements have any proper validity.

3 The presently available attempts to compare wage statistics for America with those for Europe are thoroughly unsatisfactory. The following efforts exist: 1. compilations by the Bureau of Labor in Washington in its *Seventh Annual Report*; however, in this source the non-American workers' incomes have been selected quite unmethodically and arbitrarily. [See United States, Fifty-second Congress, House of Representatives, *Seventh Annual Report of the Commissioner of Labor, 1891*, II, Part II. – Cost of Living (Washington, D.C., 1892), esp. 851–65. – *Ed.*] 2. the short presentation by Albert Schäffle in the article, „Der Geld- und der Reallohn in den Vereinigten Staaten" ['Money-wages and Real Wages in the United States'], in *Zeitschrift für die gesammte Staatswissenschaft [Journal of General Political Science]*, Tübingen, XLVI (1889) 111–71, which is not based on either the best American or the best German data: [Albert Schäffle (1831–1903) was an economist and sociologist who held professorial chairs in Tübingen (1860–8) and Vienna (1868–1871). He was an editor of the *Zeitschrift für die gesammte Staatswissenschaft. – Ed.*] 3. the relevant chapters in E. Levasseur, *The American Workman*, translated by Thomas S. Adams (Baltimore, 1900) 276–435, which, relatively speaking, are the best treatment of the subject but which naturally lack the German situation as a basis for comparison.

4 I have described the arrangement and significance of these in Items 2 to 20 of my literature review; see Sombart, in *ASS* XX 638–52.

5 Ibid., 638–42.

6 The specialist is sufficiently informed of the statistical value or otherwise of these data; see, for example, the latest detailed criticism of them by J. Jastrow and R. Calwer: „Berufsgenossenschaften" in *Schriften des Vereins für Sozialpolitik [Publications of the Association for Social Policy]* CIX, „Die Störungen im deutschen Wirtschaftsleben während der Jahre 1900 ff." Fünfter Band: „Die Krisis auf dem Arbeitsmarkte" ['The Upsets in German Economic Life since 1900', Volume 5, 'The Crisis on the Labour Market'] (Leipzig, 1903) pp. 49–76, esp. 52. [In the text the word *Berufsgenossenschaften* has been translated as 'industrial associations that administer accident insurance'. The word usually means 'professional associations', but it has also a narrower, legalistic meaning: according to this, such associations were corporate groupings of employers of an occupational sector or of several related occupational sectors that were required by law to administer employees' accident insurance. All members of these associations were required by law to file with the executive of their respective association details of the number of insured employees in their business and the salaries and wages earned by them during the relevant financial year; Jastrow and Calwer (ibid., p. 49) say that, according to legislation passed in 1900, this had to be done within six weeks of the end of the financial year. For a contemporary account in English of the German system of accident insurance existing at about the time that Sombart was writing, see 'Industrial Insurance (State) in the

German Empire', in *The New Encyclopedia of Social Reform*, ed. William D. P. Bliss and Rudolph M. Binder (New York, 1908) p. 617. – *Ed.*]

7 *Ed.* – The mention of 4 marks is a reference to one aspect of the critique of these data by Jastrow and Calwer that Sombart has already cited. Sombart has undoubtedly calculated these averages either from the data given in German Empire, Reichs-Versicherungsamt, *Amtliche Nachrichten des Reichs-Versicherungsamts [Official Reports of the Imperial Insurance Office]*, XVIII: 1 (1 Jan 1902), 15, 17, or from the same data as reproduced in *Statistisches Jahrbuch für das Deutsche Reich*, 1902, XXIII, 213–16. Both these primary sources contain notes to the same effect as Jastrow and Calwer's critique. In the first source is the following note (p. 2): 'In order that erroneous inferences may be avoided, special attention is drawn to the fact that the wages entered for the industrial associations that administer accident insurance are not the same as the wages actually paid. . . . The concern is not to establish wage statistics, but to demonstrate those wages that are chargeable and significant in the calculation of contributions. . . . It was obligatory that, for juvenile and untrained workers, the customary local daily wage of adults be used in rating contributions.' The second source makes clear that the problem in using these data to indicate wages actually paid is not merely the simple one that wages over 4 marks (a day) are not considered, as Sombart maintains. A note on p. 216 says: '. . . for the purposes of assessment the following amounts are rated at only a third: for the period from 1 January to 30 September 1900 daily wages in excess of 4 marks and for the period from 1 October to 31 December 1900 annual wages in excess of 1500 marks.'

8 For Prussia the figures have been made available annually, first in Prussia, Ministerium für Handel und Gewerbe, *Zeitschrift für das Berg-, Hütten- und Salinenwesen im Preußischen Staat [Journal of Matters Connected With Mining, Smelting and Salt-mining in the Prussian State]* (Berlin, 1853 onward); then also in Prussia, Statistisches Bureau, *Statistisches Handbuch für den Preußischen Staat [Statistical Manual for the Prussian State]* (Berlin, quinquennially from 1889 to 1904); and recently in Prussia, Statistisches Bureau, *Statistisches Jahrbuch für den Preußischen Staat [Statistical Yearbook for the Prussian State]* (Berlin, 1905) II 72–3.

9 See United States, Department of Commerce and Labor, Bureau of the Census, *Bulletin No. 9: Mines and Quarries* (Washington, D.C., 1904), which is Item 5b of my literature review; see Sombart, in *ASS* XX 642.

10 Unfortunately, the wages of the 'miner' are not given separately for the various categories of mining; instead, data for iron, copper, gold, silver and other types of mining are aggregated with those for bituminous coal-mining.

11 *Ed.* – It did not prove possible to consult Sombart's cited source for these data, but the Census Bulletin that he says he used is almost certainly a preliminary presentation of data subsequently published in greater detail in a longer report that appeared in 1905; this latter is United States, Department of Commerce and Labor, Bureau of the Census, *Special Reports: Mines and Quarries, 1902* (Washington, D.C., 1905). Wage data calculated from this latter source for the categories of worker being discussed by Sombart in this context are not quite consistent with the figures given by him. The average annual wage for all workers in mining and quarrying in 1902 was $635.97 (2671.07M), for all such workers above ground it was $564.71 (2371.78M),

for all such workers below ground it was $679.78 (2855.08M), and for all miners below ground it was $717.74 (3014.51M) (ibid., 91). The same source (ibid., 709) permits the calculation of the equivalent figures for bituminous coal-mining only (which Sombart says his source did not enable him to do); these are $646.68 (2716.06M), $597.23 (2508.37M), $654.03 (2746.93M), and $677.39 (2845.04M) respectively.

12 Davis R. Dewey, *Employees and Wages: Special Reports, Twelfth Census of the United States Taken in the Year 1900* (Washington, D.C., 1903), which is Item 2f of my literature review; see Sombart, in *ASS* xx 640. [Sombart comments there that the method of selection of the 720 business establishments sampled by Dewey, particularly in view of their relatively large size and the fact that they had to have been in existence for at least twelve years, ensures an excessively favourable picture of wage conditions in the United States. On the other hand, A. L. Bowley, in a Review of Dewey's *Employees and Wages*, in *Journal of the Royal Statistical Society*, LXVII (1904) 523–8, argues that this sampling procedure may have produced a less favourable picture because of the exclusion from the sampling frame of more progressive (and by implication more generous) firms.

A more systematic analysis of the sampling aspects of Dewey's study is contained in A. E. James, 'The Dewey Report on Wages in Manufacturing Industries in the United States', in *Quarterly Publications of the American Statistical Association*, x (New Series, No. 79) (1907) 319–44; James argues that there is an overrepresentation of manufacturing establishments in the (better-off) Central states and also a lack of fit between the distributions of those industries sampled in the Report and those in the economy as a whole. These factors combine to mean that the Report gives too favourable a picture of wages in America in 1900. – *Ed.*]

13 Massachusetts, Bureau of Statistics of Labor, *The Annual Statistics of Manufactures, 1901*, XVI (Boston, 1902). This series is Item 15 of my literature review; see Sombart, in *ASS* xx 648–9.

14 Illinois, Bureau of Labor Statistics, *Twelfth Biennial Report of the Bureau of Labor Statistics of the State of Illinois, 1902* (Springfield, 1904) 101. This report is Item 18 in my literature review; see Sombart, in *ASS* xx 651.

15 Theodor Leipart, *Beitrag zur Beurtheilung der Lage der Arbeiter in Stuttgart: Nach statistischen Erhebungen im Auftrage der Vereinigten Gewerkschaften, herausgegeben von Theodor Leipart* [*Contribution to the Assessment of the Situation of Workers in Stuttgart: Prepared from Statistical Data Collected on Behalf of the United Trade Unions, Edited by Theodor Leipart*] (Stuttgart, 1900) 60, 63, 91 and 93.

16 [Rudolf] Fuchs, *Die Verhältnisse der Industriearbeiter in 17 Landgemeinden bei Karlsruhe: Dargestellt von dem Großherzoglichen Fabrikinspektor Dr. Fuchs, Bericht erstattet an das Großherzogliche Ministerium des Innern und herausgegeben von der Großherzoglichen badischen Fabrikinspektion* [*The Conditions of Industrial Workers in 17 Communities around Karlsruhe: Prepared by Dr. Fuchs, Factory Inspector of the Grand Duchy of Baden, Report Made to the Ministry of the Interior of the Grand Duchy of Baden and Published by the Department of Factory Inspection*] (Karlsruhe, 1904) 90–1.

17 D. Fuhrmann, *Die wirtschaftliche Lage der Arbeiter Hanaus: Im Auftrage*

der Statistischen Kommission des Gewerkschaftskartells Hanau am Main bearbeitet von D. Fuhrmann [*The Economic Situation of Workers in Hanau: Compiled by D. Fuhrmann on Behalf of the Statistical Committee of the Combined Trade Unions of Hanau am Main*] (Hanau am Main, 1901).

18 *Ed.* – See Note 9 of this Section, above.

19 Baden, Ministerium des Innern, *Die sociale Lage der Cigarren-arbeiter im Großherzogthum Baden: Beilage zum Jahresbericht des Großh. badischen Fabrikinspektors für das Jahr 1889, Herausgegeben im Auftrage des Großherzoglichen Ministeriums des Innern* [*The Social Situation of Cigar-workers in the Grand Duchy of Baden: Supplement to the Annual Report of the Factory Inspector of the Grand Duchy of Baden for the Year 1889, Published on Behalf of the Ministry of the Interior of the Grand Duchy*] (Karlsruhe, 1890) 57.

20 Shortly before the appearance of the report named in the previous Note, I had prepared wage figures on the basis of careful verbal inquiries in my study of the German cigar-making industry; this appeared as „Die Deutsche Zigarrenindustrie und der Erlaß des Bundesrats vom 9. Mai 1888" ['The German Cigar-making Industry and the Bundesrat's Decree of 9 May 1888'], in *Archiv für Soziale Gesetzgebung und Statistik* [*Works in Social Legislation and Statistics*], ed. Heinrich Braun, II (1889) 107–28, esp. 113. From the calculation in the text it appears that my figures were justified, at least as they referred to that time.

The survey that the Tobacco Workers' Union made in 1900 (C. Deichmann, *Ergebnisse einer im Jahre 1900 vom Deutschen Tabakarbeiter-Verband veranstalteten Enquete, Bearbeitet von C. Deichmann* [*Results of an Enquiry Organised in 1900 by the German Tobacco Workers' Union, Compiled by C. Deichmann*] (Bremen, 1902)), which – as regards wages – covers 39,032 workers (ibid., 4), cannot unfortunately be used for a comparison, since it ascertained only the average weekly wage paid by each of 1527 manufacturing establishments. These were as follows (ibid., 14):

Less than 10.01M	182
10.01M–12.00M	306
12.01M–14.00M	588
14.01M–16.00M	308
16.01M or more	143
	1527

[Mean: 12.94M; Median: 12.94M; Semi-interquartile Range: 1.57M; and Quartile Coefficient of Variation: 0.122. – *Ed.*]

In any case, even these figures let the gap between German and American rates of pay be seen sufficiently clearly. [Several comments on the data reproduced above, as well as on those in Table 7, are required if the reader is fully to comprehend their significance.

Deichmann (ibid., 13) described the German cigar-making industry as a whole as being composed of about 50 per cent *Zigarrenmacher* (cigar-makers, who assemble filler tobacco (that of the lowest quality) inside a binder (made of tobacco of a higher quality than the filler), before enclosing this in the outside wrapper (a leaf of the highest quality) – all this being done by one person in a series of continuous operations), about 35 per cent *Wickelmacher* (who prepare the leaves used for binding and wrapping), and about 5 per cent *Zurichter* (literally, in this context, preparers, who remove veins from the raw leaves and are also called *Ausripper*), with the remainder being *Sortierer* (graders) and 'other' workers. *Zigarrenmacher* and (especially) *Sortierer* were relatively well paid; *Wickelmacher* and (especially) *Ausripper* were relatively badly paid. The data on the average weekly wages paid by the 1527 establishments that have been quoted above by Sombart cover only *Zigarrenmacher* and include both male and female workers.

However, the data in Table 7 (which in fact refer only to thirty specific cigar-making factories in Baden, not to all of them) cover all categories of adult worker in the industry. These are *Werkführer* (foremen, who are well paid and are probably all male), *Zigarrenarbeiter* (literally, cigar-workers, and undoubtedly the same as Deichmann's category of *Zigarrenmacher*), *Wickelmacher*, *Ausripper* (Deichmann's *Zurichter*), *Sortierer*, *Packer und Kistenmacher* (packers and box-makers), and 'others', a slightly less inclusive category than that with the same title used by Deichmann.

Because of an apparently unusual distribution between these job categories in the thirty factories in Baden – relative to their distribution in the occupational structure of the whole industry as described by Deichmann – it is possible that, even with the 50 to 100 per cent increase that Sombart recommends to bring these wage data up to national standards, they would still not adequately reflect the wages paid in the industry as a whole. This is a matter that can finally be settled only if one has knowledge of the sex and age distributions of each of the particular job categories in the industry as a whole, and Deichmann does not give this information. However, it does seem likely that the Baden factories were peculiar in that they contained a relative underrepresentation of the better-paid jobs in the industry and a relative overrepresentation of the poorly paid ones. *Zigarrenarbeiter* are only 43 per cent of the total labour force in the Baden factories (45 per cent of all males and 42 per cent of all females; the bases of all percentages include those workers under sixteen years old). *Ausripper* (*Zurichter*), on the other hand, are as much as 9 per cent of the total labour force in Baden (2 per cent of all males and 13 per cent of all females). Thus, if these wage data are to represent adequately the national picture, they should perhaps be increased by something more than 50 to 100 per cent that Sombart suggests. – *Ed*.]

21 This could be done only for men's wages. Separate data on the wages of women workers in the cigar-making industry of the South are not produced, and in this case I had to take the average for the country as a whole. [In Tables 7, 9 and 10 the American wage data given by Sombart are actually rates per week rather than actual earnings in a week – the difference between the two being due to such matters as overtime, which increases earnings relative to rates, and strikes or lay-offs, which do the reverse. Dewey, the author of the original data source, states at one point (p. xiv) that 'at the present stage of economic conditions, earnings are of more interest' but, while he invariably presents information on rates per week, comparable data on earnings in a week are not always given, particularly where the respective distributions are similar. In the case of the cigar-making industry, however,

earnings data for both adult men and adult women in the South in 1890 are given. The derived descriptive statistics for these distributions are shown below:

Earnings in a week	Men	Women
Mean	$9.94	$5.08
	(41.75M)	(21.34M)
Median	$9.33	$4.75
	(39.19M)	(19.95M)
Semi-interquartile Range	$2.77	$0.92
	(11.63M)	(3.86M)
Quartile Coefficient of Variation	0.276	0.193

The weekly earnings of adult female cigar-workers in 1890 in the United States as a whole had the following descriptive statistics: mean, $5.89 (24.74M); median, $5.44 (22.85M); semi-interquartile range, $1.61 (6.76M); and quartile coefficient of variation, 0.283.

In the case of adult women the picture of wage levels in these statistics is slightly less favourable than that in those statistics given by Sombart. – *Ed.*]

22   *Ed.* – Friedrich Woerishoffer (1839–1902) was first head of the Factory Inspectorate of the Grand Duchy of Baden from 1879 to 1902.

23   Baden, Ministerium des Innern, *Jahresbericht der Großherzoglich Badischen Fabrikinspektion für das Jahr 1896, Erstattet an Großherzogliches Ministerium des Innern* [*Annual Report of the Department of Factory Inspection of the Grand Duchy of Baden for the Year 1896, Made to the Ministry of the Interior of the Grand Duchy*] (Karlsruhe, 1897) 203.

24   Theodor Leipart, *Die Lage der Arbeiter in der Holzindustrie: Nach statistischen Erhebungen des Deutschen Holzarbeiter-Verbandes für das Jahr 1902 im Auftrage des Verbandes-Vorstands bearbeitet und herausgegeben von Theodor Leipart* [*The Situation of Workers in the Woodworking Industry: Compiled from Statistical Data Collected by the German Woodworkers' Union for the Year 1902 on Behalf of the Union's Executive and Edited by Theodor Leipart*] (Stuttgart, 1904) 68.

25   *Ed.* – Sombart states in his text that his data on wages in the German woodworking industry pertain to '71,054 workers'. This is incorrect. The author of the primary source says (p. 30) that 71,054 questionnaires were received in his survey, but that 356 had to be excluded as unusable. Moreover, wage data are presented on only 67,151 males and 698 females (p. 68); those workers on half-pay and receiving their board and lodging are not included in the wage data.

26   *Ed.* – It was not possible to verify Sombart's claim that his wage data for American woodworkers are based on 38,387 cases. His data source gives weekly wage rates for adult male woodworkers in 1900 in six separate categories: 11,962 workers making agricultural implements; a supplementary 2845 also making agricultural implements; 3695 making furniture; 2492 working in lumbering and planing mills; 1646 making pianos; and 2093 making wagons and carriages. (See Dewey, *Employees and Wages*, 142–3, 152, 168–9, 184–5, 194, 200–1.) These figures total only 24,733. The data on wage rates for these 24,733 workers have the following percentage distribution.

Less than $5.00 (21.00M)	4.0
$5.00–$7.49 (21.00M–31.46M)	9.0
$7.50–$11.99 (31.50M–50.36M)	51.1
$12.00–$23.99 (50.40M–100.76M)	35.0
$24.00 (100.80M) or more	0.8
	99.9

The usual derived descriptive statistics for this distribution differ significantly from those for the American data in Table 10. For the data just given above they are: mean, $11.01 (46.24M); median, $10.28 (43.18M); semi-interquartile range, $2.07 (8.69M); and quartile coefficient of variation, 0.189.

27 *Ed.* – Several writers contemporary to Sombart would have been in some agreement with this conclusion, although there would also have been some reservations. Shadwell, for example, while emphasising the variations in wages that made international comparisons difficult, concluded that for the 'unskilled day labourer, who occupies the same position in every country' the indexes of wages in German and American manufacturing centres in the winter of 1902 to 1903 were 78.6 and 142.8 respectively, these figures being standardised on an English one of 100; see Arthur Shadwell, *Industrial Efficiency: A Comparative Study of Industrial Life in England, Germany and America* (London, 1913 ed.) 378–9. Very similar ratios are repeated (p. 383) for wages in 'manufacturing industries'.

Significantly, however, in view of Sombart's later discussion of living standards, Shadwell also says (p. 466) that housing in corresponding localities was twice as dear in America as in England, with Germany in an intermediate position. Cost of living, inclusive of rent, was lowest in England and highest in America; between the United Kingdom and the United States this difference in the cost of living was large enough to neutralise wage differences, although this is not true of a comparison between Germany and the United States. (See also the article on 'Wages', in *New Encyclopedia of Social Reform*, pp. 1266–7.)

Several other writers of the period, while they say little that necessarily detracts directly from the validity of Sombart's comparison of wages in the United States and Germany, do none the less provide information about trends in American wages that belies the cosiness implicit in Sombart's statement. For example, James, in *QPASA* x 333, argues that 'wages were, on the whole, lower in 1900 than in 1890'. Peter Roberts's book, *The Anthracite Coal Industry: A Study of the Economic Conditions and Relations of the Co-operative Forces in the Development of the Anthracite Coal Industry of Pennsylvania* (New York, 1901) 103–27 *passim*, stresses both the frequently poor wage conditions in anthracite coal-mining and also the surplus labour that kept wages low.

One estimate in 1906 – in John A. Ryan, *A Living Wage: Its Ethical and Economic Aspects* (New York, 1906) 150 – was that anything less than $600 per year was not a living wage in any American city. Clearly, many American urban workers did not earn that amount, even if their wages may have been better in money terms than those of their German equivalents.

Such more recent work as that by Bry does contain comparative material on wages in Germany, Great Britain, and the United States, but it is really of limited value in elucidating comparative wage levels between these countries at a single point in time because the data are presented in index form as changes in wage rates within these countries. Even so, Bry's overall conclusion concerning the behaviour of wages in the three countries between 1871 and 1913 may still be relevant to a debate about the effects of wage conditions on working-class attitudes: 'between 1871 and 1913 real per capita income doubled in Germany and Great Britain, trebled in the United States'. See Gerhard Bry, *Wages in Germany, 1871–1945* (Princeton, 1960) 267.

28 Commission Industrielle Mosely, *Des conditions de la vie économique et sociale de l'ouvrier aux États-Unis* [*Some Conditions of the Economic and Social Life of the Worker in the United States*], translated by Maurice Allfassa (Paris, 1904), this being a translation of *Mosely Industrial Commission to the United States of America, Oct.-Dec. 1902: Reports of the Delegates* (Manchester, 1903). The former is Item 145 of my literature review; see Sombart, in *ASS* xx 684–6. [A. Mosely was an English industrialist who in 1902 financed a group of twenty-three English trade-union leaders from a variety of industries on a fact-finding visit to America. Mosely prepared a report in English from their written comments and their responses to a questionnaire that he had administered to them. Sombart was unable to locate the English original when preparing his literature review and he relied on the French translation. With considerable justification, one feels, Sombart doubted the objectivity and value of the data in the report. – *Ed.*]

29 The worker is frequently the owner of his own house, although at present this is still the exception. Among the labour élite whose household budgets were examined by the Bureau of Labor, 18.97 per cent were owners of the houses in which they lived; see United States, Fifty-eighth Congress, House of Representatives, *Eighteenth Annual Report of the Commissioner of Labor, 1903: Cost of Living and Retail Prices of Food* (Washington, D.C., 1904) 54, which is Item 7 of my literature review (Sombart, in *ASS* xx 642–4). In 1900 36.5 per cent of all American families, not counting farm families, lived in their own houses; see United States Census Office, *Twelfth Census, II*, Population, Part II, Table ciii, p. cc.

30 *The Tenement House Problem: Including the Report of the New York State Tenement House Commission of 1900*, ed. Robert W. De Forest and Lawrence Veiller (New York, 1903), 2 vols, which is Item 159 of my literature review; see Sombart, in *ASS* xx 692.

31 Massachusetts, Bureau of Statistics of Labor, *Thirty-second Annual Report of the Bureau of Statistics of Labor, March 1902* (Boston, 1902) 243.

32 It is customary for their results to be summarised in the *Statistisches Jahrbuch Deutscher Städte* [*Statistical Yearbook of German Cities*]; the most recent data are in that for the eleventh year of publication, ed. M. Neefe, xi (Breslau, 1903) 69–101.

33 Peter Roberts, *Anthracite Coal Communities: A Study of the Demography, the Social, Educational and Moral Life of the Anthracite Regions* (New York, 1904), which is Item 146 of my literature review; see Sombart, in *ASS* xx 686–8.

34 In United States, Fifty-eighth Congress, Senate, *Document No. 6, Report to the President on the Anthracite Coal Strike of May-October, 1902, by the*

Anthracite Coal Strike Commission (Washington, D.C., 1903) 43, the percentage of workers living in houses owned by the mining companies was given as less than 10 per cent for the northern and southern districts and as a little less than 35 per cent for the middle one. In *Anthracite Coal Communities*, 122, Roberts assumes it to be 16 per cent for the whole area.

The *Report of the Anthracite Coal Strike Commission* is Item 8c of my literature review; see Sombart, in *ASS* xx 645.

35 Dr [ ] Sattig, Inspector of Mines, „Über die Arbeiterwohnungsverhältnisse im oberschlesischen Industriebezirk" ['Workers' Housing Conditions in the Industrial Region of Upper Silesia'] in *Zeitschrift des Oberschlesischen Berg- und Hüttenmännischen Vereins* [*Journal of the Upper Silesian Union of Miners and Foundrymen*] (1892).

36 *Ed.* – Workers' Secretaries headed so-called *Arbeitersekretariate*; these were legal-aid bureaux in Germany that were organised and managed by workers. The first one had been established in Nuremberg in 1891. There were several hundred such local bureaux in Germany at the beginning of this century. Most, but not all, were formally organised and run by the Social Democrats.

37 *Eighteenth Annual Report of the Commissioner of Labor, 1903.*

38 Of course, we are concerned only with retail price data.

39 They are reprinted in the *Statistisches Handbuch für den Preußischen Staat* – for example, in IV (Berlin, 1904) 224.

40 *Ed.* – The data in Table 18 (*b*) are from the *Jahrbuch*, XI 421–4.

41 In a study called „Wie der amerikanische Arbeiter lebt" ['How the American Worker Lives'], which I published in the journal, *Das Leben* [*Life*], some mistakes crept into the conversion. The figures given there are therefore wrong and should be replaced by the data given here. [No further details of this reference could be found. – *Ed.*]

42 *Ed.* – Sombart's original text says 'so-called Nash houses', but this is clearly either a misprint or an example of Sombart's faulty ear for American slang terms; a 'hash house' is merely a cheap restaurant.

43 See the menu of such a restaurant in Kolb, *Als Arbeiter in Amerika*, 9. Kolb's book in Item 144 of my literature review; see Sombart, in *ASS* xx 681–4.

44 *Ed.* – Greenwich House's currently held records covering the pertinent period show no information about Mrs Charles Husted More or about her study.

Mary Kingsbury Simkhovitch (1871–1951), a social economist, was Head Worker at Greenwich House from its founding in 1902 until 1946 and Director Emeritus from 1946 till her death.

45 Massachusetts, Bureau of Statistics of Labor, *Prices and the Cost of Living: 1872, 1881, 1897 and 1902* [From the *Thirty-second Annual Report of the Bureau of Statistics of Labor, March 1902*, 239–314] (Boston, 1902), which is Item 16a of my literature review; see Sombart, in *ASS* xx 649.

46 It is admissible to infer income differences from wage differences, since the proportion of the family income made up by the earnings of the family head is somewhat larger in the United States than in Germany.

47 *Ed.* – Those derived descriptive statistics of income for May's twenty families that are not given in the text, as calculated from the ungrouped

figures in the source, are: median, 1100.00M; semi-interquartile range, 266.75M; and quartile coefficient of variation, 0.220.

If the reliability of the information about the income range of families in large cities is to be adequately evaluated, it should be known that only four of May's twenty families are in this category!

48 *Ed.* – This source contains a large number of obvious and varied errors, misprints and inconsistencies, some of which are in fact quite serious and almost none of which Sombart seems to have recognised. In such circumstances it was very difficult to perform a totally definitive check on all the figures that Sombart derived from the source and included in his text, although the Editor is almost certain that some of the data as originally given by Sombart contain errors of varying size and significance.

A major problem derives from the fact that not all forty-four families are included in some of the data-presentations. The usual method used by the author of the source in presenting data on particular commodity expenditures first shows such expenditures for all individual families for whom data are available, although the number involved is seldom forty-four and is sometimes as low as thirty-nine. Then there usually follows a summary table giving expenditure on the same commodity – as well as total expenditure – arranged according to these two types of expenditure within discrete groupings of total income or expenditure. Only in some cases does such a summary table provide a sum of total expenditures on the particular commodity, and even where this is done the figure quoted is usually different from the sum of all the individual families' expenditures on that commodity as given in the previous table. In order to obtain his average commodity expenditures, Sombart seems usually to have divided by forty-four the total expenditure on the particular item in all income or expenditure categories as given in, or summed from, the summary table. This has been done irrespective of the fact that relevant data for some commodities are available on only a smaller number of cases. Hence, almost all such averages given by Sombart are too low. Apparent errors of this sort have been corrected throughout by the Editor, but appropriate editorial comment has been made only where the errors were unusually large or affected the validity of some inference being drawn by Sombart from his data.

49 *Ed.* – The usual derived descriptive statistics of income for Nuremberg, as calculated from the ungrouped figures in the source, are: mean, 1535.11M; median, 1497.52M; semi-interquartile range, 191.43M; and quartile coefficient of variation, 0.124.

50 *Ed.* – The derived descriptive statistics of income for Berlin that are not given in the text, as calculated from the source, are: median, 1679.40M; semi-interquartile range, 258.84M; and quartile coefficient of variation, 0.152.

51 *Ed.* – The mean net surpluses or deficits of these sets of data are: May, surplus of 23.00M; Nuremberg, surplus of 47.52M; Berlin, deficit of 17.26M; Massachusetts, surplus of $31.02 (130.28M); and Washington, surplus of $50.26 (211.09M).

52 *Ed.* – Sombart says in his original text that thirty-two Nuremberg families had an average surplus of 125 marks each and twelve had a deficit of 82 marks each. However, not only did he wrongly calculate the respective averages from the given figures of individual surpluses and deficits, but he also failed to notice that two deficits are wrongly described as surpluses by the

author of the primary source. One of the latter cases is a deficit of 388.87 marks quoted as a surplus of 338.87 marks!

53 *Ed.* – In fact, the following expenditure data are based on only thirty-nine of the forty-four Nuremberg families. The following averages have been appropriately amended by the Editor.

54 Both studies give the broken-down figures for only some types of food; furthermore, the Nuremberg study does not cover all forty-four households, but twenty-one, twenty-two or twenty-four of the families provide data on the various items.

55 *Ed.* – This figure for expenditure on vegetables and the later one for expenditure on fruit do not cover all 908 Berlin families, but only the 881 containing from two to nine persons.

56 Kolb, *Als Arbeiter in Amerika*, 45–6. [However, in a passage just before the one quoted here Kolb describes the brewery workers among whom he also worked as being 'relatively dirty and scruffy'. – *Ed.*]

57 Madame John van Vorst and Marie van Vorst, *L'Ouvrière aux États-Unis* [*The Female Worker in the United States*] (Paris, 1904), this being a translation of Mrs John van Vorst and Marie van Vorst, *The Woman Who Toils: Being the Experiences of Two Gentlewomen as Factory Girls* (New York, 1903). The latter is Item 143 of my literature review; see Sombart, in *ASS* xx 681–4. [The first quotation is from p. 94 of the English-language version; it actually describes the theatre audience at a local performance of *Faust* that, somewhat unusually, was attended by a working girl. The second quotation is from p. 112 of the same version, and it is part of a direct comparison between the ostentatious clothing and the shoddiness of the diet and homes of the same female workers. – *Ed.*]

58 Roberts, *Anthracite Coal Communities*, 101–3.

59 *Ed.* – In the original text these percentages for the American studies are described as being of total income but are really of total expenditure.

60 *Ed.* – Three-tenths is the fraction stated in Sombart's text. See particularly Notes [a], [b], and [e] on Table 23 to account for the difference between this fraction of 'free' income given by Sombart and the corresponding figures that are in fact given in Table 23.

61 *Ed.* – The question of the proportions of income spent on food, housing, clothing, and sundries, for incomes of different sizes was perhaps more absorbing in economics at the end of the nineteenth and the beginning of the twentieth centuries than it is today. One of the more widely known outcomes of this interest is the so-called Engel's Law, which was propounded by the German statistician, Ernst Engel (1821–1896), head of the Royal Saxon Statistical Office from 1850 to 1858 and Director of the Royal Prussian Statistical Office from 1860 to 1882. This was first put forward by Engel in 1857 in the *Zeitschrift des statistischen Bureaus des Königlich Sächsischen Ministeriums des Innern* [*Journal of the Statistical Office of the Ministry of the Interior of the Kingdom of Saxony*] and has been discussed in English in, among other places, the *Seventh Annual Report of the Commissioner of Labor, 1891*, ii, Part iii, 860. The law states that the proportion of income spent on food declines as income increases. There have also been attempts to formulate similar laws for other items of expenditure.

Empirical assessments of Engel's Law have usually been made using intranational rather than international analyses. Certainly, Table 23 scarcely supports it, if one is comparing Germany with the United States. Even using intranational comparisons the evidence for Engel's Law in Table 23 is questionable, given the means of the incomes of the families in the studies concerned; this is particularly the case for the American studies and less so for the German ones. However, intranational analyses using individual families as the units of analysis have found the law to be correct; see, for example, H. S. Houthakker, 'An International Comparison of Household Expenditure Patterns, Commemorating the Centenary of Engel's Law', in *Econometrica*, xxv (1957), 532–51.

62 See, for example, the valuable work by Dr B. Laquer, „Trunksucht und Temperenz in den Vereinigten Staaten: Studien und Eindrücke" ['Drunkenness and Temperance in the United States: Studies and Impressions'], in *Grenzfragen des Nerven- und Seelenlebens* [*Borderline Issues Between Nervous and Spiritual Life*], ed. L. Loewenfeld and M. Kurella, v, No. 34 (Wiesbaden, 1905).

63 *Ed.* – Sombart says in his original text that the average Karlsruhe family spent 219 marks on alcoholic drinks, this being more than a fifth of its housekeeping expenses and 12.6 per cent of its total expenditure. However, these figures were calculated on the basis of what the Editor considers to be a misconception. The data source provides information both on what the average family actually *spends* for housekeeping and also on the monetary value of any food or drink consumed that was produced by virtue of the family's occupation. The average family spent 819 marks on all food and drink, including 147 marks on beer, 60 on wine and 7 on brandy – the total of 214 marks spent on alcohol given here. In addition, wine to the monetary value of 5 marks was produced in the family's occupation this amount being part of a total monetary value of 202 marks for all food and drink so obtained. Sombart uses the latter amount, plus the 819 marks actually spent, as the divisor in his calculation of the proportion of household expenditure going towards alcoholic drinks, giving the total of 'more than a fifth' that he mentions. However, 214 marks divided by the more appropriate figure of 819 is 26.1 per cent, slightly more than a quarter.

64 *Ed.* – The recalculation of the percentage of 'free' income among the Karlsruhe families performed by the Editor in Table 23 (see Note [a] on that table) seriously affects the validity of Sombart's present general inference from his German and American comparative material – certainly as regards the rural Karlsruhe families.

The percentage in parentheses here is what this entry would be if the Editor's re-estimation of the correct percentage of 'free' income in the Karlsruhe families were used. See Note [b] on Table 23.

65 *Ed.* – Sombart has probably taken these figures from United States Census Office, *Twelfth Census*, vii, Manufactures, Part i, p. cxxvi. In fact, they cover workers in manufacturing only, not in trade and transportation too. Workers in all 'productive industries' including 'hand and neighborhood industries' are covered by the data.

SECTION THREE

1 See the views of the English workers who took part in the Mosely Industrial Commission; Commission Industrielle Mosely, *Des Conditions de la Vie*, *passim*.

2 Ibid., 18.

3 See the reports of the Mosely Industrial Commission, whose members had just this point singled out to them by the organiser of the study trip; ibid., xvii, 6, 122, 152, 168, 213, 275, 354, 359, 416, etc. See also Nicholas Paine Gilman, *Methods of Industrial Peace* (Boston, 1904) 288–9.

4. *Ed.* – Full details about the Steel Trust's system are to be found in Moody, *Truth about the Trusts*, 172–91.

5 Ghent, *Our Benevolent Feudalism*, 163. This is Item 140 of my literature review; see Sombart, in *ASS* xx 678–81.

6 Abram S. Hewitt, quoted in the Editor's Introduction of *Labor and Capital: A Discussion of the Relations of Employer and Employed*, ed. John P. Peters (New York, 1902) p. xlii. This is Item 52 of my literature review; see Sombart, in *ASS* xx 659–62.

7 Tucker, in *MLB*, No. 33, 241.

8 *Ed.* – Despite the reputation of *Why is there no Socialism in the United States?* in some quarters, this present passage is really the only one in the book that explicitly introduces the argument that greater social mobility in America out of the working class reduced the propensity of workers to support a Socialist movement.

   In spite of a formidable sociological literature on social mobility in industrial societies there is still no real consensus on whether the reputation enjoyed by the United States around the turn of the century as a country where opportunity was objectively greater than in Europe has any factual basis. Sorokin's famous early study (Pitirim A. Sorokin, *Social and Cultural Mobility* (Glencoe, 1959 ed.) 414–80) did directly examine rates of vertical mobility within Western societies around the end of the nineteenth and the beginning of the twentieth centuries, and it was disposed generally to conclude that these rates were similarly high in the different countries. However, that conclusion had to be derived from a large number of individual, usually locally-based, studies in Europe and America, rather than from the national samples that a modern sociologist would want if he were satisfactorily to address the issue. Of course, the argument of Seymour Martin Lipset and Reinhard Bendix in their *Social Mobility in Industrial Society* (Berkeley, 1959) regarding similarities in rates of social mobility in different industrialised societies is well known, but their explicit conclusion is confined to the middle of the twentieth century.

   The study by Thernstrom of social mobility in Newburyport, Massachusetts, at the end of the nineteenth century (Stephan Thernstrom, *Poverty and Progress: Social Mobility in a Nineteenth Century City* (Cambridge, Mass., 1964) and his 'Class and Mobility in a Nineteenth-Century City: A Study of Unskilled Laborers', in *Class, Status, and Power: Social Stratification in Comparative Perspective*, ed. Reinhard Bendix and Seymour Martin Lipset, 2nd ed. (New York, 1966) pp. 602–15) gave a picture of comparatively small amounts of upward social mobility. Although no direct comparison with

European rates of social mobility in the same period is offered by Thernstrom in this study, the probable lack of any greater rate in America is clearly implied, especially as he argues that rates within the United States have tended to increase over time since the late nineteenth century.

Thernstrom has recently revised his position on the basis of a more recent comparative study of social mobility in Boston and Marseilles in the late nineteenth century. He believes that the Boston rates of mobility into non-manual positions were appreciably higher than the comparable rates in Marseilles; see Stephan Thernstrom, 'Socialism and Social Mobility', in *Failure of a Dream?: Essays in the History of American Socialism*, ed. John H. M. Laslett and Seymour Martin Lipset (Garden City, 1974) pp. 509–27. Lipset's 'Comment' (in ibid., pp. 528–46) and Thernstrom's 'Reply' to this (in ibid., pp. 547–52) are the latest exchange in this debate. Lipset, applying the logic implicit in the conclusions of the book he published with Bendix in 1959, argues against any general rigidity of the class structure of late nineteenth-century Europe, but Thernstrom in his turn differs with this interpretation. Clearly, the issue is still inconclusively resolved.

9 *Ed.* – Sombart espouses what must be regarded as the most naive and dubious of the several variants of the famous 'frontier thesis', and each of the several arguments that he makes in the following passages on the effects of the frontier has been criticised by one or more subsequent historians.

Among labour historians it is those of the so-called Wisconsin school of labour history, which is identified with the names of John R. Commons and Selig Perlman, who have used the frontier thesis as an explanatory tool. The so-called 'safety valve' argument Sombart adopts here finds a clear echo in John R. Commons *et al.*, *History of Labour in the United States* (New York, 1966 ed.) 1 4, and a somewhat more ambiguous use of the concept is found in Selig Perlman, *A History of Trade Unionism in the United States* (New York, 1950 ed.) 281–2.

First major doubts about the frontier thesis, at least as formulated by Frederick Jackson Turner, were offered by Goodrich and Davison as early as 1935. With some apparent incredulity at their own findings and some anguish at their import, Goodrich and Davison report their inability to find many recorded cases of wage-earners from the East who did go West to settle permanently; see Carter Goodrich and Sol Davison, 'The Wage-Earner in the Westward Movement: 1', in *Political Science Quarterly*, L (1935) 161–85, and 'The Wage-Earner in the Westward Movement: 11', in *Political Science Quarterly*, LI (1936) 61–116. Sombart's argument, which could be made only by an urbanite lacking realistic notions about the economics and practices of farming, that a wage-earner with 'no capital or hardly any' could go blithely off to farm the frontier is effectively criticised by Clarence H. Danshof in 'Farm-Making Costs and the "Safety-Valve": 1850–60', in *Journal of Political Economy*, XLIX (1941) 317–59. Perhaps the most famous of numerous essays atacking the frontier thesis is Fred A. Shannon, 'A Post Mortem on the Labor-Safety-Valve Theory', in *Agricultural History* XIX (1945) 31–7. Shannon attacks both the demographic underpinnings of the thesis and also its purported political-economic implications. More recently, Melvyn Dubofsky has argued against the importance attributed by Commons and Perlman to the frontier as a conservative influence. Dubofsky traces sources of labour radicalism in the West, particularly among miners, which owes more to the particularly oppressive character of capitalist exploitation than to anything connected with the frontier in a specifically geographical sense. See Melvyn Dubofsky, 'The Origins of Working Class Radicalism, 1890–1905', in *Labor History*, vii (1966) 131–54; this is partly reprinted in *The American Labor Movement*, ed. David Brody (New York, 1971) pp. 83–99.

Two recent anthologies of articles provide a full assessment of the current status of the various parts of the frontier thesis. See *The Frontier Thesis: Valid Interpretation of American History?*, ed. Ray Allen Billington (New York, 1966), and *Turner and the Sociology of the Frontier*, ed. Richard Hofstadter and Seymour Martin Lipset (New York, 1968). A valuable review essay on approaches to labour history in America is Robert H. Zieger, 'Workers and Scholars: Recent Trends in American Labor Historiography', in *Labor History*, xii (1972) 245–66.

10 There is a short but well-informed account in Max Sering, *Die landwirtschaftliche Konkurrenz Nordamerikas in Gegenwart und Zukunft* [*Agricultural Competition in North America in the Present and Future*] (Leipzig, 1887).

11 *Ed.* – The Homestead Act was passed in 1862 and became effective on 1 January 1863, its purpose being to open the country's vacant public lands for agricultural settlement. In fact, it extended to virtually all citizens the chance to be recipients of a land grant; such recipients had hitherto been confined to the veterans of America's wars. Provisions of the Act that Sombart does not mention were that household heads and those who had served not less than fourteen days in the American army or navy during an actual war also qualified for a grant, irrespective of their ages. In 1891 the Act was amended to exclude eligibility from those already holding 160 acres or more in any state or territory of the Union.

12 *Ed.* – This statement contains an example of Sombart's frequent *penchant* for exaggeration. In fact, the area newly cultivated between 1870 and 1890 was barely one-and-a-quarter times the size of the German Empire.

13 See especially United States Census Office, *Twelfth Census*, i, Population, Part i, pp. cxxv and 685.

14 *Ed.* – These 'divisions' are not those currently employed by the Bureau of the Census, which are: New England, Middle Atlantic, East North Central, West North Central, South Atlantic, East South Central, West South Central, Mountain, and Pacific. According to *Historical Statistics*, 41–3, 14.0 per cent of the native-born population was in 1900 living outside the division of its birth, when the present definitions of the divisions are employed.

15 *Ed.* – The Timber Culture Act, which was actually passed in 1873, was intended to encourage the planting of trees on the Western plains. The law required that 25 per cent of a maximum allotment of 160 acres of land be planted in timber and kept in good growing condition for ten years before title to the land would be given. In practice, however, many settlers received title to their holdings without full compliance, and even from its initial enactment, the law was interpreted by existing settlers as a chance to increase the amount of their holdings rather than as an obligation to plant trees. The rights of homestead and timber culture were frequently exercised by the same individual. The law was later amended and 1891 it was repealed.

16   *Ed.* – The data on acreage sold that are given by Sombart, apparently combining entries under both the Homestead Act and the Timber Culture Act, must be considered slightly misleading and should be compared with those given in more recently published standard sources. The rise in acreage sold for original homestead entries (except on ceded Indian lands) during the 1880s was neither as high nor as dramatic as Sombart implies. 6,046,000 acres were sold for this purpose in 1880, and 5,028,000 acres in 1881; the annual average for the five years from 1885 to 1889 was 7,372,000 acres. (See *Historical Statistics*, 237.)

17   *Ed.* – In the original text Sombart says 1863, but this is inconsistent with data given in *Historical Statistics*, 56–7, and by Schwegel, in *ZVSV* xiii, Table ii, 163.

18   *Ed.* – The original text says 1882 and 1883, but again, this is inconsistent with the data given in the two sources cited in Note 17, above.

19   *Ed.* – See Note 16 of this Section, above.

20   *Ed.* – A large part of the reason for the demise of the Knights of Labor was actually organisational mismanagement and, in fact, its members deserted heavily into the newly formed American Federation of Labor; see Note 47 of the Introduction, above.

21   Sering has this to say on the effect on population movement of the crisis of the 1870s: 'In the period from 1873 and 1879 whole multitudes of farmers in the Eastern, Central and older Western states sold their land, shopkeepers and manufacturers hurriedly collected together the remains of their property, and engineers, artisans and workers gathered together their savings, all with the purpose of finding themselves a new home in the West. At that time the city of New York was full of land agents who were seeking to find a purchaser for landed properties purchased in bulk by speculators in previous years. Almost every week whole colonies left the city and from Brooklyn alone 1000 families a year are supposed to have emigrated.' (Sering, *Die landwirtschaftliche Konkurrenz*, 87)

22   *Ed.* – This quotation is from Henry George's *Progress and Poverty: An Inquiry into the Cause of Industrial Depressions, And of the Increase of Want with Increase of Wealth. The Remedy*, for example, 5th ed. (London, 1883) 350–1.

23   *Ed.* – The original text says *einen*, at this juncture, but this is clearly a misprint for *keinen*, entirely reversing the meaning of the sentence.

Bibliography

All items to which Sombart refers explicitly by title in his original text have been marked with an asterisk.

A. PUBLIC DOCUMENTS

*Baden, Ministerium des Innern, *Die sociale Lage der Cigarren-arbeiter im Großherzogthum Baden: Beilage zum Jahresbericht des Großh. badischen Fabrikinspektors für das Jahr 1889, Herausgegeben im Auftrage des Großherzoglichen Ministerium des Innern* [*The Social Situation of Cigar-workers in the Grand Duchy of Baden: Supplement to the Annual Report of the Factory Inspector of the Grand Duchy of Baden for the Year 1889, Published on Behalf of the Ministry of the Interior of the Grand Duchy*] (Karlsruhe, 1890)

*—— *Jahresbericht der Großherzoglich Badischen Fabrikinspektion für das Jahr 1896, Erstattet an Großherzogliches Ministerium des Innern* [*Annual Report of the Department of Factory Inspection of the Grand Duchy of Baden for the Year 1896, Made to the Ministry of the Interior of the Grand Duchy*] (Karlsruhe, 1897)

*Berlin, Statistisches Amt, *Berliner Statistik herausgegeben vom Statistischen Amt der Stadt Berlin: 3. Heft; Lohnermittelungen und Haushaltrechnungen der minder bemittelten Bevölkerung im Jahre 1903* (Bearbeiter: Professor Dr E. Hirschberg) [*Berlin Statistics Published by the Statistical Office of the City of Berlin: Part 3; Findings on Wages and Household Accounts of the Less Well-off Population in 1903* (Compiler: Professor Dr E. Hirschberg)] (Berlin, 1904)

*Dewey, Davis R., *Employees and Wages. Special Reports, Twelfth Census of the United States Taken in the Year 1900* (Washington, D.C., 1903)

*Fuchs [Rudolf], *Die Verhältnisse der Industriearbeiter in 17 Landgemeinden bei Karlsruhe: Dargestellt von dem Großherzoglichen Fabrikinspektor Dr. Fuchs, Bericht erstattet an das Großherzogliche Ministerium des Innern und herausgegeben von der Großherzoglichen badischen Fabrikinspektion* [*The Conditions of Industrial Workers in 17 Communities around Karlsruhe, Prepared by Dr. Fuchs, Factory Inspector of the Grand Duchy of Baden, Report Made to the Ministry of the Interior of the Grand Duchy of Baden and Published by the Department of Factory Inspection*] (Karlsruhe, 1904)

German Empire, Kaiserliches Statistisches Amt, *Statistisches Jahrbuch für das Deutsche Reich* [*Statistical Yearbook for the German Empire*]; 1902, XXIII (Berlin, 1902); 1904, XXV (Berlin, 1904); *1905, XXVI (Berlin, 1905)

German Empire, Reichs-Versicherungsamt, *Amtliche Nachrichten des Reichs-Versicherungsamts* [*Official Reports of the Imperial Insurance Office*], XVIII: 1 (1 Jan 1902)

*Illinois, Bureau of Labor Statistics, *Twelfth Biennial Report of the Bureau of Labor Statistics of the State of Illinois, 1902* (Springfield, 1904)

*Massachusetts, Bureau of Statistics of Labor, *The Annual Statistics of Manufactures, 1901*, XVI (Boston, 1902)

*—— *Thirty-second Annual Report of the Bureau of Statistics of Labor, March 1902* (Boston, 1902)

*—— *Prices and the Cost of Living: 1872, 1881, 1897 and 1902* [From the *Thirty-second Annual Report of the Bureau of Statistics of Labor, March 1902*, 239–314] (Boston, 1902)

*Prussia, Ministerium für Handel und Gewerbe, *Zeitschrift für das Berg-, Hütten- und Salinenwesen im Preußischen Staat* [*Journal of Matters Connected with Mining, Smelting and Salt-mining in the Prussian State*] (Berlin, 1853 onward)

*Prussia, Statistisches Bureau, *Statistisches Handbuch für den Preußischen Staat* [*Statistical Manual for the Prussian State*] (Berlin, quinquennially from 1889 to 1904)

*—— *Statistisches Jahrbuch für den Preußischen Staat* [*Statistical Yearbook for the Prussian State*], II (Berlin, 1905)

*United States Census Office, *Census Reports, Twelfth Census of the United States Taken in the Year 1900* (Washington, D.C., 1902)

*—— *Occupations at the Twelfth Census* (Washington, D.C., 1904)

*United States Civil Service Commission, *Reports of the United States Civil Service Commission* (Washington, D.C., 1884 onward)

United States Department of Commerce, Bureau of the Census, *Historical Statistics of the United States: From Colonial Times to 1957* (Washington, D.C., 1960)

*United States, Department of Commerce and Labor, Bureau of the Census, *Bulletin No. 9: Mines and Quarries* (Washington, D.C., 1904)

—— *Special Reports: Mines and Quarries, 1902* (Washington, D.C., 1905)

United States, Department of Commerce and Labor, *Statistical Abstract of the United States*; *1904, XXVIII (Washington, D.C., 1905); 1911, XXXIV (Washington, D.C., 1912)

*United States, Fifty-second Congress, House of Representatives, *Seventh Annual Report of the Commissioner of Labor, 1891* (Washington, D.C., 1892)

*United States, Fifty-eighth Congress, House of Representatives, *Eighteenth Annual Report of the Commissioner of Labor, 1903: Cost of Living and Retail Prices of Food* (Washington, D.C., 1904)

*—— *Forty-second Annual Report of the Comptroller of the Currency, 1904* (Washington, D.C., 1904)

*United States, Fifty-eighth Congress, Senate, *Document No. 6, Report to the President on the Anthracite Coal Strike of May-October, 1902, by the Anthracite Coal Strike Commission* (Washington, D.C., 1903)

B. BOOKS

Anderson, William, Penniman, Clara and Weidner, Edward W., *Government in the Fifty States* (New York, 1960)

Bedford, Henry F., *Socialism and the Workers in Massachusetts, 1886–1912* (Amherst, 1966)

Bell, Daniel, *The End of Ideology: On the Exhaustion of Political Ideas in the Fifties* (New, Revised Edition: New York, 1962)

Bendix, Reinhard, *Nation-Building and Citizenship: Studies in our Changing Social Order* (New York, 1964)

Bettmann, Otto L., *The Good Old Days – They were Terrible!* (New York, 1974)

Billington, Ray Allen (ed.), *The Frontier Thesis: Valid Interpretation of American History?* (New York, 1966)

Bliss, William D. P. and Binder, Rudolph M. (eds.), *The New Encyclopedia of Social Reform* (New York, 1908)

*Braun, Adolf, *Haushaltungs-Rechnungen Nürnberger Arbeiter: Ein Beitrag zur Aufhellung der Lebensverhältnisse des Nürnberger Proletariats; Bearbeitet im Arbeiter-Sekretariate Nürnberg* [*Housekeeping Accounts of Nuremberg Workers: A Contribution to the Clarification of the Living Conditions of the Nuremberg Working Class; Compiled in the Office of the Nuremberg Workers' Secretary*] (Nuremberg, 1901)

Brody, David (ed.), *The American Labor Movement* (New York, 1971)

*Brooks, John Graham, *The Social Unrest: Studies in Labor and Socialist Movements* (New York, 1903)

Bry, Gerhard, *Wages in Germany, 1871–1945* (Princeton, 1960)

*Bryce, James, *The American Commonwealth*, Two Volumes (Second Edition: London, 1889)

Burner, David, *The Politics of Provincialism: The Democratic Party in Transition, 1918–1932* (New York, 1968)

Burnham, Walter Dean, *Critical Elections and the Mainsprings of American Politics* (New York, 1970)

Butler, D. E. and Rose, Richard, *The British General Election of 1959* (London, 1960)

Butler, David and Stokes, Donald, *Political Change in Britain: Forces Shaping Electoral Choice* (London and New York, 1969)

Campbell, Angus, Converse, Philip E., Miller, Warren E. and Stokes, Donald E., *The American Voter* (New York, 1960)

*Carlier, Auguste, *La République Américaine, États-Unis: Institutions de L'Union, Institutions d'État, Régime Municipal, Système Judiciaire, Condition Sociale des Indiens: Avec une Carte de la Formation Politique et Territoriale des États-Unis* [*The American Republic, the United States: Institutions of the Union, Institutions of State, Municipal Government, the Judicial System, Social Condition of the Indians: With a Map of the Political and Territorial Development of the United States*], Four Volumes (Paris, 1890)

Carr, William, *A History of Germany, 1815–1945* (London, 1969)

Chambers's Encyclopaedia, Fifteen Volumes (New Edition: London, 1950)

*Chapman, John Jay, *Government and Democracy; And Other Essays* (London, 1898); this appeared in America under the title, *Causes and Consequences* (New York, 1898)

Clague, Ewan, *The Bureau of Labor Statistics* (New York, 1968)

Coates, David, *The Labour Party and the Struggle for Socialism* (Cambridge, 1975)

*Commission Industrielle Mosely, *Des conditions de la vie économique et* *sociale de l'ouvrier aux États-Unis* [*Some Conditions of the Economic and Social Life of the Worker in the United States*], translated by Maurice Allfassa (Paris, 1904); this is the translation of *Mosely Industrial Commission to the United States of America, Oct.-Dec. 1902: Reports of the Delegates* (Manchester, 1903)

Commons, John R. *et al.*, *History of Labour in the United States*, Four Volumes (New York, 1966 ed.)

Dahrendorf, Ralf, *Class and Class Conflict in Industrial Society* (Stanford, 1959)

*De Forest, Robert W. and Veiller, Lawrence (eds.), *The Tenement House Problem: Including the Report of the New York State Tenement House Commission of 1900*, Two Volumes (New York, 1903)

*Deichmann, C., *Ergebnisse einer im Jahre 1900 vom Deutschen Tabakarbeiter-Verband veranstalteten Enquete, Bearbeitet von C. Deichmann* [*Results of an Enquiry Organised in 1900 by the German Tobacco Workers' Union, Compiled by C. Deichmann*] (Bremen, 1902)

*Fuhrmann, D., *Die wirtschaftliche Lage der Arbeiter Hanaus: Im Auftrage der Statistischen Kommission des Gewerkschaftskartells Hanau am Main bearbeitet von D. Fuhrmann* [*The Economic Situation of Workers in Hanau: Compiled by D. Fuhrmann on Behalf of the Statistical Committee of the Combined Trade Unions of Hanau am Main*] (Hanau am Main, 1901)

Gavett, Thomas W., *Development of the Labor Movement in Milwaukee* (Madison, 1965)

George, Henry, *Progress and Poverty: An Inquiry into the Cause of Industrial Depressions, And of the Increase of Want with Increase of Wealth. The Remedy* (Fifth Edition: London, 1883)

*Ghent, W. J., *Our Benevolent Feudalism* (New York, 1902)

*Gilman, Nicholas Paine, *Methods of Industrial Peace* (Boston, 1904)

Goldthorpe, John H. *et al.*, *The Affluent Worker: Political Attitudes and Behaviour* (Cambridge, 1968)

Gollan, Robin, *Radical and Working Class Politics: A Study of Eastern Australia, 1850–1910* (Melbourne, 1960)

Green, Marguerite, *The National Civic Federation and the American Labor Movement, 1900–1925* (Washington, D.C., 1956)

Hamilton, Richard F., *Class and Politics in the United States* (New York, 1972)

Handlin, Oscar, *The Uprooted: The Epic Story of the Great Migrations That Made the American People* (New York, 1951)

Harrington, Michael, *Socialism* (New York, 1972)

Hays, Samuel P., *The Response to Industrialism: 1885–1914* (Chicago, 1957)

Hicks, John D., *The Populist Revolt: A History of the Farmer's Alliance and the People's Party* (Lincoln, Nebr., 1961 ed.)

Higham, John, *Strangers in the Land: Patterns of American Nativism, 1860–1925* (Second Edition: New York, 1970 ed.)

Hillquit, Morris, *History of Socialism in the United States* (New York, 1903. Fifth Edition: New York, 1910)

Hobsbawm, E. J., *Primitive Rebels: Studies in Archaic Form of Social Movement in the Nineteenth and Twentieth Centuries* (New York, 1963)

—— *Labouring Men: Studies in the History of Labour* (Garden City, 1967 ed.)

Hofstadter, Richard, *The Age of Reform: From Bryan to F.D.R.* (New York, 1955)
—— and Lipset, Seymour Martin (eds.), *Turner and the Sociology of the Frontier* (New York, 1968)
*Hopkins, James H., *A History of Political Parties in the United States; Being an Account of the Political Parties since the Foundation of the Government; Together with a Consideration of the Conditions Attending Their Formation and Development; With a Reprint of the Several Party Platforms* (New York, 1900)
*Hunter, Robert, *Poverty* (New York, 1904); this was reprinted and re-issued in 1965 as d'A. Jones, Peter (ed.), *Poverty: Social Conscience in the Progressive Era* (New York, 1965)
Institut für Marxismus-Leninismus beim Zentralkomitee der SED, *Geschichte der Deutschen Arbeiterbewegung: Kapitel III; Periode von 1871 bis zum Ausgang des 19. Jahrhunderts* [*History of the German Workers' Movement: Chapter III; Period from 1871 to the End of the Nineteenth Century*] (Berlin, 1966)
*Jannet, Claudio, *Les États-Unis Contemporains, ou Les Moeurs, Les Institutions et Les Idées Depuis La Guerre de La Sécession* [*The Contemporary United States, or Customs, Institutions and Ideas Since the War of Secession*] (Paris, 1875); this was subsequently published in German with the title, *Die Vereinigten Staaten Nordamerikas in der Gegenwart: Sitten, Institutionen und Ideen seit dem Sezessionskriege* (Freiburg i. B., 1893), having been translated, newly revised and considerably extended by Walter Kämpfe
Key, V. O., Jr., *Southern Politics in State and Nation* (New York, 1949)
Kipnis, Ira, *The American Socialist Movement, 1897–1912* (New York, 1952)
Kleppner, Paul, *The Cross of Culture: A Social Analysis of Midwestern Politics, 1850–1900* (New York, 1970)
*Kolb, Alfred, *Als Arbeiter in Amerika: Unter deutsch-amerikanischen Großstadtproletiern* [*As a Worker in America: Among German-American Workers in Large Cities*] (Berlin, 1904)
Lane, Tony, *The Union Makes Us Strong: The British Working Class, Its Trade Unionism and Politics* (London, 1974)
Laslett, John H. M., *Labor and the Left: A Study of Socialist and Radical Influences in the American Labor Movement, 1881–1924* (New York, 1970)
—— and Lipset, Seymour Martin (eds.), *Failure of a Dream?: Essays in the History of American Socialism* (Garden City, 1974)
*Lee, Algernon, *Labor Politics and Socialist Politics* (Third Edition: New York, 1903)
*Leipart, Theodor, *Beitrag zur Beurtheilung der Lage der Arbeiter in Stuttgart: Nach statistischen Erhebungen im Auftrage der Vereinigten Gewerkschaften, herausgegeben von Theodor Leipart* [*Contribution to the Assessment of the Situation of Workers in Stuttgart: Prepared from Statistical Data Collected on Behalf of the United Trade Unions, Edited by Theodor Leipart*] (Stuttgart, 1900)
*—— *Die Lage der Arbeiter in der Holzindustrie: Nach statistischen Erhebungen des Deutschen Holzarbeiter-Verbandes für das Jahr 1902 im Auftrage des Verbandes-Vorstands bearbeitet und herausgegeben von*

Theodor Leipart [*The Situation of Workers in the Woodworking Industry: Compiled from Statistical Data Collected by the German Woodworkers' Union for the Year 1902 on Behalf of the Union's Executive and Edited by Theodor Leipart*] (Stuttgart, 1904)

Lenin, V. I. *What is to be Done?*, translated by S. V. and Patricia Utechin (Oxford, 1963 ed.)

*Levasseur, E., *The American Workman*, translated by Thomas S. Adams (Baltimore, 1900)

Lidtke, Vernon L., *The Outlawed Party: Social Democracy in Germany, 1878–1890* (Princeton, 1966)

Lipset, Seymour Martin, *The First New Nation: The United States in Historical and Comparative Perspective* (London, 1964)

—— and Bendix, Reinhard, *Social Mobility in Industrial Society* (Berkeley, 1959)

Lipset, Seymour Martin and Rokkan, Stein (eds.), *Party Systems and Voter Alignments: Cross-National Perspectives* (New York, 1967)

Lipset, Seymour Martin and Raab, Earl, *The Politics of Unreason: Right-Wing Extremism in America, 1790–1970* (New York, 1970)

Marshall, T. H., *Citizenship and Social Class; and Other Essays* (Cambridge, 1950)

Marx, Karl, *Capital: A Critical Analysis of Capitalist Production* (London, 1938 ed.)

—— *Essential Writings of Karl Marx*, selected by David Caute (New York, 1970)

—— and Engels, Frederick [*or* Friedrich], *Selected Works in Two Volumes* (Moscow, 1962)

—— *Werke* [*Works*], Thirty-four Volumes (Berlin, 1960–66)

—— *Basic Writings on Politics and Philosophy*, edited by Lewis S. Feuer (London, 1969)

*May, Max, *Wie der Arbeiter lebt: Arbeiter-Haushaltungs-Rechnungen aus Stadt und Land; Gesammelt, im Auszug mitgetheilt und besprochen von Max May* [*How the Worker Lives: Housekeeping Accounts of Urban and Rural Workers; Assembled, Abridged and Discussed by Max May*] (Berlin, 1897)

McKenzie, Robert and Silver, Allan, *Angels in Marble: Working Class Conservatives in Urban England* (London, 1968)

Michels, Robert, *Political Parties: A Sociological Study of the Oligarchical Tendencies of Modern Democracy*, translated by Eden and Cedar Paul (New York, 1966 ed.)

Miliband, Ralph, *Parliamentary Socialism: A Study in the Politics of Labour* (Second Edition: London, 1973)

*Mitchell, John, *Organized Labor: Its Problems, Purposes and Ideals and the Present and Future of American Wage Earners* (Philadelphia, 1903)

Mitzman, Arthur, *Sociology and Estrangement: Three Sociologists of Imperial Germany* (New York, 1973)

*Moody, John, *The Truth About the Trusts: A Description and Analysis of the American Trust Movement* (New York, 1904)

Moore, Robert, *Pit-Men, Preachers & Politics: The Effects of Methodism in a Durham Mining Community* (Cambridge, 1974)

Murray, Robert K., *Red Scare: A Study in National Hysteria, 1919–1920* (New York, 1964 ed.)

Münsterberg, Hugo, *The Americans*, translated by Edwin B. Holt (New York, 1904)

Musson, A. E., *British Trade Unions, 1800–1875* (London, 1972)

New English Dictionary on Historical Principles, Ten Volumes, and Introduction, Supplement, and Bibliography (Oxford, 1888–1933)

*Ostrogorski, M., *Democracy and the Organization of Political Parties*, Two Volumes, translated from the French by Frederick Clarke (London, 1902)

Perlman, Selig, *A History of Trade Unionism in the United States* (New York, 1950 ed.)

*Peters, John P. (ed.), *Labor and Capital: A Discussion of the Relations of Employer and Employed* (New York, 1902)

Philippovich, Eugen von, *Grundriß der Politischen Oekonomie [Outline of Political Economy]* (Nineteen Editions of One or Another Volumes and Parts: Freiburg i. B. and Tübingen, 1893–1926)

Pinard, Maurice, *The Rise of a Third Party: A Study in Crisis Politics* (Englewood Cliffs, 1971)

Pollack, Norman, *The Populist Response to Industrial America: Midwestern Populist Thought* (Cambridge, Mass., 1962)

Potter, David M., *People of Plenty: Economic Abundance and the American Character* (Chicago, 1954)

Riordon, William L., *Plunkitt of Tammany Hall* (New York, 1963 ed.)

Roberts, Peter, *The Anthracite Coal Industry: A Study of the Economic Conditions and Relations of the Co-operative Forces in the Development of the Anthracite Coal Industry of Pennsylvania* (New York, 1901)

*—— *Anthracite Coal Communities: A Study of the Demography, the Social, Educational and Moral Life of the Anthracite Regions* (New York, 1904)

—— *The New Immigration: A Study of the Industrial and Social Life of Southeastern Europeans in America* (New York, 1912)

Roberts, Robert, *The Classic Slum: Salford Life in the First Quarter of the Century* (Harmondsworth, 1973 ed.)

Rogin, Michael Paul, *The Intellectuals and McCarthy: The Radical Specter* (Cambridge, Mass., 1967)

Rosenblum, Gerald, *Immigrant Workers: Their Impact on American Labor Radicalism* (New York, 1973)

Roth, Guenther, *The Social Democrats in Imperial Germany: A Study in Working-Class Isolation and National Integration* (Totowa, 1963)

Ryan, John A., *A Living Wage: Its Ethical and Economic Aspects* (New York, 1906)

Samson, Leon, *Toward a United Front: A Philosophy for American Workers* (New York, 1933)

Schorske, Carl E., *German Social Democracy, 1905–1917: The Development of the Great Schism* (New York, 1955)

Schumpeter, Joseph A., *Capitalism, Socialism and Democracy* (Third Edition: New York, 1962 ed.)

*Sering, Max, *Die landwirtschaftliche Konkurrenz Nordamerikas in Gegenwart und Zukunft [Agricultural Competition in North America in the Present and Future]* (Leipzig, 1887)

Shadwell, Arthur, *Industrial Efficiency: A Comparative Study of Industrial Life in England, Germany and America* (London, 1913 ed.)

Shannon, David A., *The Socialist Party of America: A History* (Chicago, 1967 ed.)

Simmel, Georg, *Philosophie des Geldes* [*Philosophy of Money*] (Leipzig, 1900)

Smuts, Robert W., *European Impressions of the American Worker* (New York, 1953)

*Sombart, Werner, *Sozialismus und soziale Bewegung* (Fifth Edition: Jena, 1905); this was translated into English by M. Epstein from the sixth (enlarged) German edition as *Socialism and the Social Movement* (London, 1909)

Sorokin, Pitirim A., *Social and Cultural Mobility* (Glencoe, 1959 ed.)

*Spahr, Charles B., *An Essay on the Present Distribution of Wealth in the United States* (New York, 1896); the 1900 edition of this book was reprinted and re-issued in 1970

*Spargo, John, *Shall the Unions Go Into Politics?* (New York, 1903)

Taft, Philip, *The A. F. of L. in the Time of Gompers* (New York, 1970)

Thernstrom, Stephan, *Poverty and Progress: Social Mobility in a Nineteenth Century City* (Cambridge, Mass., 1964)

Turner, Frederick Jackson, *The Frontier in American History* (New York, 1947 ed.)

*van Vorst, Madame John and van Vorst, Marie, *L'Ouvrière aux États-Unis* [*The Female Worker in the United States*] (Paris, 1904); this is a translation of van Vorst, Mrs John and van Vorst, Marie, *The Woman Who Toils: Being the Experiences of Two Gentlewomen as Factory Girls* (New York, 1903)

*von Holst, H., *Verfassung und Demokratie der Vereinigten Staaten von Amerika*, Five Volumes (Düsseldorf, 1873; Berlin, 1878–91); this was published in English as *The Constitutional and Political History of the United States*, Eight Volumes, translated by John Lalor *et al.* (Chicago, 1876–92)

Webb, Sidney and Beatrice, *The History of Trade Unionism, 1666–1890* (London, 1894)

Weber, Max, *The Protestant Ethic and the Spirit of Capitalism*, translated by Talcott Parsons (New Edition: New York, 1958)

Weinstein, James, *The Decline of Socialism in America, 1912–1925* (New York, 1969 ed.)

Wells, H. G., *The Future in America: A Search After Realities* (London, 1906)

Wirth, Louis, *The Ghetto* (Chicago, 1928)

Wittke, Carl, *The Germans in America: A Student's Guide to Localized History* (New York, 1967)

Zweig, Ferdynand, *The Worker in an Affluent Society: Family Life and Industry* (London, 1961)

C. ARTICLES AND REVIEWS IN JOURNALS AND PERIODICALS

*Bishop, Joseph, 'The Price of the Peace', *The Century*, XLVIII (1894)

B[owley], A. L., Review of Davis R. Dewey's *Employees and Wages*, *Journal of the Royal Statistical Society*, LXVII (1904)

Burnham, Walter Dean, 'The End of American Party Politics', *Trans-action*, VII (1969)

Chamberlain, Chris, 'The growth of support for the Labour Party in Britain', *British Journal of Sociology*, XXIV (1973)

Clements, R. V., 'British Trade Unions and Popular Political Economy, 1850–1875', *Economic History Review*, 2nd Series, XIV (1961)

Cole, G. D. H., 'Some Notes on British Trade Unionism in the Third Quarter of the Nineteenth Century', *International Review for Social History*, II (1937)

Converse, Philip E., 'Of Time and Partisan Stability', *Comparative Political Studies*, II (1969)

——, Miller, Warren E., Rusk, Jerrold G. and Wolfe, Arthur C., 'Continuity and Change in American Politics: Parties and Issues in the 1968 Election', *American Political Science Review*, LXII (1969)

Danshof, Clarence H., 'Farm-Making Costs and the "Safety Valve": 1850–1860', *Journal of Political Economy*, XLIX (1941)

Dubofsky, Melvyn, 'The Origins of Working Class Radicalism, 1890–1905', *Labor History*, VII (1966)

Goodrich, Carter and Davison, Sol, 'The Wage-Earner in the Westward Movement: I', *Political Science Quarterly*, L (1935)

—— 'The Wage-Earner in the Westward Movement: II', *Political Science Quarterly*, LI (1936)

Houthakker, H. S., 'An International Comparison of Household Expenditure Patterns, Commemorating the Centenary of Engel's Law', *Econometrica*, XXV (1957)

Hunter, Robert, 'First Impressions of Socialism Abroad: No. 4; The Congress of the British Labour Party', *International Socialist Review*, VII (1906–7)

James, A. E., 'The Dewey Report on Wages in Manufacturing Industries in the United States', *Quarterly Publications of the American Statistical Association*, X (New Series, No. 79) (1907)

Kelley, Florence, Review of Robert Hunter's *Poverty*, *American Journal of Sociology*, X (1905)

Key, V. O., Jr., 'A Theory of Critical Elections', *Journal of Politics*, XVII (1955)

Leggett, John C., Review of Gerald Rosenblum's *Immigrant Workers: Their Impact on Labor Radicalism*, *Contemporary Sociology: A Journal of Reviews*, IV (1975)

Lockwood, D., 'Sources of Variation in Working Class Images of Society', *The Sociological Review*, New Series, XIII–XIV (1965–6)

*Pomeroy, Eltweed, 'Why I Do Not Join the Socialist Party', *International Socialist Review*, II (1901–2)

Portes, Alejandro, 'Political Primitivism, Differential Socialization, and Lower-Class Leftist Radicalism', *American Sociological Review*, XXXVI (1971)

Rosney, J. H., 'Socialism in London', *Harper's New Monthly Magazine*, LXXVI (1887)

*Sattig, [ ], „Über die Arbeiterwohnungsverhältnisse im oberschlesischen Industriebezirk" ['Workers' Housing Conditions in the Industrial Region of Upper Silesia'], *Zeitschrift des Oberschlesischen Berg- und Hüttenmännischen Vereins* [*Journal of the Upper Silesian Union of Miners and Foundrymen*], (1892)

Schafer, Joseph, 'Who Elected Lincoln?', *American Historical Review*, XLVII (1941)

*Schäffle, Albert, „Der Geld- und der Reallohn in den Vereinigten Staaten" ['Money-wages and Real Wages in the United States'], *Zeitschrift für die gesammte Staatswissenschaft* [*Journal of General Political Science*], XLVI (1889)

*Schwegel, H., „Die Einwanderung in die Vereinigten Staaten von Amerika: mit besonderer Rücksicht auf die österreichisch-ungarische Auswanderung" ['Immigration into the United States: With Special Consideration of Emigration from Austria-Hungary'], *Zeitschrift für Volkswirtschaft, Sozialpolitik und Verwaltung* [*Journal of Political Economy, Social Policy and Administration*], XIII (1904)

Shannon, Fred A., 'A Post Mortem on the Labor-Safety-Valve Theory', *Agricultural History*, XIX (1945)

Simons, A. M., 'The Socialist Outlook', *International Socialist Review*, V (1904–5)

—— Editorial, *International Socialist Review*, VI (1905–6) 369

*Sombart, Werner, „Die Deutsche Zigarrenindustrie und der Erlaß des Bundesrats vom 9. Mai 1888" ['The German Cigar-making Industry and the Bundesrat's Decree of 9 May 1888'], *Archiv für Soziale Gesetzgebung und Statistik* [*Works in Social Legislation and Statistics*], II (1889)

*—— „Quellen und Literatur zum Studium der Arbeiterfrage und des Sozialismus in den Vereinigten Staaten von Amerika (1902–1904)" ['Sources and Literature in the Study of the Worker Question and Socialism in the United States of America (1902–1904)'], *Archiv für Sozialwissenschaft und Sozialpolitik* [*Works in Social Science and Social Policy*], XX (1905)

*—— „Wie der amerikanische Arbeiter lebt" ['How the American Worker Lives'], *Das Leben* [*Life*]; no further details of this reference could be found

*Tucker, William Jewett, 'Labor and Education', *Massachusetts Labor Bulletin*, No. 33 (Sep 1904)

Turner, Frederick J., 'The Significance of the Frontier in American History', *Annual Report of the American Historical Association for the Year 1893*; this was reprinted in *International Socialist Review*, VI (1905–6)

Vorwärts [*Forward*], Review of Werner Sombart's *Warum gibt es in den Vereinigten Staaten keinen Sozialismus?* (9 Oct 1906)

Walker, Francis A., 'Socialism', *Scribner's Magazine*, I (1887)

Zieger, Robert H., 'Workers and Scholars: Recent Trends in American Labor Historiography', *Labor History*, XIII (1972)

D. ARTICLES IN BOOKS

Bottomore, Tom, 'Class structure and social consciousness', in Mészáros, István (ed.), *Aspects of History and Class Consciousness* (London, 1971)

Converse, Philip E., 'The Nature of Belief Systems in Mass Publics', in Apter, David E. (ed.), *Ideology and Discontent* (New York, 1964)

Coughlan, Robert, 'Konklave in Kokomo', in Leighton, Isabel (ed.), *The Aspirin Age, 1919–1941* (New York, 1949)

Douglas, Roy, 'Labour in Decline, 1910–14', in Brown, Kenneth D. (ed.),

Essays in Anti-Labour History: Responses to the Rise of Labour in Britain (London, 1974)

*Gainor, Edward J., 'The Government as Employer', in *Public Policy, Employers and Employes: Full Text of the Addresses Before the National Convention of Employers and Employes, with Portraits of the Authors, Held at Minneapolis, Minnesota, September 22–25, 1902* (Chicago, 1903)

Karson, Marc, 'Catholic Anti-Socialism', in Laslett, John H. M. and Lipset, Seymour Martin (eds.), *Failure of a Dream?: Essays in the History of American Socialism* (Garden City, 1974)

Kuczynski, Jürgen, Article on Werner Sombart, in Sills, David L. (ed.), *International Encyclopedia of the Social Sciences*, Volume xv (New York, 1968)

*McEwen, W. E., 'The Future Relations of Labor and Capital', in *Public Policy, Employers and Employes: Full Text of the Addresses Before the National Convention of Employers and Employes, with Portraits of the Authors, Held at Minneapolis, Minnesota, September 22–25, 1902* (Chicago, 1903)

Simmel, Georg, 'The Metropolis and Mental Life', in Hatt, Paul K. and Reiss, Albert J., Jr. (eds.), *Cities and Society: The Revised Reader in Urban Sociology* (New York, 1957)

Sturmthal, Adolph, 'Comment 1 [on an excerpt from Sombart's *Why is there no Socialism in the United States?*], in Laslett, John H. M. and Lipset, Seymour Martin (eds.), *Failure of a Dream?: Essays in the History of American Socialism* (Garden City, 1974)

Taft, Philip and Ross, Philip, 'American Labor Violence: Its Causes, Character and Outcome', in Graham, Hugh Davis and Gurr, Ted Robert (eds.), *Violence in America: Historical and Comparative Perspectives* (New York, 1969)

Thernstrom, Stephan, 'Class and Mobility in a Nineteenth-Century City: A Study of Unskilled Laborers', in Bendix, Reinhard and Lipset, Seymour Martin (eds.), *Class, Status, and Power: Social Stratification in Comparative Perspective* (New York, 1966)

—— 'Socialism and Social Mobility', in Laslett, John H. M. and Lipset, Seymour Martin (eds.), *Failure of a Dream?: Essays in the History of American Socialism* (Garden City, 1974); see also Seymour Martin Lipset, 'Comment', in ibid., pp. 528–46, and Stephan Thernstrom, 'Reply', in ibid., pp. 547–52

Thomas, Norman, 'Pluralism and Political Parties', in Laslett, John H. M. and Lipset, Seymour Martin (eds.), *Failure of a Dream?: Essays in the History of American Socialism* (Garden City, 1974)

Urwin, Derek W., 'Germany: Continuity and Change in Electoral Politics', in Rose, Richard (ed.), *Electoral Behavior: A Comparative Handbook* (New York, 1974)

Weippart, Georg, Article on Werner Sombart, in v. Beckerath, Erwin *et al.* (eds.), *Handwörterbuch der Sozialwissenschaften* [*Concise Dictionary of the Social Sciences*], Volume ix (Stuttgart, Tübingen and Göttingen, 1956)

*Whitridge, Frederick W., 'Assessments, Political', in Lalor, John J. (ed.), *Cyclopaedia of Political Science, Political Economy, and of the Political History of the United States*, Volume i (Chicago, 1882)

E. ITEMS IN SERIAL PUBLICATIONS

Crosland, C. A. R., *Can Labour Win?*, Fabian Tract 324 (London, 1960)

*Jastrow, J. and Calwer, R., „Berufsgenossenschaften" ['Industrial Associations That Administer Accident Insurance'], in *Schriften des Vereins für Sozialpolitik* [*Publications of the Association for Social Policy*], CIX, „Die Störungen im deutschen Wirtschaftsleben während der Jahre 1900 ff.", Fünfter Band; „Die Krisis auf dem Arbeitsmarkte" ['The Upsets in German Economic Life since 1900', Volume 5, 'The Crisis on the Labour Market'] (Leipzig, 1903)

*Laquer, B., „Trunksucht und Temperenz in den Vereinigten Staaten: Studien und Eindrücke" ['Drunkenness and Temperance in the United States: Studies and Impressions'], in Loewenfeld, L. and Kurella, H. (eds.), *Grenzfragen des Nerven- und Seelenlebens* [*Borderline Issues Between Nervous and Spiritual Life*], V, No. 34 (Wiesbaden, 1905)

Martin, Roscoe C., *The People's Party in Texas: A Study in Third Party Politics* (The University of Texas Bulletin No. 3308: 22 February 1933; Bureau of Research in the Social Sciences, Study No. 4)

*Neefe, M. (ed.), *Statistisches Jahrbuch Deutscher Städte* [*Statistical Yearbook of German Cities*], XI (Breslau, 1903)

*von Holst, H., *Das Staatsrecht der Vereinigten Staaten von Amerika* [*The Constitutional Law of the United States of America*] in the series, *Handbuch des Oeffentlichen Rechts: Das Staatsrecht der außerdeutschen Staaten* [*Manual of Public Law: The Constitutional Law of Non-German States*], Fourth Volume, First Half-volume, Third Part (Freiburg i. B., 1885)

F. ALMANACS AND PERIODICALS

American Federationist; Extra Number, IX: 1½ (15 Jan 1902); *Extra Number, XI: 7A (15 July 1904)

New York Times Encyclopedic Almanac (New York, 1970)

World Almanac and Encylopedia, 1902–5 (New York, 1902–5)

G. UNPUBLISHED DISSERTATION

Husbands, C. T., *The Campaign Organizations and Patterns of Popular Support of George C. Wallace in Wisconsin and Indiana in 1964 and 1968* (Unpublished doctoral dissertation, Department of Sociology, University of Chicago, 1972)

Index

The Index attempts a full coverage of all items in the Preface, the Foreword, the Introductory Essay, and the text of the translation. However, only those items in the Notes about which some substantive comment is made are referred to in the Index and these have been marked by a letter 'n' after the appropriate page number; no differentiation has been made between notes of the author and those of the Editor.